All for Love

All for Love

Seven Centuries of Illicit Liaison

VAL HORSLER

the national archives

For Jemma and Polly, intrepid research assistants

First published
in Great Britain in 2006 by
The National Archives
Kew, Richmond
Surrey, TW9 4DU, UK
www.nationalarchives.gov.uk

The National Archives (TNA) was formed
when the Public Record Office (PRO)
and Historical Manuscripts Commission (HMC)
combined in April 2003.

A CIP catalogue record for this book is available
from the British Library.

ISBN 1 903365 97 X
978 1 903365 97 7

Typographic design and typesetting by
KEN WILSON | POINT 918

Printed in the UK by
BIDDLES LTD, KING'S LYNN

Contents

Introduction

'WELL, HE WOULD, wouldn't he?' Those words have passed into modern folklore (and into the *Oxford Dictionary of Quotations*) as the cheeky, and apposite, response Mandy Rice-Davies made to prosecuting counsel at the trial of Stephen Ward in 1963 when he put it to her that Lord Astor had denied paying to have sex with her. This was at the height of the Profumo scandal, which ended Conservative minister John Profumo's career and rakish osteopath Stephen Ward's life.

Another quotation takes us back to the fifteenth century: 'And the Bishop said to her right plainly, and put her in remembrance of how she was born, what kin and friends she had ... what rebuke and shame and loss it should be to her if she were not guided by them...'. This was Margery Paston, who had defied her family by agreeing to marry Richard Calle, the family's bailiff. Banishment from the family was the penalty for a marriage regarded as unsuitable.

Scandal and intrigue have always been with us: the financial, political and sexual shenanigans of the great and the not-so-great, of those in the public eye and those whose only witnesses are their families and friends. There are those who have suffered for their sins and those who have got away with them; those who have risked all for love or gain and others who have used scandal to exploit and then turn against their victims. And of all potentially scandalous activities, sex is the one that has always penetrated through all strata of society, because it is the one that has everyone in its grip. However poor or powerless people are, they are the brothers and sisters of kings and queens when faced with the slings and arrows of sexual desire.

Which is why societies everywhere and always have sought to control it, by taboos, rules, laws and attitudes. And it is also why secrecy and concealment so often go hand in hand with sexual intrigues. This fundamental part of human life is both necessary for the continuation of the race and a cause of illicit pleasure and the guilt, jealousy and envy that run alongside. Inter-relationships between people have always resulted in affairs bubbling below the surface, sometimes needing to be hidden and at other times blatantly played out in public. Sometimes there is a lot to lose, and at others the world is worth losing for love.

There has always been a huge difference between what is preached and what is practised. The medieval Christian Church regarded sex as inherently sinful and ordained that it must be for the purposes of procreation only. Sex as fun was forbidden, and it was hedged round with all sorts of proscriptions and denials; the usual injunction applied to questions of sexual manners was 'Don't'. Yet that did not stop Chaucer celebrating the power and the comic potential of lust, and the pleasure of sex as recreation; his Wife of Bath is eloquent in her defence of the pleasures of the body. This book is called *All For Love*; but the behaviour it chronicles is often more like 'all for lust'. The heart is not always the primary organ in question.

Sex is full of contradictions: it is enjoyable – even addictive – yet consequences can be immense. Traditionally, these included children who might be illegitimate and therefore shameful, or an extra mouth to feed when money is tight. Sex is also various: love and lust between men and men, or women and women, have always been with us and were in many ages regarded as deviant and sinful; until 1861 the penalty in Britain for male homosexual sex was death. Only recently have modern societies accepted that homosexuality is part of the human condition and not something needing to be 'cured'; recently the Greek government protested against the portrayal in film of Alexander the Great as gay, although the morality of his own time had no problem with the idea. And it is not for nothing that prostitution is called 'the oldest profession': sex in exchange for money is, and has always been, an inescapable part of society.

While pregnancies could not be reliably prevented or legally curtained, financial and inheritance considerations were part and parcel of the rules about illicit sex, at least among the propertied elements of society. Marriage was a formal financial contract, visible and necessary. Wives had to be chaste, before and after marriage, because they were responsible for the sexual probity of families, communities and the whole country. It was a woman's virtue that guaranteed the legitimacy of her children and the safety of their inheritance. Women of course it was who bore the children, whose maternity could not be challenged; men's responsibility for babies has only in very recent years been provable beyond doubt by DNA testing. Women could never escape from that role; men could, and did. This is not a book about feminism; but attitudes towards women and their rights, and the central female role in matters of sexual morality, are and have always been of fundamental importance in the consideration of licit and illicit sexual behaviour.

The aristocracy in the past accepted the sinfulness of illicit lusts and atoned for them; but they also had the wherewithal to raise and care for their illegitimate offspring, many of whom led successful and prosperous lives even if they could not inherit titles and estates. At the other end of society, the formality of marriage was less necessary – apart from for religious reasons – and the coming together of men and women could be more casual and less regulated. In a world of both wider family and community ties and high death rates, children – legitimate or not – were a fact of life, provided they did not become a charge on the parish. Immorality could be shameful; but more often it was something to be shrugged off.

For centuries society was broadly polarized between the rich and mighty at one end and the poor and powerless at the other; it was when those in the middle started to respond to increased prosperity and greater knowledge by flexing their muscles and demanding a greater say in society's rules that sexual principles began to be more fixed. Terms such as 'Victorian values' and 'middle-class morality' say it all: tolerance towards impropriety of all kinds decreased, opprobrium – and the penalties that went along with it – were heaped on the heads and the reputations of those who sinned, and an upright rectitude was demanded of everyone. Whereas a fifteenth-century woman such as Margaret Paston could – and did – remember her son's illegitimate child in her will, a nineteenth-century woman like Mary Ann Evans (George Eliot) was ostracized by her family when she chose to live with a man to whom she was not married – even though he was the victim of an adulterous wife whom the laws of the time did not permit him to divorce. There were always sexual boundaries that could not be crossed; but the increased economic and social power of the middle classes defined them more tightly and spread them more widely.

And it was the decline – or seismic shift – in western middle-class morality in recent years that has let the sexual genie out of the bottle – combined with the reliable prevention of pregnancy made possible by the contraceptive pill in the 1960s, along with the legalization of abortion. Before those revolutionary innovations, children born outside the legal bonds of matrimony were both a moral and a financial affront to an institution that underpinned society's values. Once the practical need for marriage disappeared, in a remarkably short time moral and socially respectable attitudes towards marriage began to crumble. Sex became a middle-class plaything, a pleasurable activity no longer the province of a degenerate aristocracy or a hapless working class. The students who revelled in the 'summer of love' in 1967 were middle class, and they and their children continue to celebrate the freedom granted by sex without the fear of pregnancy.

There was in truth a genuine sexual revolution in the 1960s. To those of us living at the start of the twenty-first century who are old enough to remember life before that decade, it is abundantly clear that attitudes towards sexual immorality have changed beyond all recognition. Fifty years ago, sex before marriage was disgraceful, illegitimate children were ostracized and legally disadvantaged, living together outside wedlock was 'living in sin' and homosexuality was illegal. Today, marriage is declining, cohabitation is the norm, the word 'partner' is a substitute for 'husband' or 'wife', children often carry names different from one or both of their parents or from their siblings, and homosexual relationships of both sexes can be validated by legally binding 'marital' agreements. In western secular society at least, we no longer have to hide our sexual activity for fear of society's censure or because of material implications.

But what is it that makes this old, old story so perennially fascinating? It is true that there is nothing new under the sun – but the ways in which humans down the centuries have dealt with and responded to their emotions, their feelings, their yearnings, their passions have differed according to when and where we have lived. Society has always shaped us; and the importance of sexual morality and its opposite has always been fundamental to society's rules and attitudes.

Despite the prurience of religious and sometimes secular authorities down the centuries, sex has never been just about making babies; it is a human compulsion, stronger in some than in others, taking little regard of gender or class, impossible to deny or ignore. Poets and philosophers have struggled to define its impact; Byron considered erotic love 'a sort of hostile attraction' while Simone Weil regarded it as 'hunger and repletion'. Moreover, despite its sometimes disastrous consequences (venereal disease, unwanted pregnancies, social ostracism or worse for those whose sexual needs were different) it is enjoyable, fun and titillating – and if forbidden fruit then doubly so. The very danger of illicit sex adds to the spice of life, as we recognize today when we ask about yet another politician caught with his pants down: 'Why did he do it? Surely he knew he'd be found out?' The randiness of men in the mould of Pepys and Boswell and women such as Margaret, Duchess of Argyll; the bold effrontery of Oscar Wilde; the appalling debauchery of the Earl of Rochester along with the insouciant womanizing of his king, Charles II; the celebration in John Donne's sensual poetry of his mistresses and his much-loved wife; the determination of Victorian women to have done with male domination of families and children and to control their own sexual destiny – all add up to a story of achievement, enjoyment and sinfulness at one and the same time.

Love has always defied rules that seek to constrain it, and celebrated the human spirit in the process; it is small wonder that 'libertine', 'liberal' and 'liberty' all come from the same root. Thom Gunn's poem 'Adultery' sums up the simplicity and freedom of stolen passion, which serves our natural instincts and yet moves beyond them:

> Hot beautiful furless animals
> Played in a clearing opened by their desire.

Perhaps our fascination with the lives and loves of others – stronger than ever in our vicarious age – is no more than a desire to enter that same clearing and find our own glorious, albeit fleeting, place in the sun.

One · Medieval romances

BRITAIN seven hundred years ago: a feudal society where kings and noblemen ruled with fists of iron and the laws of State and Church favoured the strong. A much emptier land, too, than the overcrowded islands of today, where people stayed put for most of their lives, living and dying in the place they were born, enduring pestilence and famine in the bad years, but making the best of what nature had to offer and carrying on their existence as well as they could. Life was short for most people, circumscribed by dirt and disease. Infancy and old age were perilous, and childbirth highly dangerous for both mother and baby. Girls were marriageable when they reached puberty, and among those with property boys and girls of good family were valuable commodities, forging useful alliances through tactical marriages and keeping wealth within the tight circle of kin and influence.

We know relatively little about medieval daily life, and still less about the manners and morals of the vast bulk of the population – those below the topmost ranks of society. A certain amount can be deduced from demographic data and from some of the literature of the time, but direct evidence is sparse. The letters written to each other by members of the Paston family in the fifteenth century are a remarkable survival; but the Pastons were upwardly mobile, and their concerns and interests were those of the landed gentry. We can, however, make certain assumptions; people then, after all, were in many ways much like people now – and never more so than in the area of life covered here: sex and love. Chaucer's audience, for example, could engage with tales of sexual and marital intrigue, and men and women did risk a great deal for the naughty pleasure of an affair. Passion and attraction seem to have been just as potent then as they are now, judging by the fears of the Church and moralists. And on the other hand we can also assume that for many husbands and wives life together was contented, mutually supportive and chaste.

Of one thing we can be sure: that in the Middle Ages everything was underpinned by the thundering authority of the Church, with profound consequences for those who chose to sin against God's and the Church's laws. Hell was very real to medieval people, and religion a daily presence in their lives – actions in life had eternal repercussions, and it was all too easy to follow a tempting path towards damnation. The story of Adam and Eve – thrust out of Paradise because they succumbed to the allure of knowledge and sexual sin – provided a dire warning of the perils of disobedience, and of the female sex. Life, with its loves and losses, was a mere prelude to the reality of eternity.

That reality found expression in Dante's *Inferno* (written between 1308 and 1321) and his recital of the story of Paolo and Francesca – a grim reminder of what might happen to those who died in a state of mortal sin without the chance to repent. Francesca had been tricked into a political marriage to the ugly Gianciotto Malatesta by his comely younger brother Paolo, but had then fallen for Paolo and found her feelings returned. They started an affair but were caught by Gianciotto; he drew his sword to kill Paolo, but instead impaled Francesca, who had thrown her body between the two brothers. He then went on to kill Paolo, and the lovers were buried in the same grave. But Dante finds them in the first circle of hell where they are condemned to burn for ever – together – for the sin of adultery.

Yet sex and sexuality were necessary, too, a part of daily life and – despite the strictures of the Church about the sinfulness of sex as fun – an acknowledged part of keeping the human race going. In medieval times, as ever, relationships could be complex, involving love and pleasure on the one hand and lust and sin on the other. And in that multi-layered society, there were aspects of courtship and romance that seem strange to us now – the idea of courtly love, for example, epitomized by the tales of King Arthur, Queen Guinevere and the Knights of the Round Table. Geoffrey of Monmouth and, later, Sir Thomas Malory bring us a golden world of chivalry, 'parfit, gentil knyghts', fair maidens, damsels in distress, quests for honour. Yet there was a dark side to those tales which was accepted by their audience. It was a rape at Camelot that started the sequence of events in Chaucer's *Wife of Bath's Tale*: one of Arthur's knights, while out hawking, met a maiden walking alone and ravished her, despite her putting up a desperate fight. Even Arthur himself was not the saintly king who features in later views of the legends. Like many flawed heroes, he nurtured the seeds of his own destruction within himself – and realized it through sex. He knew when he slept with Morguase that she was the king's wife, though he did not know the much more grievous fact that she was his half-sister: in Malory's words, 'all thys tyme kynge Arthure knew nat kynge Lottis wyff was his sister'.

[13]

Not just adultery, then, but incest, too, although he only discovered it when Merlin reproved him. 'Ye have done a thynge late that God ys displeased with you, for ye have lyene by youre syster and on hir you have gotyn a childe that shall destroy you and all the knyghtes of youre realme.' This child was Mordred, both son and nephew, who was to betray Arthur and cause his death.

Arthur's queen, Guinevere, and Lancelot, noblest of knights, were culpable as well. Although Lancelot embarked on quest after quest in a vain attempt to stay away from the queen, he succumbed in the end — and in the process, through his loss of virtue, he condemned himself to exile from the select band of knights who could pursue the Holy Grail. It was Mordred's catching them together in the queen's room that led to the end of the Arthurian romance: Guinevere was sentenced to be burnt at the stake, Lancelot returned to save her, and Mordred's rebellion resulted in Arthur receiving a mortal wound and being carried off to Avalon.

The idea of romantic love has its roots in the courtly love codes fostered by the troubadours and brought to England from Europe. They are set within a Christian framework yet have violence and moral ambiguity at their heart. The story of Tristan and Isolde is a chivalric tale of illicit love: sent to Ireland to escort Isolde back to Cornwall to marry King Mark, his nephew Tristan falls passionately in love with her after they both drink a love potion. Despite her marriage they carry on an adulterous affair until the king exiles Tristan to Brittany, where he marries another Isolde. But his true love never fades, and when he falls sick he sends for the first Isolde in the hope that she can cure him, asking the captain of the ship to hoist white sails on the return journey if she is on board, and black if she is not. His jealous wife, however, looks out for the ship and reports that the sails are black, whereupon Tristan sickens and dies in a dramatic Liebestod, where love and death become one. Despite their often tragic outcomes, courtly love tales were revered as 'guides to conduct', though perhaps the military prowess and knightly quests were the real draw.

Courtly love in this sense was an art to be mastered, with codes and patterns of behaviour that had to be strictly obeyed. And the fundamental rule was that true love was secret — and therefore different from anything felt for a wife, the woman who was openly acknowledged and shared a legitimate bed. It had to be another man's wife who inspired the sighs of unrequited affection, the tears of frustration, the pallid complexion, the frail, thin body of the true lover who could neither eat nor sleep. For Malory, love in his own time was flawed: 'But nowadays men can nat love sevennyght but they muste have all their desires… But the olde love was nat so. For men and women could love togydirs seven yerys, and no lycoures [lecherous] lustis was betwyxte them.' *The Romance of the Rose* embodies these principles: love in this context is refined and exclusive, an artificial ritual for a chosen few. It is as far from the tough everyday reality of medieval life as it is possible to be.

Chaucer's *Franklin's Tale* depicts both the conventions of courtly love and the emotional turmoil that could lie at its heart. Arveragus is a noble knight who falls in love with Dorigen and marries her. They are blissfully happy together in their home in Brittany until Arveragus decides to go to England to seek knightly renown in arms. She pines for him miserably, constantly fearing that when he does return his ship will come to grief on the harsh rocks of Brittany's coast. Her friends try to distract her from her grief by planning a dance in a beautiful garden, where she comes face to face with Aurelius, a squire who has loved her hopelessly for years. He blurts out his feelings, and she is taken aback: '"Is this youre wil," quod she, "and say ye thus? Nevere erst," quod she, "ne wiste I what ye mente."' She protests her everlasting love for her husband, but then promises wistfully that if Aurelius can make the rocks on the coast disappear she will give herself to him.

Arveragus returns and the two are blissfully reunited, while Aurelius sickens yet further with unrequited love. Then his brother persuades him to seek out a magician to make the rocks disappear; the spell works and he asks Dorigen to fulfil her vow to him. She is distraught and confesses all to her husband, who is deeply saddened but tells her that 'Trouthe is the hiyeste thing that man may kepe' and that she must do as she promised. She goes to the garden to meet Aurelius, but when the squire sees her deep misery, he releases Dorigen from her vow:

> …heere I take my leve
> As of the treweste and the beste wyf
> That evere yet I knew in al my lyf.

So all is well; even the magician refuses to accept his payment after Aurelius tells him what he has done. And:

> Arveragus and Dorigen his wyf
> In sovereyn blisse leden forth hir lyf.
> Nevere eft ne was ther angre hem bitwene.
> He cherisseth hire as though she were a queene,
> And she was to him trewe for everemoore.

The Franklin's Tale moves from the principles of courtly romance to the emotions of the real world – and as it might be experienced in a real love triangle. Chaucer's psychological understanding extends to lovers in more exotic locations, such as *Troilus and Criseyde*, set in the pagan past of the Trojan War. It tells the story of love lost through circumstances and expediency, charting the betrayal of Troilus, a prince of the city, by his lover Criseyde, a Greek who has been taken captive. Criseyde promises undying love, but when she is returned to the Greeks as part of a hostage exchange she eventually falls to the Greek warrior Diomedes. Criseyde is usually portrayed as a paradigm of female inconstancy, but Chaucer paints a gentler portrait and talks of her distress at what she sees her future reputation will be:

> But trewely, the storie telleth us,
> Ther made nevere woman moore wo
> Than she, when that she falsed Troilus.
> She seyde, 'Allas! for now is clere ago
> My name of trouthe in love, for evermo!
> For I have falsed on the gentileste
> That evere was, and oon the worthieste!

Despite the tragic consequences, Chaucer celebrates the rapture at the core of the poem as a pinnacle of human experience, rather than castigating it as fornication and sin:

> O blisful nyght, of hem so longe isought,
> How blithe unto hem bothe two thow were!
> Why nad I swich oon with my soule ybought
> Ye, or the leeste joie that was there?
> Awey, thow foule daunger and thow feere,
> And let hem in this hevene blisse dwelle
> That is so heigh that al ne kan I telle!

Our increasingly secular, twenty-first-century society has chosen to ignore many of the rites of passage that once delineated sexual relationships. Oddly, though without the secularity, this was also the case in the early Middle Ages. A formal marriage required only a public commitment by the two people involved. Oddly also, divorce and remarriage were by no means uncommon. When property and power were involved things were more complicated; but for the majority of 'ordinary' people marriage was a pretty casual affair.

It was only when the Christian Church began to assert its authority over the institution of marriage that formality and legality began to creep in. Moreover, medieval relationships were constrained by four factors that are not always issues in today's world. The first was procreation, something that could not be reliably controlled; the second was property, a vital element of all marital arrangements except among the very poor; the third was the formal inequality between the sexes, both legally and financially.

And the fourth was sex. Regarded by the Christian Church as essentially sinful, it was ordained to be for the purposes of procreation only. Within the new church rules, brought in during the thirteenth century, proclaiming the principle that marriage was monogamous and for life, and excluding illegitimate children from inheritance, sexual conduct, too, was to be controlled. Enjoyment was not part of the bargain, and Lust, one of the Seven Deadly Sins, was taboo inside marriage as well as out. Sexual play or modes of intercourse regarded as deviant were forbidden; the missionary position was the best, not least because it avoided the dangers of women appearing dominant or men imitating beasts. In a world where celibacy for a man and virginity for a woman were the loftiest planes attainable, matrimonial chastity was a lower, but still desirable, virtue. Making love to your wife as if she was your mistress, or even a whore, was not only disgusting but sinful. Sensuality was evil, and sex as fun was deplored.

There were religious reasons for this attitude, based on early Christian views of sex as impure and unclean. For St Paul the best of all states, for both men and women, was celibacy; he did not regard procreation as necessary given the imminent Second Coming of Christ and the end of the world. He did not echo God's command to Adam and Eve that they should 'go forth and multiply', but rather acknowledged that if a man and a woman could not contain their sexual desire for each other, 'let them marry, for it is better to marry than to burn' (I Cor. 7:9). Marriage for St Paul was simply to prevent fornication, allowing him to present his disciples to the returned Christ in a pure state.

Since the world had clearly not yet ended, however, the medieval

Church sought to restrain sexual behaviour by restricting its role to pro-creation. Sex was thus not allowed when a woman was pregnant, since conception was not a possibility at this time. Sexual abstinence was also expected of devout married couples during Lent and Advent, or on feast days, fast days and Sundays – at least during the hours when good Christians ought to have been at their devotions. Some were prepared to poke fun at such requirements, however – and the naughtiness of breaking them may have given an added spice. In *The Family, Sex and Marriage in England 1500–1800*, Lawrence Stone quotes an obscene poem which ends with the lines:

> And for which I am sure she will go to Hell,
> For she makes me f**k her in church time.

Another fifteenth-century poem boldly celebrates a seduction carried out by a cleric, Jankin, against the background of the Christmas Day Mass. Each verse ends with 'Kyrieleison' (the Greek words for 'Lord have mercy' from the Kyrie at the beginning of Mass) and the phases of intimacy reflect the stages of the Mass. The 'pax-brede', for example, was the article kissed during Mass while the kiss of peace was being exchanged among the congregation. It clearly has another meaning here, and as the service proceeds, matters heat up:

> Jankin at the Agnus
> Bereth the pax-brede:
> He twinkled but said nowt,
> And on my foot he trede,
> Kyrieleison.

> Benedicamus Domino,
> Christ fro shame me shilde:
> Deo gracias, therto –
> Alas! I go with childe,
> Kyrieleison.

There were more secular reasons, too, for demanding sexual restraint, based on the medical view at the time that ejaculation and over-indulgence in sexual activity diminished the life forces and weakened men who succumbed too often. Male semen was vital to good health and a strong physique, so was to be expended only in moderation. Over-lustful women were regarded as responsible for their men becoming thin, pale

and weedy. The ability of women to achieve multiple orgasms reinforced the belief that they were insatiable, carnal predators who were
responsible for the evils of erotic incontinence. Husbands were expected
to achieve a balance in their sexual relations with their wives – enough
to satisfy the woman's desires so that she would not seek to satisfy her
passions elsewhere, but not so much that she would become oversexed
… and seek to satisfy her passions elsewhere!

Demons known as succubi were another manifestation of the evils of
incontinent sexuality. They took on the female form in order to
infiltrate men's dreams and cause them to have sexual intercourse.
Monks were particularly vulnerable, it seems; and the succubi could be
so insistent that they drew out all the energy from their victims and
sometimes led them to the point of death. They would collect seed from
the men and give it to incubi, who would then use it to impregnate innocent women. Useful devices, perhaps, to explain wet dreams and surprise pregnancy; but they were all too real in a fearful and superstitious
world.

Women since Eve were viewed with suspicion as potential tempt-
resses who could lead men astray. The only acceptable path was to
remain a virgin before marriage and be monogamous within it. Men, on
the other hand, were expected to indulge in sexual adventures before
marriage, and later unfaithfulness to their wives was a mere peccadillo.
The double standard roared loud and clear! There were reasons for this,
of course, rooted in the need to be sure of a child's legitimacy, but also
resulting from women's second-class status in society. A chaste reputation was essential for a woman, and equally for her husband; to be
branded a cuckold was to be ridiculed and reviled, both because a man's
sexual ownership of his wife had been stolen, and also because he was
unable to control his own household.

There are numerous examples of women turning a blind eye to their
husbands' – or their sons' – extramarital affairs. In the fifteenth century
Margaret Paston left ten marks to her son's illegitimate child, and
another woman left two valuable items of clothing to her husband's bastard daughter. Some men asked their wives to take on the responsibility
of bringing up their illegitimate children, and the wives often agreed.
Women, of course, were not allowed the same licence, and could be
thrown out of the house if they were even suspected of adultery, let
alone having it proved against them.

Hypocrisy undoubtedly ruled. Medieval attitudes towards sex and the sexes are suffused with it. On the one hand, women are the spawn of the devil, their lusts the perennial downfall of men. Yet the codes of courtly love set women on pedestals as models of chastity, beauty and purity which the lover, in desiring, imperilled. The paradoxes also embraced men – celibacy for both sexes was the ideal, yet motherhood was a woman's highest calling.

And then there was prostitution. Officially sanctioned brothels, or 'stews', were to be found everywhere, owned and managed by male 'stewholders'. They often paid rent to landlords such as the Bishop of Winchester, who owned land in Southwark, on the south side of the Thames in London, well known for its brothels. Prostitutes here were known as 'Winchester geese' because of the connection. A named procuress, Margaret, was active in this area in 1438; one of her girls was Isobel and another was Joan, who, records tell us, received twelve pence for sex with a client, out of which she had to give Margaret four. The appropriately named Cock Lane, at Smithfield in London, was another centre of the 'oldest profession'. A statute of 1384 condemned any prostitute found living outside the designated area of Cock Lane to be 'carted': taken from prison in a striped hood, carrying a white wand and accompanied by minstrels, to a pillory at Aldgate where her offence would be publicly proclaimed before she was escorted back to Cock Lane. Sometimes women were flogged at the back of the cart as well. Men found guilty of procuring prostitutes were made to stand in a pillory until set free by the mayor.

The Church and the landowning gentry were making a fortune from the trade; but when the prostitutes who were the basis of their profits died they could not be buried in consecrated ground. Echoes of this widespread and profitable activity are to be found to this day in the street names of cities and towns all over the country. The explicitly named Gropec**t Lanes in London, Oxford, York, Shrewsbury, Bristol, Newcastle and many other cities are now to be found hiding under much more respectable identities, such as Grape Lane in London and many other places, and Grove Lane in Oxford. Shrewsbury still has a Grope Lane, and Southwark still has Horselydown ('whores lie down') Lane. It was clearly a city-centre activity, central to urban life and important in both social and financial terms, while those who indulged in it were reviled and punished.

Despite all the occasions of sin that marriage and sex offered, and despite chastity being the highest calling for both women and men in a society of powerful religious institutions, marriage was still the norm at all levels of society. But in the days before parish registers and efficient communication, neither the secular nor the religious powers had full control over the process: cohabitation before marriage, bigamy and secret marriage were by no means uncommon.

Moreover, at this time the rituals of marriage were still unclear: there was no formal need to invoke the Church, and the initial 'spousals', or betrothal, were a binding contract, provided they took the form of a declaration before witnesses and were followed by consummation and cohabitation. Such marriages were irrevocable, unlike the vaguer form of spousals which were a promise to marry some time in the future; those agreements, provided there was no consummation, could be overturned later and were no impediment if one or other party decided to marry someone else. Family and neighbourhood peer pressure had its part to play in keeping things on the straight and narrow; but the rigidity of later regulations about marriage was yet to have any force.

Where property was involved, of course, matters were considerably more complicated, and status within society was also a fatal impediment to any matches felt to be injudicious or unsuitable. Margery Paston suffered in this way in 1469. A letter from her mother, Margaret, to Margery's brother, John II, tells the story. It seems that Margery had exchanged vows with Richard Calle, who was the family's bailiff and was therefore certainly not the husband Margaret wanted for her daughter. Margery was, however, adamant that she regarded her vows as binding, and nothing that her family or the Bishop of Norwich could say would make her change her mind. The consequence was predictable; as Margaret wrote to John, 'I charged my servants that she should not be received in mine house ... and I sent to one or two more that they should not receive her if she came.' Banishment from the family was the penalty for a marriage regarded as unsuitable; and, as her mother went on to say, 'remember you, and so do I, that we have lost of her but a brethel [a good-for-nothing].'

Her other brother, also John, assured his brother that he, too, was against the match: 'he should never have my good will for to make my sister to sell candle and mustard in Framlingham.' But in the same letter he asks his brother 'to send to Richard Calle to deliver me money...'. It seems that the family were unwilling to lose the services of an efficient and trusted bailiff; they could repudiate Margery but would continue to employ her husband, clearly putting their own convenience before their repugnance at their daughter's choice of husband. Another Paston servant was less fortunate. The continuation of his dalliance with Margery's sister, Anne, was successfully prevented when he was fired.

Margery Paston's story illustrates another aspect of marriage at this time, certainly among the moneyed classes: marriage for love was rare; money and position were considerably more important in marital affairs than any sort of compatibility between men and women. It was a deal, a matter of politics and financial gain, together with the need to carry on the line. A good wife was a brood mare and an efficient housekeeper; if she was easy on the eye and a pleasing sexual partner, that was added value. Men took mistresses for sexual gratification if their wives did not satisfy them in that department – and often when they did as well. In other words, most marriages among those with some sort of property to worry about were arranged.

This did not necessarily mean that affection, tolerance and even love itself failed to blossom once the deal had been done. The word 'love', however, must be treated with caution; it rarely carried any explicit sense of erotic desire, since such feelings were regarded as potentially sinful; nor was it to do with 'romance' in the modern sense. In the context of marriage as a transaction, it could only be hoped that the couple would grow to like and trust each other and be faithful and kind; of such pragmatic emotion did successful marriages consist. And although the wife was invariably expected to be obedient to her husband, her role was as a partner in the family business – managing the household, dealing with affairs in her husband's absence, bearing the children and keeping the whole enterprise up and running.

Yet another Paston, Elizabeth, daughter of Agnes Paston, is an example of what could happen to women who defied their parents' wishes in matters of matrimony. When Elizabeth expressed an obstinate wish to marry for love, she was confined to the house, forbidden to speak to any visitors or male servants and beaten 'once in the week or twice, and sometimes twice on a day, and her head broken in two or three places.'

There were occasions where a woman's preference was taken into account, provided the man chosen was of a fitting rank and rich enough. Margery Brews reaped the benefit of such indulgence, when both her mother and her prospective husband's mother approved of her choice of John Paston III; she fared rather better than her namesake and sister-in-law. There are even a few cases where a doting father suggested that his daughter and her young man marry in secret, despite the objections of the man's family. One suspects here that the financial advantage of the match was on the side of the daughter!

However, even in cases such as Margery Brews' where there appears to have been affection on both sides (although one suspects her feelings ran rather deeper than his), the matter of money appears to have been the absolute bottom line. John III tried until he was thirty-three to find the 'right' wife – a woman of good family, reasonably attractive and rich. Her wealth was the crucial element: when he started to despair of ever finding someone suitable, he told his brother that he would settle for 'some old thrifty draff wife [ale wife]' as long as she had enough money. When he finally met Margery, who was seventeen, the prospects for the match were not great as her family was not as rich as he hoped. Moreover, there were other daughters so her dowry would be small.

Her letters to her 'Valentine' are poignant: 'I commend myself to you with all my heart, desiring to hear of your happiness... And if it please you to hear how I am, I am not in good health in body nor in heart, nor will be until I hear from you... And my lady my mother has pursued the matter with my father very industriously, but she cannot any more than you know of, because of which, God knows, I am very sorry... But if you love me, as I truly believe you do, you will not leave me because of that. Because even if you did not have half the wealth that you do, and I had to undertake the greatest toil that any woman alive should, I would not forsake you...'.

Margery's next letter makes it clear that mutual liking was not enough for John. 'As for myself, I have done and endured in the business as much as I know how or am able to, God knows. And I want you to understand clearly that my father refuses to part with any more money than 100 [pounds] and 50 marks in this business, which is far from fulfilling your wishes... For which reason, if you could be content with that amount and my poor person, I would be the happiest maid on earth. And if you do not consider yourself satisfied with that, or believe that you could get more money, as I have understood from you before, good, faithful and loving Valentine, do not take the trouble to visit anymore on this business. Rather let it be finished and never spoken of again, on condition that I may be your faithful friend and petitioner for the duration of my life.'

Mainly because their mothers intervened, John and Margery did indeed marry and had several children. But, like most men of the time, he seems to have spent much time away, as another letter testifies: 'It seems to my mother-in-law that she has not heard from you for a long time. She is in good health, blessed be God, and all your babies are too. I am surprised that I hear nothing from you, which greatly troubles me. I sent you a letter by the son of Brasier of Norwich, of which I have not heard a word... Sir, I entreat you that it will please you to send for me, if you remain long in London, because it seems to me a long time since I lay in your arms.'

Chaucer's *Wife of Bath's Tale* illustrates a deeper aspect of women's role in the medieval world, and one which has resonances with modern feminism. It tells of an errant Arthurian knight, convicted of rape and condemned to death, but reprieved at the urging of the queen, who gave him a year and a day to seek out the answer to the question, 'What thing is it that wommen moost desiren?' Far and wide he ranged, getting so many different answers that he despaired of saving his life – until he met an ugly old woman, 'a fouler wight ther may no man devyse', who promised to give him the answer if he in turn would agree to do the first thing that she required of him after he had successfully gained his freedom and his life. The answer she provided – that women desire to have dominion over their husbands and their lovers – was something no woman at the court could deny: 'ne was ther wyf, ne mayde, ne wydwe, that contraried that he sayde.'

He duly gained his life and his freedom; but the demand the old woman made was that he marry her. He tossed and turned in bed on their first night together, unable to carry out a husband's marital duty towards this abhorrent creature, berating her for being hideous, old, poor and low-born. She replied to him at length and with eloquence, pointing out the innate contradictions in his stance: that noble birth does not always result in nobility of mind or action; that it is churlishness that makes a churl; that poverty can often draw one close to God; and that he is unlikely to become a cuckold if he has an aged wife. She then offered him the choice of having her old and ugly but faithful to him, or young and beautiful and the object of jealous adoration. Chastened, he left the choice to her, and was overjoyed to hear that she would be both beautiful and faithful. He really didn't deserve her; one is reminded of Elizabeth Bennet's reproach to Mr Darcy in *Pride and Prejudice*, that he had not 'behaved in a more gentleman-like manner'. Yet *The Wife of Bath's Tale* was written over four hundred years earlier.

The Wife's plea at the end of the tale, that 'Jhesu Crist us sende Housebondes meeke, yonge, and fresh abedde', is echoed in her own life story, as told in the Prologue to her tale. Now on her fifth husband, she makes a passionate case for the pleasures of the bed, and is completely open about the wiles and stratagems she used to entwine her husbands. She also argues long and forcefully against the apparent superiority of virginity over the condition of being a wife, and a wife who has buried four husbands at that. Genitalia, she affirms, were not made just for the emission of urine; and even if wives are mere barley-bread in comparison to the pure wheat seed of virginity, 'In wyfhod I wol use my instrument as freely as my Makere hath it sent.' She rails against the double standard, too, tearing pages out of the misogynist book her husband has been reading and forcing him to cede control of the household to her. Altogether, the Wife of Bath's narrative is a neat illustration of the contradiction between women's formal subservience to their husbands and the power of their dominance within the home. And her tale makes it clear that widowhood was one of the few states for women in the Middle Ages where they could arrange to hold all the cards. It was Magna Carta that underpinned the strength of their position: before the new laws contained in that charter were imposed on him, the king had the right to sell off widowed noblewomen to the highest bidder. Some were even kidnapped so that the king could be sure of collecting his fee.

The Wife of Bath is a bawdy creature, too, her obvious eroticism echoed in the Anglo-Saxon words she uses. At least her sexual exploits were within marriage (on the whole – there are sly hints that she may not always have trodden the way of faithfulness). Two of the tales that precede hers in *The Canterbury Tales* are bawdy, too, but these are about infidelity and cuckoldry. The Miller first relates the story of a carpenter who was tricked by his young wife and her lover, and the Reeve (who happens also to be a carpenter, and is therefore rather aggrieved by the Miller's aspersions on a member of his own profession) then gets his own back on the Miller by recounting the tale of a miller whose wife and daughter were both seduced in his own house by two young men.

The carpenter in *The Miller's Tale* has a young wife, Alison, who is lusted after by the lodger, a clerk called Nicholas. They make a plan to dupe the carpenter so that they can spend all night in bed together, and the plan duly works. But Alison has another admirer, Absolon, who chooses the night they are together to serenade her and will only go away when she offers him a kiss. He does not get quite what he wants:

> Derk was the nyght as pich, or as the cole,
> And at the wyndow out she putte hir hole,
> And Absolon, hym fil no bet ne wers,
> But with his mouth he kiste hir naked ers
> Ful savourly, er he were war of this.
> Abak he stirte, and thoughte it was amys,
> For wel he wiste a womman hath no berd.
> He felte a thing al rough and long yherd,
> And seyde, 'Fy! allas! what have I to do?'
> 'Tehee!' quod she, and clapte the wyndow to…

The Reeve's Tale is a farce by comparison, with two young Cambridge men staying in the carpenter's house while they are collecting corn from him and bed-hopping the whole night through, making love to both his young daughter and his wife who, it seems, had not enjoyed such passionate sex for a while: 'So myrie a fit ne hadde she nat ful yore.'

Chaucer's lusty language and open celebration of these affairs may be fiction; but his works are one of the very few ways in which we can catch a glimpse of daily life as it was for the ordinary people of the time – the artisans, tradesmen, wives, travellers, pilgrims who do not make it into the documents and records of the period and hence into the history books. These stories tell us that young women married old men – the Wife of Bath was twelve when she was first married, and her first three husbands were all much older than she was; that these older men could often be relied on to predecease their wives – so wives turned into widows with regularity, and often rich widows who could dictate their terms to any new suitor; that the puritanical and prurient views of the Church about sex and marriage were not always reflected in the behaviour and needs of those to whom the preaching was addressed. Fines imposed on village women for fornication and bearing illegitimate children were a useful source of income for the lord of the manor in the Middle Ages.

As Lawrence Stone points out, sexual behaviour among the lower classes can often only be deduced from such records as exist of children born less than nine months after marriage; and for this early period such records are rare. However, he relates a story told by the Italian diplomat and cleric who later became Pope Pius II, of an incident that happened to him when he was travelling through Northumberland in the middle of the fifteenth century. Stopping for the night in a remote village in the border country where raiders were common, he found himself abandoned with the women after dark while the men and children took themselves off to a fortified tower. The reason given was that the worst that could happen to the women was that they would be raped, which was not seen by the village men as anything reprehensible or to be feared. Chastity was clearly not valued by either sex, as he further found when two of the women offered to sleep with him; he declined, in case he might have his throat cut by night raiders while in a state of mortal sin. Almost as shocking is that these people seemed to acknowledge no duty of care to a casual guest who had thrown himself on their hospitality; no invitation to join the other men in the tower was forthcoming.

We know more, of course, about the morals and activities of the nobility and gentry; their lives and actions had a strong influence on the development of all aspects of history – political, financial and cultural. These were the literate classes, men and women both, who wrote letters to each other, who disposed of their property in wills which have survived, whose marriage settlements are recorded. At the very top of society, among royalty and the powerful barons, marriages were great affairs of state, negotiated carefully and tightly as the means of building power bases, forging useful alliances, amalgamating land and wealth and repairing damaging feuds and rifts.

As with other levels of society, however, the political and financial basis of such marriages did not always preclude affection and even love. Edward I was famously enamoured of his wife, Eleanor of Castile: the crosses he had erected wherever her body rested on its journey back to London after her death near Lincoln in 1290 are still extant testimony to his feelings, though only three originals now survive.

But monarchs and lords also regularly took mistresses and their illegitimate children were usually acknowledged by their fathers, brought up as part of the royal or baronial household with the full knowledge and agreement of the legitimate wife and went on to well-regarded positions in high society – even if they could not, after the Church began to impose its will on the laws of marriage and inheritance in the thirteenth century, automatically inherit titles or property. The records that survive show that, at this level of society, illegitimate daughters usually married well, and sons were granted land and honours and led successful, high-profile lives. It is worth remembering that William the Conqueror, taunted through life as William the Bastard, was able to inherit the dukedom of Normandy from his father despite his birth – and from that strong power base to invade and conquer Saxon England.

Mistresses frequently had almost as much influence as wives – unsurprisingly, perhaps, since they were chosen for their beauty and/or charm rather than for their connections, though many of them, as it happened, were also high-born. Henry II's famous mistress, Rosamund Clifford, was the daughter of marcher lord Walter Clifford. Fair Rosamund, as she was known in later legend, was openly acknowledged by the king after his powerful wife, Eleanor of Aquitaine, supported her sons in rebellion against their father, and her relationship with Henry continued until she retired to a nunnery at Godstow, near Oxford, shortly before her death. Her tomb in the convent's church, paid for by Henry and the Clifford family, became a place of local pilgrimage until the Bishop of Lincoln condemned her as a harlot and ordered her remains to be moved outside the building.

Tales about her abounded for centuries, especially the one where Henry built her a retreat within a maze and marked the path through to the centre by a hidden silver thread. As the story goes, Eleanor found the thread and followed it through to discover Rosamund, whom she then had poisoned. Fair Rosamund's name lives on to this day in roses named after her.

Henry's other mistresses included Ida, Countess of Norfolk, who bore him a son, and a woman known only as Ykenai whose son, Geoffrey Plantagenet, one of Henry's favourites, became Archbishop of York. No barrier to progress, or shame indeed, it seems, in being the illegitimate son of a king and a woman whose family may not have been of the highest rank. The Bishop of Durham and the Abbess of Barking were also Henry's illegitimate children, and after his wife's defection to the cause of her sons against her husband, he started negotiations to annul his marriage to Eleanor and marry Alys, daughter of the king of France – even though she was already betrothed to his son, Richard. Nor did he wait until the marriage was agreed before taking her to his bed and allegedly making her pregnant. One wonders whether his antipathy towards his son played some part in this affair; he is reported as whispering to Richard, while apparently giving him the kiss of peace, 'May the Lord never permit me to die until I have taken due vengeance upon you.'

It could undoubtedly be a good career move to become a king's mistress in the Middle Ages. Edward III's mistress, Alice Perrers, was a lady-in-waiting to his queen, Philippa of Hainault, and after her death became his semi-official consort. Edward lavished gifts on her, including Philippa's jewellery, and she bore him at least four children, one while Philippa was still alive. The story goes that, as he lay on his deathbed, Alice forced the rings off his fingers, and she certainly had to endure years of litigation after his death while the authorities tried to wrest back some of the wealth he had bestowed on her.

It may have been an illicit liaison during Edward III's long reign that occasioned the foundation of that most noble and august institution, the Order of the Garter. It seems that Edward was dancing with the Countess of Salisbury at a ball when her garter fell onto the floor. While those around stood sniggering, Edward picked it up and fastened it round his own leg with the words '*Honi soit qui mal y pense*' ('shamed be he who evil thinks'), which remains the Order's motto to this day. This may have been just a chivalrous action, or it may be that the Countess was his mistress; in either case it is intriguing that the origins of England's premier order of chivalry may lie in the medieval version of 'no laughing up your sleeve, please'.

It seems clear from many of these stories that there was some tension between the precepts of the Church at this period and real life as it was lived among high society. Although birth outside the bounds of matrimony was usually no barrier to progression within all the careers then open to young men of nobility, even the Church, Rosamund Clifford could still be denounced as a harlot by a bishop. Perhaps the reality was that, just as the double standard in sexual behaviour between men and women was never questioned, so the deference accorded to birth and power meant that men of rank could do more or less as they pleased. After all, their wealth could buy prayers and indulgences while they were alive to ensure that their immortal souls were forgiven their earthly sins after death. As ever, it was the poor and the 'ordinary' folk who were made to abide strictly by the formal laws of the Church.

No matter how inclined they were to take and maintain strings of mistresses, kings and great lords married for status and property, and in

accordance with the wise counsel of their advisers. And in many cases –
at least where there was compatibility between the parties – these marriages were successful and affectionate. But there was one royal marriage, at the height of the Wars of the Roses, which was nearly the ruin of
the king and had enduring political effects. This was the marriage of
Edward IV to Elizabeth Woodville, conducted in secret and as a consequence of love (or lust). Edward fell head over heels for Elizabeth, whose
fair beauty was legendary, and who was a widow with children. But she
knew where her best interests lay and refused to become his mistress.
Their secret marriage in 1464 infuriated the powerful Earl of Warwick,
whose support had been vital during Edward's tussles for the throne
with Henry VI and who had been in the throes of arranging a match for
Edward with the French royal family. Warwick promptly took Edward
prisoner, forced him into exile and restored Henry VI to the throne.
After Edward's return and defeat of Warwick at the Battle of Barnet,
Elizabeth's Woodville family found themselves in a position of high
influence, which they used to the full.

Edward IV's own legitimacy has been called into question in recent
years, and with it that of the British monarchy. Recent research seems to
indicate that his father, Richard of York, may have been away campaigning during the crucial time of Edward's conception. Similar charges of
illegitimacy were made against Edward's sons, Edward V and Richard –
the Princes in the Tower – though these are usually regarded as fabri-
cated by the supporters of Richard III's right to the throne. The claims
are based on yet another secret marriage that Edward is supposed to have
entered into, this time to Lady Eleanor Talbot, a year or so before his
slightly less secret marriage to Elizabeth Woodville. Lady Eleanor and
the child she had borne to Edward, a boy called Edward de Wigmore,
died three years after his marriage to Elizabeth. Like other medieval
monarchs, Edward had several illegitimate children by a variety of mistresses, and all took the surname Plantagenet. One daughter is recorded
as being present at the funeral of her stepmother, Queen Elizabeth, and
another married Sir Thomas Lumley in 1477. Once again, being the 'bar
sinister' children of the monarch appears to have been no impediment
to acceptance in society at this time.

However, kings also had mistresses of lowlier rank. One of Edward's,
Jane Shore, was the first of the three whom he described respectively as
'the merriest, the wiliest and the holiest harlots in the realm'. She was

relatively low-born, being the daughter of a London merchant, and was a small, round-faced woman who was reputedly more captivating for her conversation than her beauty. Edward was obviously sufficiently entranced to have maintained his dalliance with her until his death, and she lived on until the late 1520s, still – according to Sir Thomas More, who met her – showing signs of her old allure. After Edward's death she took up with other lovers, notably Thomas Grey, first Marquess of Dorset, who was the oldest son of Elizabeth Woodville and thus one of Edward IV's stepchildren. Another lover was Lord Hastings, later to be executed over a log in the courtyard of the Tower of London – the first actual recorded execution there – probably because he would have opposed plans to depose Edward V in favour of his uncle, Richard III.

Jane Shore was made to do a public penance for her promiscuity, and was also imprisoned. However, the King's Solicitor, Thomas Lynom, became so enamoured of her while she was locked up that he entered into a contract of marriage with her, despite Richard III's attempt to persuade him against the match. Marry they did, and had a daughter. Her charms must have been spectacular.

For those with property, marriage was a contract that – if all went well – resulted in children to carry on the line and the consolidation of great estates. But for those whose wealth and position were compromised in some way – perhaps by being younger sons – marriage was not always a viable option. It cost money to maintain a wife and family in accustomed comfort and state, and money for those lower down in the family pecking order was not always available. Nor was marriage always an attractive option. John Paston II was regarded by his parents as rather feckless because he preferred to hang around in London, on the edges of the court of Edward IV, rather than settle to his responsibilities. An engagement was arranged between him and Anne Haute, a cousin of the queen, Elizabeth Woodville, but nothing came of it and he died unmarried. He did, however, have at least two mistresses and two illegitimate children.

For others, the Church was a good career option, though probably after they had sown their wild oats since a vow of celibacy was required, even if it was not always adhered to. Prelates were often rich and powerful officers of the state, and monasteries were crucial to the economic and social infrastructure of medieval society, so membership of a religious order was not at all the total revocation of worldly goods that the vows of poverty, chastity and obedience might have indicated. For women, too, a nunnery could offer a happy refuge after widowhood, or a retreat for those for whom marriage was not an option – though there were also recorded instances, including notorious places in Venice for example, where the nuns were infamous for dissolute living. In societies where younger sons were dissuaded from marriage in order not to spread the family wealth too widely, the lack of husbands meant that many young women were dispatched to convents as the only respectable places for them. It is perhaps not surprising that they often failed to accept the celibacy that such institutions demanded. San Lorenzo convent in Venice was particularly well known in the medieval period for the lustiness of its inmates. The Council of Venice sought to check some of the fornication by passing laws in the fourteenth century to ensure that convent chaplains had to be at least fifty years of age and confessors – an even more tempting prospect, apparently – at least sixty. Assignations between the nuns and their lovers, known as *monachini*, continued nonetheless.

There was a long tradition of gossip about what went on behind the monastery grilles – with, one suspects, some justification. St Aelred, Abbot of Rievaulx, has been adopted as a patron saint of today's gay Catholic fraternity, particularly in America, where websites are devoted to 'St Aelred the Queer'. Celibate he may have been, but his lyrical writings on friendship between men seem to indicate that he recognized his own sexuality and chose to subordinate it to the higher love of God. He was indeed one of the first who is recorded as regularly taking cold baths to subdue his carnal desires.

As he wrote to his sister, a nun: 'Do not imagine that men in the absence of women and women in the absence of men cannot defile themselves, for the detestable sin that inflames a man with passion for a man (*vir in virum*) or a woman for a woman (*femina in feminam*) is judged more serious than any other crime.'

It seems that he was castigating himself for his own misspent youth, and he went on to scold two old monks who, although they still slept together in the same bed, cuddling and kissing, nevertheless believed themselves still to be chaste since at their age they were powerless to commit sin.

Aelred had strong spiritual friendships with the younger monks of Rievaulx, in particular one Simon, who was fourteen when he entered the monastery. Simon was of high birth and exceptionally devout, and had given up all his wealth and prospects in favour of his calling to the monastic life. He was frail, and very beautiful, and Aelred was heartbroken when he died young. He went into transports of sorrow for the young monk, whom he called 'my gentlest friend', 'my beloved brother', 'the one-in-heart with me' and 'sweeter to me than all sweet things in life'. Death had torn Simon from 'my embrace, from my kisses, from the sight of my eyes. It was as if my body had been eviscerated and my helpless soul rent in pieces... Oh wretched life, Oh grievous life, a life without Simon.' But he remained chaste in his own eyes, likening his love for Simon with Christ's love for John, 'the beloved disciple', whose virgin love for the virgin Christ was a paradigm of holy masculine adoration.

Homosexuality – or sodomy, which was the word for it in the Middle Ages on the basis that it was the sin that caused the destruction of the cities of Sodom and Gomorrah – was of course illegal, unchristian and reviled. But it seems to have been widely practised, though hard evidence is difficult to come by for this early period. The word 'sodomy' had a wider meaning than just that of same-sex relationships; it also referred to sexual practices that could not result in conception, whether heterosexual or homosexual, so that it was perfectly possible to commit sodomy within marriage. It also seems that, for many men, it was their role in the sex act rather than the sex of their partner which was important: it was masculine to be dominant, regardless of whether the dominance was over a woman or a man. Adolescent boys, therefore, acted the passive role with older men until they were in their twenties, when they took over as the active partner. Then often, once they reached their thirties, they settled down and took wives.

One remarkable document, which came to light only in the 1990s, is the earliest known account of same-sex intercourse, though some at least of the men in the case believed themselves to be sleeping with a woman. Dating from 1395, it concerns a prostitute brought before the City of London aldermen. She had been found with a man called John Britby, who knew her as Eleanor. However, when she was examined she turned out to be a man whose name was John Rykener. When he was asked who had taught him to 'practice this detestable vice in the manner of a woman' and with whom he had committed that 'libidinous and unspeakable act', Rykener was admirably frank. A whore called Anna had taught him, another woman called Elizabeth had dressed him in women's clothes and the same Elizabeth had procured her daughter as a substitute for Rykener in bed in a dark room at night. Reading between the lines, it seems that some of Rykener's customers indulged in sex with him, though it is not clear whether they realized that he was a man in women's clothing, while others had ordinary sex with a woman who they believed was Rykener but was not.

He named names, too – and many of them were clergymen. One was Phillip, a rector, and there were also two Franciscans, one called Brother Michael and the other Brother John, three chaplains in London and a Carmelite friar. Many more priests had 'committed that vice' with him, and he was particularly happy to accommodate them because they gave him more money than other men. He also named three Oxford scholars who had done it with him several times: one was Sir William Foxlee, another Sir John and the third Sir Walter. He also confessed that he often had sex as a man with nuns and with other women, married or not. The outcome of this case is, regretfully, unknown; but it was buried in the reference works under a short and uninformative summary, presumably to suppress the homosexual and transvestite content.

There was plenty of it about, however. Richard I is widely thought to have been homosexual, despite being 'the Lionheart'; his sexual preferences defied the stereotype of camp effeminacy if his bloody deeds are any guide. But a century later, Edward I had to expend a great deal of paternal and political effort to put some masculine grit into his son, later to become Edward II. Although the young man was dragged into his father's Scottish wars, and entered into an arranged marriage with Isabella, daughter of the king of France, he preferred sport and plays to warfare and spent as much time as possible away from his wife. They did produce children, and Edward also had at least one illegitimate child, but he much preferred to spend his time with Piers Gaveston, a young lord from Gascony, who had been part of his household from boyhood. Edward was much influenced by Gaveston, and they are assumed to have had a homosexual relationship. Whatever the truth, after Edward demanded favours and honours for Gaveston which were far greater than his station in life warranted, the king banished him, and it was only after Edward I's death and the accession of his son that Gaveston was allowed to return.

His influence over the weak and vacuous Edward was unabated, and after the disaster of the Battle of Bannockburn, when Edward lost most of his father's gains in Scotland to Robert the Bruce, Gaveston attracted the enmity of the powerful English barons. He was eventually forced to surrender to the Earl of Warwick with the promise of a safe-conduct, but was taken to Warwick Castle and beheaded. Contemporaries certainly believed both that Gaveston had exerted undue influence over Edward and that they had enjoyed an illicit relationship. The sixteenth-century poet Michael Drayton wrote explicitly about the nature of their friendship in his poem *Peirs Gaveston* [*sic*]. Gaveston first describes his seduction of Edward:

> This *Edward* in the Aprill of his age,
> Whil'st yet the Crowne sate on his fathers head
> My *Jove* with me, his *Ganimed*, his page,
> Frolick as May, a lustie life we led:
> He might commaund, he was my Soveraigns sonne,
> And what I saide, by him was ever done.
> My words as lawes, Autentique he alloude,
> Mine yea, by him was never crost with no,
> All my conceite as currant he avowde,
> And as my shadowe still he served so,
> My hand the racket, he the tennis ball,
> My voyces echo, answering every call...
> My breast his pillow, where he laide his head,
> Mine eyes his booke, my bosome was his bed...
> His love-sick lippes at every kissing qualme,
> Cling to my lippes, to cure their griefe with balme.

Then follows Edward's lament for his dead lover:

> O end my dayes, for now my joyes are done
> Wanting my Peirs, my sweetest Gaveston.
> Farewell my love, companion of my youth
> My soules delight, the subject of my mirth,
> My second selfe if I reporte the truth,
> The rare and onely *Phenix* of the earth
> Farewell sweete friend, with thee my joyes are gone,
> farewell mv *Peirs*, my lovely Gaveston...

After Gaveston's death, Edward came under the influence of even more baleful advisers in the form of Hugh le Despenser and his son. Queen Isabella and the barons had had more than enough, and eventually forced the king to abdicate in favour of the young Edward III. The

Despensers died horrible deaths and Isabella — now glorying in the nick-name 'the She-Wolf of France' — reigned in her son's name with her lover, Roger Mortimer. What happened to Edward II is disputed, but the goriest story is that he was killed at Berkeley Castle by murderers who demonstrated their dislike of his homosexuality by inserting a red-hot poker into his intestines. It is an unlikely scenario, even given the brutal-ity of the age, and he was later very much avenged by his son after he ascended the throne; Edward III banished his mother to her country homes (where she led a comfortable life), but condemned Mortimer, without a trial, to be ignominiously hanged at Tyburn — a form of execu-tion not normally the fate of noblemen.

Within Edward III's many progeny lay the seeds of the Wars of the Roses which were to divide England in the fifteenth century. These civil wars ended only with the coming of the Tudors, the dynasty which was to make huge changes to religious and marital customs. The complexity of reconciling emotional turbulence and the rules of courtly love with daily life was fading away, along with other medieval attitudes. Life at the end of the fifteenth century was still short, still local, still firmly set within a Christian perspective of eternal damnation for mortal sin. One side of the coin was still the sort of family life as had been lived a century earlier by the Pastons, affectionate, loyal and friendly but working firmly within the rules of property and class; the other side still echoed Chaucer's celebration of bawdy comedy within an amoral world. But for some, at least, the world was about to widen, offering challenges to reli-gious values and social mores alike. New questions would soon be asked, and many would be put in danger for asking them, but all across society people would go on loving and lusting, just as they always had.

Two · Making merry in Merrie England

THE SIXTEENTH and seventeenth centuries were dramatic times. They saw a breakaway religious movement with sometimes dire effects for people at all levels of society; rapid exploration and expansion overseas; the union of England and Scotland under a single monarch; a bloody civil war during which the son of that monarch was beheaded; a decade of Commonwealth rule; and finally the restoration of the kings and the court. For those in high places there was both the splendour and the uncertainty of change and movement within royal and political spheres; while for the ordinary people daily life went on much as before — apart from the consequences of the religious upheavals which affected them just as much as they did their masters. Above all, these were centuries when religion — always at the heart of life — became no longer the trusted given it had always been, but something perilous and frightening.

It is hard for modern people, who live in both a secular and a multi-faith world, to understand how groaningly fearful sixteenth-century folk would have been of Henry VIII's repudiation of Rome, the seat of the power of God as expressed through his Church, the ultimate controller, in that religious world, of everything. Henry's dissolution of the monasteries removed a fundamental plank of the economy, and threw out into the world men and women whose role as educators, farmers, industrialists and hoteliers had always been vital both nationally and locally. Most of them received pensions or returned to their families; but it is questionable how individuals, and the society which had nurtured them and their way of life, were able to deal with their new secular circumstances. For those who had taken full vows, marriage was no longer an option and any relationship would be mortal sin. And for all there was continual religious change: Catholicism was driven underground; Protestantism took on extreme forms under the Commonwealth; and the fear of a Catholic resurgence under the restored Stuarts prompted the banishment of King James II and the eventual establishment of a whole new dynasty.

While it is still difficult to piece together much about the daily lives of ordinary people, public records were beginning to become the norm. In 1538 Thomas Cromwell ordered every parish to keep a record of its weddings, christenings and burials; they were to be entered into a book each Sunday after the service and kept in a 'sure coffer' with two locks. Towards the end of Elizabeth I's reign a new ruling ordered that the records should be entered on longer-lived parchment, and that a complete copy of the previous records from the beginning should be made. At the same time bishops' transcripts were established – an annual return to the bishop of each parish's records for the previous year. These records, together with those of both the ecclesiastical and the civil courts, begin to give a broader picture of life as it was lived day to day. And, as ever, marriages and morals were to be found at the centre of such daily life, whether within high society – Henry VIII's multiple marriages, followed a hundred and fifty years later by the profligacy of Charles II's restored court – or among the more local stories of humbler people.

It is perhaps ironic to recall that it was Henry's urgent need for a legitimate male heir which drove his repudiation of papal sovereignty over the laws of marriage. The need for a new governance on annulment and divorce was at the root of Henry's assumption of the role of Supreme Head of the Church of England – a role subsequently undertaken by much more strait-laced recent monarchs. Henry's England was still tied firmly to the old faith. Yet politics triumphed over religion, and created a new dispensation where barren – or unsatisfactory – wives could be cast away and serial marriages undertaken.

The fates of Henry's six wives are recalled through the chant 'Divorced, Beheaded, Died, Divorced, Beheaded, Survived'. Even his first marriage was unconventional, in that Catherine of Aragon had been married to his older brother Arthur, but only for a few months before Arthur died. Henry, still loyal at this point to Rome, got a papal dispensation to marry his brother's wife on the grounds that the marriage had never been consummated, and they duly wed when Henry became king in 1509. She endured six pregnancies, but only one child survived – and she was a girl.

Henry, of course, like kings before and after him, had had several extra-marital liaisons, and his roving eye now settled on Anne Boleyn, younger sister of Mary, one of his mistresses. He later said that Anne had 'bewitched' him, and his feelings for her were both lustful and charmed: she was a spirited and intelligent woman, accomplished in all the arts needed by ladies of the time. However, she resisted following her sister into Henry's bed, and held out for marriage. This time the pope was not so accommodating, and refused to annul the marriage to Catherine. So Henry resorted to the logic-chopping at which he and his advisers were so adept, and cited the stricture in Leviticus whereby 'If a man shall take his brother's wife it is an unclean thing... and they shall be childless.' His marriage, on that basis, was clearly incestuous and illicit so he now proclaimed an annulment on his own account. He had already secretly married Anne anyway in early 1533. Catherine was never reconciled to the situation, and steadfastly withstood either accepting the title of princess dowager or acknowledging the Act of Succession and the Act of Supremacy. Nor would she quietly retire to a nunnery. But the deed was done and Anne was now queen.

The annulment of Henry's first marriage meant that his daughter, Mary, was now illegitimate. However, it was only among those who had accepted the new Protestantism that Anne and the daughter she bore to Henry, Elizabeth, were legitimate in their turn; to those who continued in their allegiance to Rome – including the whole of Catholic Europe – Henry's marriage to Anne was bigamous, she was a mere concubine and her daughter was a bastard. Moreover, she failed to produce the longed-for male heir; and when the birth of a stillborn son coincided with Catherine of Aragon's death, Henry realized that he could make himself technically free to marry again. So he accused Anne of treason, adultery and incest with her brother and she was condemned to the headsman's block. Henry was free to marry again, in the eyes of both Catholics and Protestants, and his next wife, Jane Seymour, finally produced a male heir, though she died in the process.

The convolutions of Henry's marital adventures now meant that both his daughters were illegitimate, their status as such confirmed by an Act of Parliament in 1536. But he continued to care for them, and after Edward's birth – perhaps in recognition that he was unlikely to have more children – he included them in the succession: first Edward and any heirs, then Mary, then Elizabeth. Mary took care to reverse her own illegitimacy when she became queen; Elizabeth didn't bother.

Henry's marriage to wife number four, Anne of Cleves, lasted a mere six months and was never consummated, which gave valid grounds for an annulment. Catherine Howard now entranced the fifty-year-old king with her youth and high spirits, but she was a silly young girl and was certainly guilty of the adultery of which she was accused. To her credit, when offered the option of a divorce on the grounds of a previous betrothal, she refused. She was beheaded, aged only nineteen or twenty, in the Tower – a fate rather more merciful than that suffered by the two young men who were accused of being her lovers. Francis Dereham and Thomas Culpepper were hanged, drawn and quartered.

Wife number six, Catherine Parr, already twice widowed, survived the king, who died in January 1547, and married Thomas Seymour, brother both of the late Queen Jane and of Edward, Duke of Somerset, who had been appointed Lord Protector during the new young king's childhood. Thomas Seymour was a man inclined to take his chances where he could. Before his marriage to their stepmother, he is said to have made passes at both princesses while they were living with her, and later to have indulged in the sort of horseplay with Elizabeth that might be regarded as introducing her to the pleasures of courtship. But when Catherine caught him and the princess in a rather more compromising position, there was a furious row and Elizabeth was sent away. He went too far, however, when, after Catherine died in childbirth only eighteen months after Henry VIII's death, he resumed his advances to Elizabeth and suggested marriage. His brother, the Lord Protector, was furious and had him arrested for treason, one of the charges being that he had plotted to marry the king's sister. Elizabeth found herself having to deny that she had been seduced and even that she was carrying Seymour's child. He was executed.

Catherine Parr's pregnancy by Seymour – she was still only in her thirties – fuelled rumours that it may have been Henry's infertility that led to his last three queens all being childless by him. For many years before he died he suffered from badly ulcerated legs, which has led to speculation that he may have suffered from syphilis, a disease that could also have caused him to be infertile. He did, however, have one acknowledged illegitimate son, born in 1519 to Elizabeth Blount, who had come to court as a maid of honour to Catherine of Aragon. The child was named Henry Fitzroy and was later created a duke. 'Bless 'ee, Bessie Blount' was a common saying at the time, in acknowledgement of her role in proving that Henry was not totally impotent when it came to producing sons.

Mary Boleyn is much less well known than her younger sister, but like Bessie Blount she was one of Henry's few long-standing mistresses – most of his affairs were very short-lived – and she, too, may have borne him a son. Lady Bullen, Mary's and Anne's mother, was a high-born

Howard, but their father came from lowlier stock and so relied very much on the charms of his daughters for worldly advancement. He may have first managed to get Mary into the entourage of Henry's sister, Mary Tudor, when she went to France to marry Louis XII, who lived for only three months after the wedding, and it is rumoured that she stayed on as part of the court of the new king, Francis I, and in due course became his mistress; his affectionate name for her was 'my English mare'. Both Mary and Anne Boleyn were present at the Field of the Cloth of Gold, after which the sisters returned to England. But Mary had caught Henry's eye, and her speedy marriage to William Carey freed her up to become his bedfellow. Her husband was duly given a role at court which allowed the newlyweds to live there so that she was close at hand.

The relationship with the king persisted for six years, and it was during these years that she produced her first child, a son named Henry. Whatever the truth of his paternity, the king chose not to acknowledge him, but he did take care to provide for him after William Carey's death and the boy grew up to become a favourite at the court of Elizabeth I. Mary later went on to create yet more scandal – and to antagonize her sister – when she secretly married Sir William Stafford, a young man of unsuitable rank. It was only when she became pregnant, two years later, that the marriage became public knowledge. Her family were scandalized. Mary had married a man of lower standing for love, and she also had the temerity to be carrying a child when her sister, the queen, desperately needed to be in the same situation. She and her husband were banished from court and she was disowned by her family. She was probably lucky: not only, as she later wrote to Thomas Cromwell, 'could I never have had one who loved me so well, nor a more honest man', but her new obscurity probably saved her from the effects the rest of her family felt after Anne's downfall.

Sexual attraction was still frowned on as a basis for marriage; but in some cases at least, love and affection were recognized, and widows seem generally to have been free to choose their next husbands, even when their choice was contentious. The king's sister, Mary Tudor, Queen of France for a mere three months while her elderly husband lived, immediately after his death secretly married Charles Brandon, Duke of Suffolk. Her usefulness to Henry as a political wife was at an end, but as she reminded him, she had agreed to the French match on condition that he would allow her to choose her next husband freely. This marriage was 'the thing which I desired most in the world' though, as she hastened to assure him, she had not acted 'carnally, or of any sensual appetite'. A later Duchess of Suffolk scandalized Elizabeth I when she married a member of her household who was not only of a lower class but was also fifteen years her junior; and the widow of the heir to the earldom of Bath ran off with her stepfather's land agent. The kidnapping and forced marriage of wealthy widows who chose not to remarry was, however, not uncommon; the power and influence their wealth offered was not to be squandered.

Few aristocratic men of this era were censured for infidelity, and many of the surviving wills contain bequests to mistresses and their children; the legitimate family members were usually well aware of the arrangements made for their illegitimate counterparts, and they often formed a regular part of the extended household. Patronage and influence were powerful arguments against upsetting apple carts: Henry, Lord Stafford, was furious with his sister, the Duchess of Norfolk, when she complained about her husband moving his mistress into their main residence, particularly since she was also defying the king in objecting. Stafford was deeply fearful of losing such important support, to the extent that he refused to give his sister a home on the grounds that housing her would greatly jeopardize him and his family. Other women were more compliant, as a later example demonstrates: the Countess of Pembroke was on excellent terms with her husband's bastard son, and stipulated only that he should not be allowed to take the family name. He went on to enjoy a successful naval career and had a good relationship with his half-brother, the legitimate heir. It seems to have been generally the case at this period that the illegitimate sons of well-placed fathers were able to lead prosperous and successful lives; girls did less well, since their only option was marriage and here their birth told against them.

There is one instance when a man was forced to take the sacrament as demonstration that he had not committed adultery with the wife of another nobleman while his own wife was still alive. This was Sir William Compton, and the woman was Anne, sister of the third Duke of Buckingham and wife of George, Lord Hastings. Whatever the truth of what happened between them, there was clearly a strong attraction; her husband had consigned her to a nunnery after her brother found Sir William in her room only a short time after her marriage, and she also benefited in Compton's will both financially and by being included in the prayers for which he was paying. In another case, Sir Thomas Wyatt was released from the Tower in 1541 on condition that he repudiate his mistress, Elizabeth Darrell, with whom he was openly living, and return to his wife. Whether he complied or not is unknown, though it seems that he had left his wife twenty years earlier on the grounds of her adultery; and he certainly later provided for his mistress and his son by her in his will.

Women who committed adultery received short shrift by comparison, and punishments could be grievous, particularly when, in order to secure the survival of the true line, a woman suspected of adultery suffered the bastardization of her children. She could also be thrown out, like the wife of the Earl of Suffolk suspected of bigamously marrying Sir Edmund Knyvett, without 'money, men, women, meat, nor more than two gowns of velvet'. But on the other hand, many of them went on to marry their lovers after the death of their husbands. Joan Courteney, daughter of Sir William Courteney of Powderham, had a child during her marriage to William Beaumont by another man, Henry Bodrugan, and went on to marry him after Beaumont's death. Another case was that of Mary Darcy, who had no fewer than four children by Sir Richard Southwell when both he and she were married to other people. When her husband and his wife died, they married, and Sir Richard provided for all his children, legitimate and illegitimate, both while he was alive and in his will.

Some women resorted to elopement in order to be with their lovers, and resisted all efforts to bring them back to the straight and narrow. One such was the Duke of Suffolk's daughter, Anne, who left her husband, Lord Powys, to live with her lover, Randall Haworth. Although Lord Powys petitioned the Privy Council to punish her for persevering in her 'abomination and whoredom', she refused to comply and stayed with her lover until Powys's death, when she married him.

Others resisted the social conventions in other ways. It was during the reign of Henry VIII that the first legislation was passed outlawing homosexuality. The Buggery Act of 1533 made sodomy with man or beast punishable by hanging, a penalty that persisted until 1861. In line with medical ignorance of the time, fear of cross-species births may have motivated the inclusion of animals within this law. The first person to die under its provisions may, however, have been executed more for treason than for proven sodomy. He was Walter Hungerford, first Baron Hungerford of Heytesbury, an ally of Thomas Cromwell's who was arrested in 1540. The charges against him included inciting two people to witchcraft in order to procure the king's death; and the coincidental fall from grace of his protector, Cromwell, allowed his wife to pursue him for charges of keeping her prisoner for four years at Farleigh Hungerford Castle in Somerset, and for 'unnatural vices'. Convicted of these offences, he was at least spared the indignity of the hangman's rope; he and Cromwell were beheaded next to each other on Tower Hill on 28 July 1540.

Nicholas Udall was luckier. A teacher and writer (his play, *Ralph Roister Doister*, is often described as the first comedy written in English) and headmaster of Eton College from about 1534 to 1541, he was accused by two of his young ex-pupils of being complicit in stealing some candlesticks from Eton. It emerged during questioning that he had also sexually and physically abused many of his pupils, including one of those involved in this theft. He confessed and was convicted under the Buggery Act, but received a relatively lenient sentence – a year in Marshalsea prison. His poetry later won him the support of Catherine Parr and Edward VI, so it seems that devotion to art was able to overcome any repugnance that may have been felt about his sexual inclinations.

Apart from the death penalty for buggery (not always, as we have seen, enforced), punishment for sexual offences at this time was a matter for the ecclesiastical courts –known as the 'bawdy courts' because they dealt with so many sexual misdemeanours. Unlike the civil courts, they recognized women as people in their own right, so many of their cases were brought by women who were also often witnesses. In one example from the 1570s, at St Paul's in London, a woman charged the local parson that he 'had thy pleasure and use of me, and in occupying me [a euphemism for sex] thou didst use me more ruffianlike than honestly.'

Another, from Appleby in Leicestershire, concerned one John Petcher who was brought before the Leicester Archdeacon's Court on 29 October 1597 charged with committing adultery with Sara Winter, wife of Robert Winter, a neighbour. Petcher was a widowed sheep farmer, and the Winters were tenants of a smallholding, though Sara appears to have been living away from her husband with Nicholas Taylor and his wife; there is an implication that Sara was a bit of a philanderer, and it was also probably true that she loved going to fairs and spending time enjoying herself away from home. The chief witness against Petcher was another member of the Taylor family, Edward, who claimed to have taken the couple in adultery, and moreover refused to accept sixpence from Petcher to keep quiet. But his reputation was a bad one: he had spent time in prison (as had his wife, for stealing a pair of shoes), and much of the evidence on behalf of Petcher consisted of bringing depositions about Taylor's criminal past. It seems that the Taylor family had also seen Sara and Petcher together in an alehouse during a fair at Atherstone. But others who were there testified that they were in a public place where they could not have got up to anything; and moreover, Edward Taylor had spent most of the day drinking in another alehouse, so was completely unreliable as a witness.

There are all sorts of undertones to this case, which perhaps typify the ways in which these 'bawdy courts' operated. There is also evidence that Robert Winter had bribed Taylor 'to watch Sara and Petcher to take them in adultery together', and thus more than a suspicion that Winter was trying to entrap his wife. And it seemed that some of the neighbours disapproved of this sort of spying, since three local farmers testified that they had been at the alehouse in question and had seen no wrongdoing. However, the court did listen to a great deal of hearsay evidence from neighbours who had seen Sara with Petcher, and it was regarded as 'common knowledge' that he had visited her at her house while her husband was away.

Whatever the truth, it was reported that John Petcher 'purged himself' of this offence 'as well by his own oath as by the oaths of four of his honest neighbours', and was acquitted of the charge and 'restored again to his good name'. Perhaps the most interesting element of this case (beyond the fact that we can never know what happened to the principal actors) is the light it throws on village communities of the time. This was a tightly knit world, where attitudes towards illicit behaviour varied between indifference and strong condemnation; where knowledge of one's neighbours' doings was an inescapable part of daily life; where petty intrigues and surreptitious behaviour were commonplace, but where the villagers had their own ways of dealing with such things. To quote the researcher of this case (Alan Roberts): 'We are left with the impression that they lived socially more eventful, emotionally more unsettled and sexually more active lives than one might at first suppose from studying economic records alone.'

The problem with the ecclesiastical courts was that they had no real teeth when it came to punishment. Their only sanctions were based on public shaming, which was a disgrace but could be survived. Fornicators and adulterers could be made to stand in the market place dressed in a white robe and holding a white wand, and those who became pregnant before marriage frequently only had to make an open confession of their sin. And although religious law had always forbidden it, bigamy was not a civil crime until 1603. Difficulties of communication meant that people who ran away from home could often marry again without anyone ever knowing anything about it. But it was impossible to do so openly. As Lawrence Stone reports, one John Loggan sought to marry Mary Hewitt in 1578 on the grounds that his first wife was 'gone from him and married to another man now dwelling in Kent, wherefore he thinketh he might marry again.' The Church disagreed, of course. As ever, financial considerations provoked the worst punishments: the production of a bastard child who would be a monetary drain on the parish could result in both father and mother being stripped to the waist, tied to a cart tail and whipped through the streets.

Henry VIII's direct line was not destined to flourish, despite his endeavours. It was the son of Mary, Queen of Scots, who, after being crowned king of Scotland at the age of only thirteen months in 1567, became king of England as well on Elizabeth's death in 1603. James I and VI produced three sons and four daughters by his wife, Anne of Denmark, but he is also well known for his open and self-confessed homosexuality. He appears indeed to have had no mistresses but to have confined his extra-marital liaisons to young men. In 1617 the Privy Council, concerned at the growing influence over James of George Villiers, Duke of Buckingham, held a debate about the situation. Sir John Oglander testified, 'I never yet saw any fond husband make so much or so great dalliance over his beautiful spouse as I have seen King James over his favourites, especially Buckingham. The King is wondrous passionate, a lover of his favourites beyond the love of men to women. He is the chastest prince for women that ever was, for he would often swear that he never kissed any other woman than his own queen.'

From the beginning of his reign 'Long live Queen James' was a shout often heard in London, and many ordinary people knew and openly recited the epigram '*Rex fuit Elizabeth: nunc est regina Jacobus*'; 'Elizabeth was king: now James is queen.'

James himself testified before the Privy Council: 'I, James, am neither a god nor an angel, but a man like any other. Therefore I act like a man and confess to loving those dear to me more than other men. You may be sure that I love the Earl of Buckingham more than anyone else, and more than you who are here assembled. I wish to speak in my own behalf and not to have it thought to be a defect, for Jesus Christ did the same, and therefore I cannot be blamed. Christ had John, and I have George.' He openly referred to Buckingham as his wife and to himself as Buckingham's husband.

James's first male love, when he was fourteen, appears to have been Esme Stuart whom he created Earl of Lennox; but the favours heaped on the earl inevitably led to jealousy, and he was eventually forced by a conspiracy of noblemen to leave the country. But there were others: George Gordon, Earl of Huntley, was conveniently married to Lennox's sister, Lady Henrietta Stuart, which made it possible for Huntley to be made Captain of the Guard with a role as personal bodyguard and lodgings in the king's own chambers. There was also Alexander Lindsay, Lord Spynie, the boy nicknamed 'Sandie' who was James's vice-chamberlain; and Francis Stewart Hepburn, Earl of Bothwell, whom James nonchalantly kissed and embraced in public, causing great scandal.

Robert Carr, a Scots lad who came to England with James as a page, had a chequered history with the king; he was also to be involved in one of the age's most celebrated scandals and murders. Carr had been sent back to Scotland after James had settled into London society, but later returned and was recognized by the king when he fell off his horse at a festival in front of the royal box, breaking a limb. James ordered the best medical treatment for his former page, and then had him appointed a Gentleman of the Bedchamber. As a courtier wrote: 'The Prince constantly leaneth on his cheek, and smoothes his ruffled garment. Carr hath all favours; the King teacheth him Latin every morning (and Greek every night?). I tell you, this Scottish lad is straight-limbed, well-favoured, strong-shouldered, and smooth-faced, with some sort of cunning and show of modesty.' Their relationship continued until 1615 when they had a falling-out, the king apparently complaining that Carr had removed himself from the king's chamber despite him 'soliciting to the contrary'.

Several years before, in about 1609, Carr had started an intrigue with Frances Howard, daughter of the Earl of Suffolk, whose marriage to the Earl of Essex was subsequently annulled on the grounds that he was impotent with her – the blame for the marriage's sexual failure was, of course, laid at Frances' door. Significantly, the Archbishop of Canterbury was loath to grant the nullity, fearing to be deluged by other petitioners – as he observed, 'If I yield unto them, here will be strange violations of marriages; if I do not, I must tell them it was fit for my Lord of Essex, but it is not so for you.'

He overcame his reservations, however, and Carr, now Earl of Somerset, married Frances in 1613. But before the marriage Carr had been strongly advised by his friend and mentor, Sir Thomas Overbury, not to go ahead, on the grounds that she was 'noted for her injury and immodesty'. He went so far as to use a highly insulting word of her, which Carr repeated to her. She and her family, incensed and deter-mined to pursue the advantageous connection with Carr, had Overbury accused of disrespect to the king and thrown into the Tower. There, through accomplices, Frances Howard arranged for him to be murdered by sending poisoned tarts and jellies. The crime was not discovered until two years later, and at the celebrated trial that followed the accomplices were found guilty of murder and hanged. Frances herself was portrayed as a notorious whore who had been adulterous with Carr before their marriage and probably with many others, too. 'She ran at random and brought herself into the contempt of all the world ... almost all men spake of the looseness of her carriage,' claimed one witness. Needless to say, Somerset's reputation was not shredded to the same degree.

Lady Somerset pleaded guilty to murder and was pardoned, though she was imprisoned in the Tower for several years more. Carr was also disgraced and imprisoned there, though it never became clear how deeply he was involved. He subsequently abandoned his wife, apparently more resentful of his wrecked career than appalled that she could com-mit murder.

Buckingham was probably the king's most favoured lover, and they maintained their liaison from 1614 until James died in 1625. Buckingham was universally regarded as one of the most beautiful young men in Europe, and many letters survive professing the king's love for him. Buckingham called himself James's dog and addressed him as 'Dear Dad', and James reciprocated with passionate avowals: 'I naturally so love your person, and adore all your other parts, which are more than ever one man had, that were not only all your people but all the world besides set together on one side and you alone on the other, I should to obey and please you displease, nay, despise them all.' In another letter, the king confesses that, 'I desire only to live in the world for your sake, and I had rather live banished in any part of the world with you, than live a sorrowful widow-life without you. And so God bless you, my sweet child and wife, and grant that ye may ever be a comfort to your dear dad and husband.'

Many courtiers sought to seduce James away from his affection for Buckingham, notably Sir William Manson, who would gather up from the streets a troupe of handsome young boys and scrub them up in the hope that one of them would entice the king. They would process round the throne every day in a routine that became known as the 'mustering of the minions'; but James quickly realized that he was being manipulated and ordered the court to be cleared. He arranged a starry marriage for Buckingham with Lady Catherine Manners, but even this appears to have had an ulterior motive in that he expressed the hope that they would soon have many children so that 'I may have sweet bedchamber boys to play with me.'

The sixteenth and early seventeenth centuries saw a great flourishing of the arts in England, fostered by Elizabeth I and James I, both of them intelligent, educated and cultivated monarchs. Theatre, in particular, bloomed; this was the age of Shakespeare, of course, and before him of Christopher Marlowe, whose talents were cut off early by his untimely death in 1593 at the age of twenty-nine. Marlowe was an enigmatic figure, an atheist when it was illegal, and possibly a homosexual, whose writings included passages dealing with both heterosexual and homosexual love. He was accused of believing Christ to be a bastard and his mother a whore, and of claiming that Christ had illicit relations with the women of Samaria (also whores, it seems) and that John was his bedfellow: 'he used him as the sinners of Sodom.' The same accuser – whose notes were handed to the authorities just three days before Marlowe's death – also quoted him as saying that 'all those that love not pipes and boyes are fooles.'

Marlowe's play *Edward II* deals with the homosexual relationship between Edward and Piers Gaveston, and elicits sympathy towards the declining king; and his poem *Hero and Leander* has the sea god Neptune aroused to lust by Leander during his swims across the Hellespont to woo Hero. Whether Marlowe was gay will never be certain; the lack of evidence for a marriage or liaisons with women is inconclusive, and the later testimony that he was killed in a tavern brawl by 'a bawdy serving-man, a rival of his in his lewd love' can never be proved. But he was undoubtedly brave for the time in openly celebrating same-sex relation-ships in his plays and poems.

It is known that Shakespeare got Anne Hathaway pregnant before they were married, and had to apply to the bawdy court in Worcester for a special licence exempting them from the normal requirement for banns to be proclaimed three times before the wedding. But there has also been speculation about Shakespeare's sexuality, on the basis mainly of the sonnets, the majority of which are addressed to an unknown young man whose beauty and charms are feted. Elizabethan poetry did tend to extravagant, flowery language on friendship, but even so the sus-picion remains that the emotion expressed in these poems may have been something rather more. There was also the mysterious 'Mr W H' to whom the sonnets were dedicated as their 'onlie begetter'; it may have referred to patronage, but could have been love or affection. The plays themselves provide some fuel for speculation. The plots frequently revolve around the cross-dressing of heroines into male clothes – an obvious dramatic device to exploit, as women were played on the Elizabethan stage by boys, but also one full of erotically charged ambigu-ities (despite the heterosexuality of the actual plots). This cross-dressing was partly the reason for the Puritans' disapproval of the theatre of the time, which might stir lascivious thoughts in men watching these young beardless boys.

Shakespeare has, of course, given us many of the images of love, both licit and illicit, that eternally define the emotion. Romeo and Juliet are the archetypal doomed lovers, the anguish of whose passion was based not on sex but on their defiance of the feud between their families; Othello is the ultimate jealous husband, convinced by the treacherous Iago of the infidelity of his faithful wife, Desdemona; Viola in *Twelfth Night* woos the icy Olivia for Duke Orsino while falling headlong in love with him herself. *Measure for Measure*, indeed, is founded on the notion of illicit sex, with the Duke of Vienna appointing a deputy to enforce harsh laws against promiscuity, only to hear that this hypocritical deputy has propositioned a virtuous woman and promised to spare her brother's life – he has been sentenced to death for impregnating his fiancée before they were married – if she will only sleep with him. All's well that ends well, of course!

In *Antony and Cleopatra* — the play from which Dryden's *All for Love* derives — the Roman general Antony takes romance to a heroic extreme. He surrenders everything — status, empire, his very life — for the love of a bewitching Cleopatra:

> Age cannot wither her, not custom stale
> Her infinite variety; other women cloy
> The appetites they feed, but she makes hungry
> Where most she satisfies...

Thus Cleopatra's allure — undying, everlasting, unlike that of other women whose charms may seduce a man into a love affair in the first place but are likely to erode with familiarity. For Antony, desire for Cleopatra can never die and is worth any price. A different tack is taken in Shakespeare's more cynical *Troilus and Cressida*, which exposes and deplores the limitations of love. Troilus himself acknowledges the paradox of their illicit amour that echoes across centuries of passion: 'this is the monstruosity in love, lady, that the will is infinite, and the execution confined; that the desire is boundless, but the act a slave to limit.'

Shakespeare's plays have become timeless tales, celebrated in modern cinema through romances such as the real-life passion of Richard Burton and Elizabeth Taylor, who met when he was playing Antony and she Cleopatra, and echoed in a cross-dressing Gwyneth Paltrow in *Shakespeare in Love* pretending to be a boy so that she could play Juliet on the stage of the Rose Theatre, and allowing the playwright into her bed on the side.

John Donne was the great poet of physical desire of this period. Before his marriage and his return to religious belief, he had been a young man-about-town whose witty poetry celebrated his attempts at seduction. 'The Flea' is essentially a proposition to a young woman whose virginity he desires. When both of them are bitten by a flea, he asks her why, since the flea has mingled both their bloods in its body, they should not do the same: the marriage service makes a man and a woman 'one flesh', the bites of the flea have made them 'one blood' and so they are practically married:

> Marke but this flea, and marke in this,
> How little that which thou deny'st me is;
> Me it suck'd first, and now sucks thee,
> And in this flea our two bloods mingled bee;

Confesse it, this cannot be said
A sinne, or shame, or losse of maidenhead,
   Yet this enjoyes before it wooe,
   And pamper'd swells with one blood made of two,
   And this, alas, is more than wee would doe.

Donne's early life was bedevilled by both religious controversy and illicit love. Born a Catholic – his uncle was a Jesuit who was hanged, drawn and quartered for his faith – he repudiated the Church and only reluctantly agreed to become an Anglican cleric when James I refused to grant him any preferment unless he did so. Before that he had been secretary to Sir Thomas Egerton, but lost that job after he secretly married Egerton's niece, Anne More, in 1601. Her father, Sir George More, Constable of the Tower, was furious and had Donne thrown into the Fleet prison for several weeks, together with the two friends who had helped with the clandestine affair and witnessed the wedding. When he was released he was reunited with his wife, but without the help of her family had to struggle to support her and the children they were beginning to produce. It was not until 1609 that they were reconciled with her father, who then agreed to pay her dowry. The marriage had for a while ruined him; as he summed it up, 'John Donne, Anne Donne, undone.'

His wife died in 1617, aged only thirty-three, after giving birth to their twelfth, stillborn, child. The poet who wrote 'No man is an island, entire of itself,' and 'Never send to know for whom the bell tolls; it tolls for thee,' was devastated. His love for his wife, despite the controversy they created when they married, is celebrated by the sensuality of some of his poetry, like the lines from 'The Good Morrow':

I wonder, by my troth, what thou and I
Did, till we loved? Were we not weaned till then?
But sucked on country pleasures childishly?
Or snorted we in a Seven Sleepers' den?
'Twas so; but this, all pleasures fancies be.
If ever any beauty I did see,
Which I desired, and got, 'twas but a dream of thee.

Civil war and the ascendancy of the Puritans during the Commonwealth closed theatres and restricted the arts during the middle decades of the seventeenth century – though Milton and Marvell flourished, and Marvell could entreat his 'coy mistress' with the words 'Had we but world enough, and time, This coyness, Lady, were no crime…'. But it was a time when fidelity and morality in all walks of life were promoted; the Commonwealth Parliament even, for a short time, made a second offence of adultery punishable by death, and one woman, Ursula Powell, was hanged for it. But the restoration of the monarchy in 1660 saw extravagant pleasure flourish again, led by the decadent, epicurean example of the 'Merrie Monarch' himself. Like Henry VIII, Charles II had trouble conceiving a legitimate heir with his wife, Catherine of Braganza – though, unlike Henry, he stayed married to her. He proved his own potency by fathering countless illegitimate children, fourteen of whom he acknowledged, including one daughter who was almost certainly not his but the child of John Churchill, later Duke of Marlborough. These children bore surnames such as Fitzcharles and Fitzroy, and many of them were later ennobled and went on to found prominent dynasties.

Lucy Walter was the mother of Charles's eldest son, later created the Duke of Monmouth in England and the Duke of Buccleuch in Scotland. Claiming that his mother and father had been secretly married, Monmouth tried to get his father to acknowledge him as his legitimate heir, but Charles refused. Monmouth was later executed after a failed uprising against James II. Charles also had a long dalliance with Louise de Kérouaille, whom he created Duchess of Portsmouth; she was regarded as an unsavoury French influence and much disliked. One of his most notorious (and fecund) mistresses was Barbara Palmer, Countess of Castlemaine and Duchess of Cleveland, who bore him six children. She described the king to her friend, the Earl of Rochester, as magnificently well endowed, a comment which Rochester turned into one of his witty epigrams:

> Nor are his high desires above his strength
> His sceptre and his pr*ck are of a length.

Charles spread his favours across all levels of society; although many of his mistresses were the wives of noblemen, he also had frequent dalliances with lower-born women including Mary 'Moll' Davis, actress and courtesan, Jane Roberts, the daughter of a clergyman, and Winifred Wells, one of the queen's maids of honour. He is even rumoured to have seduced Cristabella Wyndham, his former wet-nurse, when he was only fourteen. The renowned Nell Gwynn was another, an orange-seller who bore him two sons, Charles and James Beauclerk; Charles was later made Duke of St Albans.

Although relaxation of the harsh regime imposed by the Puritans was generally a relief, the riotous debauchery at court began to repel ordinary citizens. The king's mistresses often had to endure public abuse; Lady Castlemaine was called a 'vile whore' on one occasion when she was taking the evening air in St James's Park, and later found an insulting note pinned to her door after she had given birth to one of her children by the king. When, in 1668, the London apprentices went on one of their regular rampages against brothels, they threatened to pull down 'the biggest brothel of all', Whitehall Palace. Louise de Kérouaille was particularly reviled, not just as a foreigner but as a Catholic mistress in a Protestant country; indeed, Nell Gwynn once saved herself from a mob who were attacking her carriage in the belief that Mme de Kérouaille was inside by sticking her head out of the window and saying, 'Pray, good people, be civil; I am the Protestant whore.' Nell Gwynn herself was derided for her lowly birth; when the dowager Duchess of Richmond complained to Charles that she could not stand talking to Nell, he replied that 'those he lay with were fit company for the greatest woman in the land'.

It is from this period that we begin to acquire some insight into the lives of 'ordinary' people through court records, particularly those from the Old Bailey. One rather spectacular case to be found in these records is of the trial on 11 July 1677 of a woman who was accused of having carnal relations with a dog. The account of the trial begins, 'One of the first and most talkt of tryals at this Sessions, was for such an abominable crime, attended with such odious circumstances, as 'tis thought scarce any story can parallel it, especially in this our more modest and chaster climate, hitherto a stranger to such unnatural wickedness; and we hope the justice executed on this wretched criminal will deter all others from any the like detestible inclinations for the future.'

This unnamed married woman, living near Cripplegate in London, was charged 'for that she having not the fear of God before her eyes, nor regarding the order of nature, on the 23 of June last, to the disgrace of all womankind, did commit buggery with a certain mungril dog, and wickedly, divellishly, and against nature had venerial and carnal copulation with him.' She seems to have been a woman of loose morals, and moreover had the misfortune to live in a house which offered her neighbours several places through which they could peep at her activities.

On that June day, it seems that a young woman looking through one of these holes saw the accused with the dog, at which she called on two others to witness what was happening. These witnesses testified before the court as to what they had seen, and the dog was also brought into court and sealed the woman's fate by wagging his tail and 'making motions as it were to kiss her, which 'twas sworn she did do when she made that horrid use of him.' The prisoner denied the charge, alleging malice in the witnesses, and her husband supported her. But it was to no avail: she was found guilty and sentenced to death. As the summary of the sessions reported: 'Two men and five women received sentence of death, amongst whom that monster who prostituted her self to a dog was one; the rest incorrigible thieves.' The dog's fate is unrecorded.

Bigamy – now illegal and punishable by death – makes a frequent appearance before the courts at this time, sometimes the result of ignorance or happenstance, but sometimes malicious and profiteering. An example of the latter was tried on 10 May 1676. The writer of the account of the trial evidently took great pleasure in his own intellectual capacities, for he described the unnamed defendant as '*sutor ultra credipam*' ('cobbler, stick to your last') and a 'knight of the order of St Crispin', in other words a shoemaker. This man was reckoned to have had seventeen wives, though he was indicted for only four. It seems that he roamed the land, pretending to be a person of quality, and seduced rich young women or wealthy widows into marrying him; whereupon he would enjoy their persons for a while before making off with as much of their fortune as he could inveigle out of them and trying his luck elsewhere.

The record of the trial laments the fact that he was canny enough to plead guilty and 'so prevented all farther disquisition of the circumstances, and we are sorry we are forced to fail the readers expectations in a relation which would certainly have been very rare and divertiseing...'. His guilty plea was a clever one: not only did he cheat the avid followers of criminal proceedings of the details of all his crimes, but he was thereby able to gain 'benefit of clergy', remission of sentence of death. This benefit had long ceased to be open only to genuine members of the clergy; by the seventeenth century it was possible for anyone indicted of most crimes to claim the benefit provided they could read verses of the Bible offered by the judge. Most judges used lines from the 51st Psalm, which became known as the 'neck verse' since it saved so many people from the gallows.

Benefit of clergy could, however, only be invoked once. This shoemaker therefore ensured that he would be tried for one crime only by pleading guilty to the first indictment. However, his cleverness seems to have deserted him at this point, as the court record narrates: 'but however subtilly he behaved himself heretofore, I conceive he fail'd in his politicks, when being brought to the Bar and demanded what he could say for himself why judgment should not pass upon him, whereas 'tis believed he might have had the benefit of the clergy, he obstinately waived that, and insisted for transportation, which being not thought convenient to be granted, because he stood charged in the Sheriffs custody with an action of a thousand pounds, he thereupon received sentence with the rest to be hang'd.'

A case in 1701, during the reign of Queen Anne, involved a plea for a reprieve from the death sentence; the trial had been held on the island of Jersey where benefit of clergy was unavailable, and the petitioner, Thomas Messervy, therefore found himself stuck on the mainland and unable to return home while the sentence stood against him. His case was that he had returned to Jersey after a stint in the navy to deal with some property matter and 'he was unfortunately trapped by some seamen into the company of one Ursula Ellwick and being made drunk easily decoyed to marry her, though [he] remembers nothing of it. That after having cohabited with her four or five days and still kept hot with drink by pernicious company whereby [he] could not know what he did, he then came to himself...'. He fled and then married one Mary Mourant and lived with her in Jersey, until during his absence on business in England Ursula Ellwick reappeared and entered a case against him for having two wives.

When he heard of this, Messervy fled to France and 'in his absence and without being heard Your Majesty's Royal Court of Jersey ... have proceeded against him and upon Ursula Ellwick's producing of certificates of her being married with [him] sentenced him to die. That there is no benefit of clergy in the said island, which [he] would be allowed... in England whereby [he] without Your Majesty's most gracious pardon is hindered from ever going to Jersey, and the little estate he has liable to be forfeited after a year and one day after the date of the sentence... [He] therefore humbly beseeches Your Majesty to grant him your most gracious pardon for his offence which he most heartily repents of and that he may return to the quiet possession of his inheritance.'

The petition was presented to the court of St James on 11 June 1702 and referred to the Attorney General to examine. The response was delivered on 27 Oct 1702 and seems to suggest that he should be pardoned: 'the petitioner appears to be a very weak, sickly and ignorant man and is an object of Your Majesty's royal mercy, and if Your Majesty shall graciously please to extent the same to him, by granting him your royal pardon for the said offence Your Majesty will not thereby any way prejudice the said Ursula Ellwick as to any right she may claim as being his wife. All which is humbly submitted to Your Majesty's great wisdom.' The documents outlining this case are held in the National Archives [PC 1/1/70].

Women were also charged with bigamy; in one case, the woman appears to have meant to deceive. Mary Stoakes was tried on 31 August 1692 for marrying two husbands, both of whom were in court. She was accused of pretending 'to be a maid' and to have a large estate. She was found guilty and sentenced to be 'burnt in the hand'.

Written accounts of their lives by people who would, in modern times, be regarded as members of the 'chattering classes' now begin to appear. Samuel Pepys is perhaps the most well known of these, but we also have the autobiography of Lady Anne Halkett, which interestingly presents a female perspective on the trials and temptations she had to withstand. She was a pious and obedient daughter to a strict mother, but she had the misfortune to find herself in love with, and passionately loved by, Thomas Howard, the son of Lord Howard of Escrick, a young man whom she would never have been allowed to marry as she was not rich enough. She was determined to obey her mother's commands that she never see him again, an order she obeyed by agreeing to a secret meeting while she was blindfolded. Her mother threatened to turn her out of the house and disown her if she continued with her faithful – though quite chaste – entanglement with Thomas, a situation that eventually resolved itself when he married someone else. It is not known whether he consented to the match.

This was in the 1640s, and Anne then met an Irish royalist called Joseph Bampfield who was not only a dashing secret agent – he had helped to smuggle James, Duke of York, out of the country – but also convinced her that his wife was dead and that she should agree to marry him. He was clearly both a highly romantic figure and a rogue: imprisoned and threatened with execution, he made a daring escape and fought a duel with Anne's brother-in-law, who challenged him with planning to commit bigamy. Anne continued to believe that Mrs Bampfield was dead, and refused other offers on the grounds of her previous engagement. When she received incontrovertible proof that the wife was indeed still alive, she agreed to marry Sir James Halkett; but Bampfield turned up yet again – by now acting as a double agent for both Oliver Cromwell and Charles II. Anne, however, was by this time ready to give up on her romantic would-be lover and settle down to become a dutiful wife and mother.

The diaries of Pepys provide an invaluable insight into life in the middle of the social scale during the second half of the seventeenth century. He was quite open about his sexual desires, using coded language that when deciphered can be startlingly explicit. One complication was that his wife, Elizabeth, was often sexually unavailable, because she suffered from severe menstrual pain and also developed a vaginal abscess. Another problem was that, unlike many other women of the time, she was jealous of her husband's promiscuity, so he had to keep it hidden. The double standard still prevailed, however: she was a great beauty who received much attention from other men, although she faithfully rebuffed their advances; but Pepys had grave suspicions about her relationship with a young dancing master and kept a close watch on her behaviour while she was having lessons with him. They were, in truth, a bourgeois, rather puritanical couple whose sensitivities would not allow them to indulge in the sort of antics that were quite normal among the aristocracy. But Pepys was also highly sensual and found himself irresistibly attracted to pretty young women.

He was a notable voyeur, and would often follow attractive women in the street and try to touch them. His diaries record over fifty women with whom he had some sort of sexual congress between 1660 and 1669. He could not keep away from his own servants who, while combing his hair for lice, would find him pawing their breasts and putting his hands up their skirts. Tavern girls, too, were his prey, whom he would kiss and fondle, as well as the wives of his business partners whom he would play with for hours. Pepys was so sensual that he would often achieve orgasm just by thinking about sex with a current fantasy; he did it once in church.

However, Pepys was mortally afraid of illicit pregnancy, so he rarely engaged in full intercourse except with married women whose husbands were away, but not for too long. In that way, if they became pregnant he could not be blamed. His first mistress, Betty Lane, was unmarried when he met her, so they contented themselves with fondling while Pepys sought to find a husband for her. After she had married a Mr Martin they were lovers for many years – and it is more than likely that her husband was complicit in the arrangement since it did no harm to his career. Pepys, as Commissioner of the Navy Board, had much patronage at his beck and call and he used it fully to buy himself sexual favours. He notes on one occasion that Mr Martin went out to buy wine for them while they were in bed together, and that he was going to do his best to get him a position as a naval purser (which he successfully did).

Indeed, it became well known that favours and promotions could be best got from Pepys by sending him a pretty wife or daughter to kiss and caress. Mrs Bagwell's husband progressed from the lowliest position as a ship's carpenter on a fifth-rate man-of-war to master carpenter on a first-class ship of the line while his wife was leading Pepys on to ever more intimate embraces. Neither party to any of these dalliances seems to have felt that there was anything reprehensible going on, on the level either of sexual promiscuity or of the blatant use of what would now be called sexual harassment to obtain favours. A woman's body was a bargaining tool at the disposal of her menfolk, whether husband or employer. And although Pepys suffered with a conscience that sometimes made him remorseful, his shame was never strong enough to persuade him to stop. It took him three weeks to bring himself to dismiss from the house a young companion whom Elizabeth had discovered him feeling up, because he could not give up the hope that she would yield her maidenhead to him. It was perhaps his undeserved good fortune during those three weeks that his wife's passionate denunciation of his behaviour led to equally passionate performances with her in bed.

Today he would be condemned as the ultimate in sleaze; yet to himself he was a gay dog whose randiness was normal and whose luck in having a position of patronage allowed him to indulge in his favourite pastime at will. To his credit, he did pay his debts and the men whose women he used duly found themselves employed and promoted. And when his wife died aged only twenty-nine, he formed a liaison with Mary Skinner, whom he never married but who openly lived with him until his death, and he left her £200 a year in his will.

To be fair to Pepys, there were many far more debauched men around – mostly, however, among the aristocracy, and from the king down. One of the most notorious of these was John Wilmot, second Earl of

Rochester, who combined personal bravery in battle and considerable literary skills with lewdness, extravagance and drunkenness. Pepys describes Rochester's attempt to abduct Elizabeth Malet, an heiress whose family were seeking a suitably rich husband for her. Rochester's lack of fortune disqualified him from being a suitor, even though the king himself, according to Pepys, had pressed his suit with her; so he simply tried to make off with her. Pepys describes '…my Lord Rochester's running away on Friday night last with Mrs Malet, the great beauty and fortune of the North, who had supped at Whitehall with Mrs Stewart, and was going home to her lodgings with her grandfather, my Lord Haly, by coach; and was at Charing Cross seized on by both horse and footmen, and forcibly taken from him, and put into a coach with six horses, and two women provided to receive her, and carried away. Upon immediate pursuit, my Lord of Rochester … was taken at Uxbridge; but the lady is not yet heard of, and the King mighty angry and the Lord sent to the Tower.'

Two years later she eloped with Rochester of her own accord and they married; his access to her wealth now freed him to carry on his debauched life in London while she was left behind, with their children, at his house in the country. He was a prominent member of the 'Merry Gang' who led a riotous existence at court and within society. Pepys describes one of their excesses when Sir Charles Sedley and Lord Buckhurst acted out 'all the postures of lust and buggery that could be imagined' while playing around naked on a Covent Garden balcony, in full view of the crowds.

The king eventually tired of Rochester's excesses and his scatological satires on court life, and stopped protecting him. After one episode when he could have been arrested for murder Rochester disguised himself as 'Doctor Bendo', whose skills in curing barrenness appear to have consisted of his own intercession as a secret sperm donor. He took as his mistress the prominent actress Elizabeth Barry, whose career he enhanced and who was probably the love of his life; but he was also openly bisexual, as his writings show. His poems include many denunciations of ordinary sex, extolling instead the joys of three-in-a-bed sex with a woman and a pageboy. And one of his plays, *Sodom, or the Quintessence of Debauchery*, is widely regarded as the first example of printed pornography. After his death the play was denounced as obscene and copies of it were destroyed (though one sold at Sotheby's for over £40,000 in December 2004).

Rochester died in 1680 at the age of thirty-three, from syphilis and from the mercury he had taken for years to combat it. He concealed his rotting nose under a silver nasal mask and wore thick make-up to hide the lesions on his face caused by the disease. For all his debauchery he was clearly a one-off: famously atheistic, he is supposed to have made a deathbed conversion to Christianity; and many later literary figures admired the fire and wit of his writing. In truth, the scale of his promiscuity was not at all unusual; it was his additional atheism and contempt for the hypocrisies of the time, expressed in his often vicious satirical poetry, that gave rise to his later reputation as the most degenerate figure of that degenerate age.

Venereal disease was endemic, treated by a variety of quack pills and potions to be found advertised in the broadsheets of the time. Charles Churchill, who in the early 1760s contracted gonorrhoea along with his mistress, took the dangerous course of trying to cure it with mercury; and in the 1780s Lord Herbert, after contracting the pox, suffered from a large wound in his groin which took weeks and much medical intervention to heal. Other diseases, too, took their toll on sexual habits: women suffered from a wide range of gynaecological problems, and the impossibility of reliably preventing pregnancy sometimes deadened women's wish to have sex. The dangers and discomforts of continually giving birth were a contraceptive of sorts.

One of Rochester's verses alludes to a besetting problem of the time: the sheer dirtiness of people of all classes:

> Fair nasty nymph, be clean and kind
> And all my joys restore
> By using paper still behind
> The sponges for before.

Personal hygiene was not a high priority. Pepys only agreed to go to a bath-house after his wife refused to let him into her bed until he did; and comments now and later about general smelliness and filth indicate that, even though everyone must have been much more used than we are today to living among noxious odours of all kinds, they still did not like it.

Somewhat oddly, however, some notoriously smelly men would only bathe if they wished to pick up a woman; their wives, it seems, had to put up with whatever state their husbands chose, whereas whores could be more demanding. Women were often counselled on marriage to expect their husbands' behaviour towards them to deteriorate once they were safely wed; indeed, the custom of the women retiring to the drawing room after supper appears to have arisen mainly because the men wanted the freedom to drink, talk bawdily and relieve themselves freely in the chamber pots kept for this purpose in the dining room sideboards.

Prostitutes abounded, of course, in all cities and towns, and in rural areas, too: some poor families would let out a room to the local whore, and married women would agree to sex in the fields in order to earn a little money. In an age when the younger sons of high-ranking families could often expect never to marry, and when young men of the middle and lower classes were often sent away from home to be apprenticed to a trade, brothels were an essential tool in the easing of tension and frustration. There were between twenty and thirty thousand apprentices in London in the seventeenth century, and they required a lot of servicing. Once again, even at this level, the double standard prevailed: the young men needed these women, but they would regularly riot on Shrove Tuesday and destroy the brothels, ostensibly to prevent illegitimate sex during Lent but more probably because they needed to let off steam. It is an interesting fact that statistics show a dip in births nine months after Lent; abstinence at that time was clearly expected.

Prostitution was, for many poor young women, the only way to relieve their poverty; if they found themselves thrown out of a job in service, or became an unmarried mother, there was little alternative to selling their bodies apart from taking on the drudgery of long hours in cramped, ill-lit workshops. And the market for their wares was a broad one, whether they allowed themselves to be picked up in the street, roamed public places such as the new Vauxhall Pleasure Gardens with other masked women of ill repute, or found themselves ensconced in one of the many brothels that abounded in all town and city centres.

These were mostly run by notorious bawds like Elizabeth Holland, who came from a respectable background but was wild and ambitious and soon found that life as a whore could be highly profitable. As Fergus Linnane relates in *Madams, Bawds and Brothel-Keepers of London*, Holland was also shrewd enough to get out before venereal disease caught up with her and her looks deteriorated; and her next step was to open her own brothel in the City of London offering good food, plenty to drink and lots of willing women. But she fell foul both of the authorities and of rival brothels whose custom she was taking, and was sentenced to the public 'carting' that had been the punishment for vice for centuries. She also had to endure a spell in Newgate until she could pay a hefty fine, and when she got out she took her business across the river to the less well-regulated district of Southwark, famous for bawdy houses and all kinds of vice. There she bought a building with a moat and a gatehouse which she felt she could defend against anything the authorities might send against her, and she set up a new brothel which became known as Holland's Leaguer.

Surrounded by taverns, arenas for bull- and bear-baiting, theatres such as the Globe and the Swan and rival whorehouses, this was an ideal spot; and Elizabeth Holland soon established herself with four fine whores, augmented when necessary by other girls. These four – Beta Brestonia, Eliza Caunce, Longa Maria and Maria Pettit – all had different things to offer and between them they satisfied anything that a client could want. Mother Holland controlled her girls and her clients with a rod of iron, allowing no credit to anyone, however grand, and never tolerating abusive or wild behaviour. The authorities tried several times to close the Leaguer down, once sending a troop of soldiers who were enticed onto the drawbridge which was then collapsed, flinging them into the putrid waters of the moat. The whores, led by Mother Holland, emptied their chamber pots over them and threw all manner of missiles at them until they retreated. But in the following year, 1632, her house was finally closed down.

By the 1660s, when Restoration London was full of revel again, the area of London around the Strand and Covent Garden was where the best brothels were to be found, run by famous bawds such as Mother Cresswell. Charles II himself honoured her with a visit; and she also ran houses of assignation where both men and women could meet their lovers and where impoverished gentlewomen, perhaps from royalist families ruined in the Civil Wars, could sell their favours. Those who wished could even pay for a 'royal' encounter, with one of Charles II's daughters by his mistress, Moll Davis.

The last decades of the seventeenth century were clearly a riotous time, perhaps as an antidote to the Puritanism of the first half of the century. There was a great deal of entertainment to be had in London, at places such as Vauxhall, on the south bank of the Thames, and Ranelagh in Chelsea, where the respectable could promenade and listen to music accompanied by a dish of tea, and those in search of less reputable pleasures could pick up a girl or find a suitable bush behind which to cavort with a lover. The popularity of Vauxhall at times caused traffic jams on the few bridges over the Thames, and the shilling entrance price ensured that the gardens were always crowded with a cross-section of society, from royalty and the gentry to the thieves and prostitutes who were hoping to profit from them. Other pleasure gardens included Cuper's Garden – often known as Cupid's Garden – and later Cremorne; but their popularity and their respectability declined, until towards the end of the eighteenth century most of them had closed their gates or been shut down, in Cuper's Garden's case because of 'the profligacy of the company by whom it was frequented.'

The end of the seventeenth century echoed the beginning of the sixteenth, in that once again there was a succession crisis and challenges to royal legitimacy – the son of James II and Mary of Modena was declared 'supposititious', i.e. substituted for a stillborn child, by a nervous Protestant Parliament. It had been two hundred turbulent years, in which people had witnessed changes in law, religion and mores that affected their ordinary, everyday lives. At the end of the period we can recognize our modern world with its virtues, vices and social duplicity, further modified in the following century by new forms of industry and radical ideas. The Georgian era saw its share of rakes and rebels, not least in the kings and princes who gave it their name, but it also saw the beginning of a new industrial age.

Above [1] THIS PAINTING from *The Romance of the Rose,* dated to *c.* 1500, encapsulates the idealism of medieval love. A lady and her lover are about to enter a beautiful medieval garden, where they will find music, literature and water gently playing. Love for the exclusive few was a noble ritual, delicate and refined.

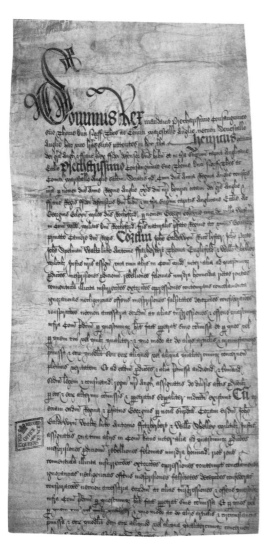

Above [5] A STUDY by Rubens for his portrait of George Villiers, First Duke of Buckingham. He became the lover of King James I, and remained his favourite from their first meeting in 1614 till the king's death in 1625. **Left** [6] THE DOCU-MENTS in the care of the National Archives are invaluable original sources for some of the trials and scandals of the past. This one forms part of the court roll recording the trial of Anne Boleyn, Sir George Boleyn and Lord Rocheford on charges of high treason, adultery and incest [KB8/9].

To the Queens Most Excell.^t Majesty

May it please your Majesty

In humble Obedience to your Majestyes Order
of Referrence of the 11th of June last, I have
Considered of the Annexed petition of Thomas
Messervy whereby he does Acknowledge himselfe
guilty of Bigamy in haveing Marryed Mary
Mourant in the life of Ursula Ellurick, to whom
he was before Marryed, and who is yet living,
Alledging for his Excuse, that he was drawn to
Marry the said Ursula Ellurick when he was
Drunk, and that he did not Cohabit with her
but while he was under that disorder;

And that in his Absence out of the Island
of Jersey without being heard he hath for such
his Offence in yor Majestyes Royall Court of
Jersey been proceeded against and Sentenced to
dye; And it does Appeare to me by a Copy of the
Record of the said Court, that the said Thomas
Messervy hath been Indicted for the said Offence,
and hath been severall times duly called to
Answere to the same in the said Royall Court
of Jersey, And for not Appearing is Adjudged
to dye such Sentence being in the Nature of
an Attainder by Outlawry by the Laws of
England;

That by the Laws of Jersey benefitt of
Clergy is not allowed for such Offence, as it is
by the Laws of England, And therefore the
petition^r unless relieved by your Majestyes
Mercy will suffer death if he be taken within
the said Island

That—

Left [7] A PETITION to Queen Anne in 1701 concerning the case of a Jerseyman, Thomas Messervy. He had been sentenced to death *in absentia* for bigamy after entering into a marriage while drunk and later marrying another woman. Unable to return home, he pleaded for mercy because of the facts of the case and because a mainland trial would have offered 'benefit of clergy' [PC1/1/170]. **Above** [8] FRANCES HOWARD, Countess of Somerset, was convicted with her husband for plotting the murder of Sir Thomas Overbury after he had warned the earl against marrying her because of her bad reputation. Those who abetted her in the crime were condemned to death, while the Somersets were imprisoned in the Tower of London for several years.

Right [11] THIS 'BAWDY
COURT' document, dated
15 January 1754, records the
sentence passed on Anne
Jilman of the parish of
Lenton, Nottinghamshire,
for having given birth to an
illegitimate child. Her punishment was to do public
penance in church dressed
in a white robe and carrying
a white wand.

Below [10] THIS PLATE
from Hogarth's *Marriage a
la Mode* in 1743 depicts the
beginnings of the descent
into disaster of the newly
married young couple. He

Above [9] SAMUEL PEPYS by Sir Godfrey Kneller. The famous
diary that Pepys kept from 1660 to 1669 covers such events
as the Great Plague and the Great Fire as well as London
life during the first years after the Restoration. It also deals
revealingly with his own life, from his hard work for the
Navy Board to his marriage and his many dalliances.

has come home late after a
night of revelry, while his
wife is exhausted after her
own party. On the right,
their steward leaves the
scene of disorder in disgust.

Pennance Enjoin'd to be performed by Anne Jilman
of the parish of Lowton

in the Archdeaconry of Nottingham as followeth

Scrop Bidmore

The said Anne Jilman ____ is to be present in the
parish Church of Lowton aforesaid upon some
Sunday ____ in Time of Divine Service
where immediately after the Niceen Creed she shall stand
upon some Seat or form before the pulpit or place where the
Minister readeth prayers having a white Sheet wrapped
about her from the Shoulders to the Feet being bare headed
bare footed and bare Legg'd with a white Wand in her Hand
shall say after the Minister as followeth

Whereas I good people forgetting my Duty to Almighty God have
committed the Detestable Crime of Fornication ____ with
James Smith ____ and have hereby most justly provoked
the heavy Wrath of God against me to the Danger of my own Soul
and evil Example of others I do earnestly repent and am heartily
Sorry for the same Desiring Almighty God for the Sake of Jesus
Christ to forgive me this and all other my offences and to Assist me
with his Holy Spirit that I never fall into the like grievous Sin
again Desiring You all to take Example of this my punishment
and You here present to pray with and for me saying

Our Father which art, And so forth

And of the performance hereof she is to Certify under
the Minister and Church-Wardens Hands or under the
Hands of two or more Credible Witnesses at the Register's
office in Nottingham on or before the fifth day of
February ____ next Ensuing together with these
presents Dated the fifteenth Day of January
in the Year of our Lord 1754 /.

Tho: Bennett
Register

27th of July 1754 further time was
given for the return of this
til the 24th of September next.

PN 369/12

Above [12] A STUDY for a caricature of James Boswell (on the right) with Samuel Johnson during their tour of the Hebrides, published in May 1786. Boswell is celebrated both for his biography of Johnson and for his revealing and explicit diaries. **Below** [13] ENJOYING the popular gardens of Vauxhall in the late eighteenth century could expose a fashionable woman to the leering gaze of men. In this engraving of 1780, the alluring lady shields herself with her fan, though she does not appear to be too unhappy at the attention she is receiving.

Three · 'Fooles for love' in the 'Age of Reason'

THE EIGHTEENTH century – the 'Age of Reason' which saw flowerings of the arts, the sciences, knowledge and culture generally. Yet it was also an age of contrasts – between the integrity of artistic and scientific enquiry and the immorality of the daily lives of some of those who conducted it. As ever, the monarchs set a bad example in their unhappy family lives. The largely absentee King George I – who much preferred his home in Hanover to his kingdom of England – had divorced his first wife for adultery and had an extremely tempestuous relationship with his eldest son, who would become George II. He in his turn was happily married, though he took numerous mistresses, and had such a poor relationship with his eldest son, Frederick, that he banished him and his family from court. Frederick died before his father, so the next king was George II's grandson, George III. He was to prove remarkably uxorious, too; unlike his grandfather and so many kings before him, he took no mistresses and all of his fifteen children were legitimate. However, his long reign, marred in later years by a 'madness' probably caused by the disease porphyria, saw him engage in recurring conflict with his eldest son – this seems to have been a Hanoverian trait – and exerting tyrannical control over his daughters, who were denied the pleasures of a normal life and resorted to secrecy in their often doomed liaisons.

For those outside the royal family, the new precepts of the 'Age of Reason' were to have a beneficial effect. The dominance of religion over civil life was beginning to wane as society became more secular and scientific discoveries began to impact. Sexual behaviour was one of the areas of life affected by these changes in attitude and approach. No longer were people willing to be bound either by the Christian Church's long-standing antipathy to sexual enjoyment or by the excesses of Puritan austerity which had provoked bitterness and defiance. Within this climate, it became possible even for religious teaching to explore the notion that marital sex could be enjoyable and could contribute to the happiness and togetherness of husband and wife. Companionate marriages were increasingly the norm, celebrated in paintings like those of Gainsborough featuring contented-looking spouses with or without their broods of children.

But despite popular disapproval of the excesses of the post-Restoration court, the reaction against enforced sobriety under the Commonwealth provoked a backlash. This expressed itself in part through an increase in sex before and outside marriage. Demographic evidence of the time points to a reversion to the medieval custom of 'spousals', whereby the promise of marriage was all that was required to legitimize consummation. Once again, however, the double standard persisted: all was well for both man and woman in cases where spousals had been exchanged, sex had taken place and a child had been conceived before marriage – provided the man kept his word and married the woman; if he did not, the woman's reputation was ruined while the man's remained untainted, although he could still be made to relieve the parish of the cost of the child's upbringing.

The laws and customs surrounding marriage were still, at this point, confused. A church wedding, solemnized by a priest, had for decades been regarded by the religious authorities as essential for a valid marriage. Since 1604 it had been stipulated that banns had to be proclaimed for three consecutive weeks before the wedding, and that the ceremony had to take place between the hours of eight o'clock in the morning and noon in a church connected to the residence of one of the partners. For those under twenty-one, the rules also stipulated that parental consent was necessary. Marriages performed at night or elsewhere, without banns, perhaps by wandering clergymen, could result in severe punishment for the clergymen who officiated.

The problem was that marriages that broke these ecclesiastical laws did not contravene civil law and were both legal and binding. This conflict between religious rules and the authority of the state led to a strange situation in which marriage became engulfed in a sort of sleazy subculture, where dubious clergymen touted their services for a fee and indissoluble contracts could be entered into quickly, easily and perhaps while drunk. Unscrupulous officials would sometimes, for an extra fee, backdate the proceedings to legitimize a child already born, or would seek to procure a husband for a woman who was in urgent need of one. Increasingly, young couples whose parents disapproved were resorting to these arrangements, leading to growing numbers of disputes and family feuds over property. A further complication was that these marriages were rarely recorded, so one or other of the parties could abscond with ease and bigamy was all too likely.

These transactions became known as 'Fleet marriages' because the area round the Fleet prison in London was notorious for them, particularly during the first half of the eighteenth century when there were heavy taxes on official weddings. The area seethed with touts inviting passers-by to 'come in and be married', and alehouses and other public places were festooned with signs announcing that marriages were performed within. Some unlicensed churches were also well known for quick, cheap weddings. The trade was becoming scandalous.

It ended with Lord Hardwicke's Marriage Act of 1753 which came into effect in 1754 – with a final flurry of 217 Fleet marriages taking place the day before. At a stroke it removed all the confusion and laid down civil laws for marriage and clear procedures that had to be followed. From now on all marriages had to be conducted in a church and recorded in parish records signed by both bride and groom. In addition, both parties had to be over twenty-one to marry without their parents' consent. These rules were to be enforced by the secular courts, and any clergyman caught breaking the law was liable to fourteen years' transportation.

There was still, however, a way out for young couples desperate to marry without parental knowledge or permission. This was Scotland, where the law allowed marriage at the age of sixteen. Increasingly now, therefore, couples fled to Scotland – and specifically, since it was the first town over the border, to Gretna Green. Marriages here were conducted by the local blacksmith, who would marry the couple 'over the anvil', as a symbol of the two being joined as one in the same way as two metals are fired together on the anvil.

There are countless stories of young women sneaking out of their bedrooms at night to join their young men on the flight to Gretna Green, and of furious fathers pursuing them. Horses drawing coaches carrying the happy couple were flogged mercilessly to keep ahead of the pursuit, and if the angry father arrived before the ceremony could be conducted, the couple were hastened into bed to convince him that he was too late – only for them to emerge and be married properly once he was out of the way. These marriages may have been legal and indissoluble; but they were still scandalous and could have dire social and financial consequences for the couple. Many an heir or heiress found themselves disinherited as the result of what may well have been an impulsive flight; and one can only speculate about the regrets that might have set in once the excitement of elopement and marriage yielded to the reality of day-to-day life with someone who was probably a virtual stranger.

The introduction in 1857 of a change to the law enforced a three-week residence in the locality before the wedding could take place. This 'cooling-off period' greatly reduced Gretna Green elopements, though determined young couples still went to live there for the necessary time. Gretna Green continued to be a focus for runaway marriages until 1940, when the law changed again. And it is still a place where romantic couples can go to get married 'over the anvil'.

Jane Austen has the wayward Lydia Bennet planning a flight to Gretna Green with Mr Wickham in *Pride and Prejudice*. As Lydia wrote to her friend, Harriet Forster, 'You will laugh when you know where I am gone, and I cannot help laughing myself at your surprise tomorrow morning, as soon as I am missed. I am going to Gretna Green, and if you cannot guess with who, I shall think you a simpleton, for there is but one man in the world I love, so think it no harm to be off.' The dastardly Wickham had previously planned a similar flight with Georgiana Darcy, though on that occasion his plan had been to marry the girl and get his hands on her considerable fortune. This time he had no intention of tying himself to the penniless Lydia, merely of seducing her. (It was, of course, the noble Mr Darcy who intervened and forced Wickham, through a substantial financial settlement, to marry Lydia.) Fortune hunters must have been a constant peril in fashionable places such as Bath and Harrogate where young women of good family went to take the waters. Unscrupulous men, preying on young heiresses and wealthy widows, were not above compromising women in order to achieve their ends, as the fictional Mr Wickham makes plain.

Pride and Prejudice provides us with many insights on attitudes towards love, sex and marriage among the gentry of the eighteenth and early nineteenth centuries. The need to marry off at least some of their five daughters was a pressing one for Mr and Mrs Bennet, since the estate was entailed away from their family; Mr Bennet's death would leave his wife and daughters in dire financial straits unless there were husbands to help. The heir was to be the unctuous Mr Collins, who was quite sure that his position as the ultimate inheritor of her home would induce Elizabeth to accept his proposal of marriage with gratitude and pleasure. Her rejection of him astonished and appalled him, as it did her mother, for whom it seemed the height of selfishness. Mr Collins' immediate

approach to Charlotte Lucas, and her swift acceptance, are a clear indica-
tion that a young woman of no great beauty or fortune could usually be
relied on to take what was offered, regardless of love or affection. Time
was running out for Charlotte as it did for other girls of her time. Those
who failed to contract a suitable match in their first flush of youth were
on the cusp of inevitable spinsterhood, and likely to be withdrawn from
the social circuit in favour of younger sisters.

The Bennet daughters' lack of financial prospects was a severe hin-
drance to their chances of good marriages; their mother's stupidity and
position within society were others; and Lydia's elopement with
Wickham could have been a final blow to the prospects of the whole
family, taint by association making it highly unlikely that the other
daughters would marry well. Darcy's declaration to Elizabeth that his
feelings for her were against his better judgement, though repellent to
modern eyes, was the norm for the time: 'Could you expect me to
rejoice in the inferiority of your connections? To congratulate myself on
the hope of relations, whose condition in life is so decidedly beneath my
own?' Status within society and worldly wealth were of high importance; like Mr Collins, Darcy was amazed when Elizabeth turned him
down. Modern feminists cheer her on; but she was unusual for her age,
and she is fictional – a real young woman in her position may well not
have been in a position to follow her own inclinations so readily.

Moll Flanders, by contrast, aspired to a status in life that she was not
entitled to, and went to great lengths to achieve it. Daniel Defoe's novel,
published in 1722, concerns a woman whose convict mother 'pleaded
her belly' to avoid being hanged and who was left with foster parents
when her mother was transported to America. Moll embarks on a life of
serial marriage, passing herself off as a rich widow to attract men but herself falling prey to both misfortune and fraud. It is a story replete with
criminality and illicit liaison: bigamy after one husband goes bankrupt
and leaves her with the suggestion that she assume he is dead; incest
when she marries a good man who takes her to America and turns out
to be her brother; thievery which leads her to Newgate prison. Along the
way she abandons her children and falls in love with a man who is con-
ning her in his turn into believing that he is wealthy. However, like
Elizabeth Bennet, Moll's life has a happy ending when she is reunited
with the man she loves and ends up in America possessed of a plantation
left to her by her mother and reunited with her son. An anti-morality

tale perhaps; but one where the social and financial constraints of the time are well explored – and one which points up the perhaps greater freedom of lower-class women to live on their wits and to move around within the social scale.

Attitudes towards arranged marriages began to soften later in the century, with many parents prepared to take their daughters' inclinations into account. The dutiful Sophia Western, in Henry Fielding's *Tom Jones*, resolves that, while she will not marry without her father's consent, she will nevertheless hold out for a man whom she herself has chosen. Samuel Richardson's Clarissa is unfortunate when she takes a similar line: after refusing the unpleasant men picked for her by her parents, her choice falls on a dissolute man who rapes her while under the influence of drugs; her subsequent death is a bit of a morality tale. And it was still the case, in both literature and real life, that property and status were absolutes when it came to the necessities surrounding marriage. As a wealthy man lamented in 1704, when faced with the dilemma of whether or not to marry a poor young woman whom he loved and who returned his feelings: 'If I marry her, I am ruined; if I lie with her, she is.' A woman, by contrast, could bewail, 'I do not like to be married in a week to a man I never knew, but I am two and twenty ... and I am likely to go off soon. It is dangerous to refuse so great a match.' Such marriages didn't always work either: Sir William Stanhope is reported as alighting from his coach at his front door and saying to his wife, before she was driven off elsewhere, 'Madam, I hope I shall never see your face again'; to which she replied, 'Sir, I will take all the care I can that you never shall.'

Some arrangements did turn out well despite unpromising starts. In 1719 the son of the Duke of Richmond was married to the daughter of the Earl of Cadogan as part of an arrangement aimed at cancelling a gambling debt. Both were young children, the boy still at school, the girl still in the nursery. 'They are surely not going to marry me to that dowdy,' he exclaimed when he arrived for the ceremony. Afterwards she returned to her mother, he to his school and then on to the Grand Tour. When he returned after several years, he noticed a beautiful young woman at the theatre in London, and was overjoyed to discover that he was married to her.

There are other examples during the eighteenth century of unlikely matches. One concerned a penniless but clever clerk to a lawyer in Banbury who fell in love with his master's daughter but was spurned when, after completing his apprenticeship, he asked for her hand. When it was revealed that they had anyway got married secretly, they were turned out of the house. But the people of Banbury came to their rescue and helped him to set up in business, even giving him the work that had previously gone to his master. In another case, the impoverished Earl of Pembroke urged his son to find himself a rich bride so that the family fortunes would be restored. The alternative, as he put it, was 'nous sommes tous foutus'. One possibility was the daughter of the fabulously wealthy banker Sir Richard Child: 'Have you ever seen her, and do you think you could bring yourself to lay your chaste leg over her for the dirty consideration of two or three hundred thousand pounds?' It was not to be, however, and the young man found himself in love with an equally impoverished young girl, whom he married. Moreover, he even had his father's blessing: 'It would have been lucky for us had you found a thirty thousand pounder as agreeable to you as Elizabeth'; money mattered, but it seems that love, in this case at least, mattered more.

Sexual attraction, too, was increasingly recognized as an essential part of a successful marriage, and a couple's inclinations in this area were important. Moreover, women were beginning to be counselled both that such attraction tends to wane with time and that they should seek to keep it alive and not 'let themselves go' once safely married – advice modern women will also recognize. In other words the distinction between a wife, who was a housekeeper and the mother of heirs, and a mistress, who was there for sexual pleasure and companionship, was beginning to wane, and wives were being urged to maintain their 'mistress' role in the relationship.

Pleasure, meanwhile, continued to take many forms. There was an extensive subculture of male homosexuality during this period, much of it centred on 'molly houses', vibrant clubs where men could get together to sing, dance and drink, and have sex with each other in private rooms at the back. Those who frequented these clubs often crossdressed, gave each other female names and used effeminate language. In addition, the men-only public institutions of the time offered a climate where sexual interactions between men could find outlets, and the libertarianism of popular culture encouraged some rather rackety behaviour.

During most of the eighteenth century morality organizations actively pursued homosexual men, using spies and agents provocateurs, and aided by thief-takers like Jonathan Wild – later himself to be hanged to great public acclaim, having amassed a fortune by extortion of various kinds. One of the leaders of these moral reformers was the Reverend Bray, who seems to have been obsessed with sodomy and frequently preached against it as 'an evil force invading our land'. The result of one of his campaigns was the raid on Mother Clap's notorious molly house in London in February 1726: the house was apparently betrayed to the police by a disaffected 'molly' and over forty men were arrested and taken to Newgate. Many of them were discharged for lack of evidence, but several committed suicide rather than face trial and seven or eight were prosecuted and found guilty. Three of them – Thomas Wright, William Griffin and Gabriel Lawrence – were hanged at Tyburn, and Mother Clap was also convicted and sentenced to the pillory in Smithfield as well as a fine and two years' imprisonment.

Executions for sodomy were not infrequent. Lord Audley, Earl of Castlehaven, and two of his menservants were executed for it in 1631, and there was another in Ireland in 1640, when John Atherton, Bishop of Waterford and Lismore, was hanged in Dublin; his lover, John Childe, was also hanged a little later. The Old Bailey records several cases: William North, aged fifty-four, was sentenced to the gallows in 1822, and in the same year John Holland and William King, aged forty-two and thirty-two, were tried together and both sentenced to death; presumably they had been caught in the act with each other. One Henry Nichols was hanged for sodomy in August 1833, repudiated by his family who would neither visit him in prison before his execution nor claim his body afterwards. The death penalty for the offence remained in force until 1861.

In practice the crime of sodomy was hard to prove, since there had to be at least two witnesses and evidence of both penetration and ejaculation. As a result the charge was often reduced to 'assault with sodomitical intent'. It does seem in addition that there was a certain reluctance on the part of judges and juries to convict defendants of full sodomy, even quite early in the eighteenth century. George Duffus is an example, tried on 6 December 1721 for committing the 'unnatural sin of sodomy' on the body of Nicholas Leader. After Duffus had persuaded Leader to let him stay for the night because he lived a long way off, the graphic evidence describes how Duffus began to embrace him and tried to have sex with him, with Leader resisting and – according to his account – at the same time being anxious not to disturb his grandmother who lay ill in the next room. Similar evidence came from a Mr Powel who was also duped into allowing Duffus to stay with him. The verdict, however, was that Duffus should be retried on the lesser charge of attempting to commit sodomy, and when the retrial took place early the following year, he was fined twenty marks, sent to prison for two months and made to stand in the pillory near Old Gravel Lane, where he had committed the offence. It appears that George Duffus and others like him – one John Dicks, for example, who seems from the evidence to have been guilty of homosexual rape – were treated leniently by the courts; but some historians suggest that the pillory was by no means a light punishment and could be a virtual death sentence if the baying crowd got out of hand. Certainly it seems that tolerance of homosexuality among the louche upper urban classes was not echoed within the rural and working classes, so severe physical harm while penned in the pillory was to be feared.

Many of the trials reveal that extortion and blackmail based on the threat to expose homosexuals was widespread. George Skelthorpe was hanged in 1709 on two charges of theft, on both of which he pleaded innocence right up to the gallows; it seems that the charges had been brought by two men from whom he had extorted money in exchange for keeping quiet about homosexual encounters. His protestations of innocence were therefore a little disingenuous; he may not technically have been guilty of theft, but he was certainly guilty of extortion on these and on many other occasions.

Blackmailers preyed on the genuinely innocent, too. In 1724 Robert Wise found himself the victim of extortioners who threatened to accuse him of sodomy unless he paid them. According to his testimony at the trial, he was relieving himself against a wall when a man came up to him and thrust his hand into Wise's breeches, at which two others reared up from behind some hogsheads and cried, 'Now by God, we have got him. A sodomite!' They extorted increasingly large sums from him until he finally handed over a diamond ring worth eight pounds which they shortly afterwards tried to sell; but they had the bad luck to offer it to the goldsmith who had originally supplied it. He called the constable and had the men arrested. Two of them skipped bail, but the remaining prisoner was found guilty and sentenced to the pillory and a fine as well as imprisonment. He was luckier than William Cane, who was tried in 1810 for theft with violence; he had threatened a Mr Price that he would denounce him for sodomy unless he gave him money. When asked why he did not raise the alarm, Price replied, 'I considered myself at the mercy of the prisoner, I did not know with whom he might be connected, and that he might have persisted in carrying into execution the horrid charge of accusing me publicly with a crime which my nature shuddered at.' After several more meetings at which the price got higher and higher, peaking at £1,000, Price set a trap for the blackmailer and he was apprehended. Cane's defence was that he had been propositioned by his accuser: 'I own that Mr Price gave me the money, I never extorted a shilling from him.' His plea was in vain; he was sentenced to death.

A prominent victim of blackmail in 1822 was Lord Castlereagh, then Foreign Secretary and Leader of the House of Commons. 'I am accused of the same crime as the Bishop of Clogher' was the admission he made to George IV, who advised him to consult a doctor. Shortly afterwards he killed himself by slitting his throat with a letter opener. This was only a week or so after Percy Jocelyn, the said bishop, had been caught in a compromising position with a soldier in the back room of the White Lion pub in central London. Despite the case causing a massive scandal, the 'buggering bishop' was released on bail and escaped to Scotland where he worked as a butler under an assumed name. He was the most senior British cleric to be involved in a homosexual scandal in the nineteenth century, and was deposed from his post shortly after his disappearance for 'the crimes of immorality, incontinence, Sodomitical practices, habits and propensities, and neglect of his spiritual, judicial and ministerial duties'. It was later discovered that the bishop, over ten years before, had successfully prosecuted his brother's coachman, who had accused him of sodomy, and had caused him to be imprisoned for two years and flogged almost to death; a public subscription was now raised for the coachman to make up for this injustice.

Lesbianism was not, by contrast, a crime at all, and can often only be inferred from accounts of women cross-dressing as men. Sometimes this resulted in a charge of fraud, as with one woman in 1777 who was convicted at the Guildhall in London of passing herself off as a man, marrying three women in turn and defrauding them of money and clothes; her punishment was the pillory at Charing Cross and six months in prison. There are also several reports of women dressing as men in order to join the militia, one of whom was Barbara Hill of York in the 1750s. She was recognized while trying to enlist and exposed as a woman, but carried on dressing as a man and took jobs as a farm servant and a bricklayer's labourer. She then 'married' a woman and lived with her happily enough for five years; when she was again outed, her 'wife' appeared in great distress, begging that they should not be parted. The parish record of their wedding still exists, showing that a later hand had scored it across.

One famous possible instance of a lesbian relationship at the end of the eighteenth century was that of the 'Ladies of Llangollen', though they themselves sued a newspaper which raised questions about their relationship. Lady Eleanor Butler was twenty-nine when she met thirteen-year-old Sarah Ponsonby in 1768. Daughters of two aristocratic Irish families, they lived near each other, and soon developed a close and intense friendship. Both their families were trying to force them into arranged marriages, or in Lady Eleanor's case into a convent when it seemed that she might be too old to attract a suitable husband, and they decided to avoid this fate by running away together. Their first attempt in April 1778 was thwarted by their families who found them and made them return home. They persisted, however, and by 1780 the couple had crossed the Irish Sea – seemingly disguised as men – and were living near the small town of Llangollen in Wales. They had to live frugally because their families refused to provide them with anything more than basic subsistence, but they set up home in a cottage which they renamed Plas Newydd and transformed into a Gothic-style manor house, where they entertained many of the literati of the time. Visitors included the Duke of Wellington and the poets Wordsworth and Byron, the latter of whom compared their relationship with his love for the choirboy John Edlestone. The two aristocratic women lived in their house for nearly fifty years before their deaths (Butler in 1829 and Ponsonby two years later). They were never explicitly open about their relationship, and while it was certain that they shared a remarkable closeness, it was never sure whether or not they were actively lesbian. Interestingly, despite the fact that they were unusual for their time in eloping together as two women, they were still rather conservative. They strongly disapproved of the French Revolution, and sacked a maid for conceiving a child out of wedlock.

For noble, rich young men of the time, the Grand Tour was the opportunity not only to broaden their minds by travel on the Continent, but also to develop their education in the arts of sex and seduction. Direct evidence of what they got up to is not always easy to come by, since their letters home and their journals tended not to mention some of their more sleazy activities; but indirect evidence in the form of the treatment they had to undergo for venereal disease is a pointer. The young Henry Digby, then in Hanover, was sent a box containing 'an injection which … will cure his present disorder, and condoms, which if he pleases … may prevent future ones.' But he still had a 'persistent clap' later in the year. Money was another worry for those at home; the son of an English duke gave £1,000 to 'one little piece of readymade love' in Paris, whereas 'in London the same woman, and consequently the same charms, would not have produced a tythe of such liberality'. And another young noble-man's generosity to 'a certain Mlle Adeline' in Paris later made it essen-tial for him to restore his and his family's fortunes by seeking a rich wife. Italy was regarded as the place where most temptation was likely to be met, both heterosexual and homosexual, though Parisian whores were reported as being most put out by the growing numbers of young boys hanging around the theatres waiting to be picked up, and a young man visiting Portugal was offered prostitutes of both sexes. Beyond disease and over-generosity with money, almost the greatest danger, for those who were concerned about the regular conduct of suitable marriages, was when a young man fell hopelessly in love with a woman abroad, be she a fellow Englishwoman on her own Grand Tour or – worse – a for-eigner. Some of these alliances did end up in marriage, but more had to be broken up by family or friends descending on the couple and separat-ing them.

Like Pepys before him, James Boswell wrote diaries that are extremely illuminating on life as observed by the literati and the prosperous classes in the middle of the eighteenth century. On the double standard, for example, he describes a conversation with an unnamed intelligent woman who stated that, as she well knew her husband had been un-faithful to her many times, she ought to have no scruple in engaging in an affair herself: 'I argued that the chastity of women was of much more consequence than that of men, as the property and rights of families depend upon it.' When she replied that the objection would not count if a woman had affairs only when she was pregnant, Boswell could not answer: 'Yet she was wrong, and I was uneasy…'. The woman was clearly beginning to question the normal assumptions about sexual freedom of the time, in common with many others of her sort.

Boswell was himself a sexual libertine, yet one who was torn by his own religious inclinations and by the disapproval of his Calvinist mother and his aloof Scottish father, Lord Auchinleck. He flirted with Catholicism and enjoyed talking to sceptics such as John Wilkes and mystics, like Rousseau. But his sexual appetite was enormous, and between the ages of twenty, when he was introduced to sex by a friend on his first visit to London, and twenty-nine, when he married, he had a huge number of sexual liaisons. As well as frequenting brothels in almost every major European city, he had at least six mistresses, some of them respectable married women while others were of lower class, plus liaisons with several actresses; and he produced at least two illegitimate children. In addition, he contracted gonorrhoea several times and eventually died of a tumour in the bladder after suffering for years with urinary problems, probably brought on by his frequent bouts of venereal disease as well as the highly dangerous mercury pills he swallowed to combat it.

One of his mistresses, while he was on one of his return trips to Scotland, was the seventeen-year-old Jean Heron, the wife of one of his friends and the daughter of a friend of his father's. She appears to have been very clear, for herself at least, about sex and marriage: one was for enjoyment, the other for convenience, and she had no scruples about throwing herself at Boswell only a few weeks after her marriage and enjoying the liaison with him. He hoped to find a similar mistress when he went to London, but his first attempt – with a young Covent Garden actress – led to another bout of gonorrhoea. His failure to find a 'safe' mistress led him eventually to buy condoms, which he called his 'armour'. He regarded them as protection more against venereal disease than against conception, since they allowed him to consort with whores with lessened danger of infection. He seemed to have no scruples about producing illegitimate children: he argued to Rousseau that, provided he gave any daughters dowries and married them off to peasants who would be happy to have them, he would be justified in enjoying the favours of large numbers of potential mothers. Rousseau disagreed. But Boswell was of his time when it came to providing for illegitimate children; he felt it was his duty, though he did not, like some of his contemporaries, treat them equally with the legitimate offspring. This tolerance towards by-blows was not, however, universal: Boswell discovered that a prostitute he frequented in Edinburgh was the illegitimate daughter of Lord Kinnaird, who had clearly not found it in himself to support her in a more respectable profession.

Boswell writes frankly in his diaries both about his sexual liaisons and about his parallel struggles to live a less bawdy life. While on the Grand Tour he decided on a plan of moral reform, to counter the fact that up to now he had been 'idle, dissipated, absurd and unhappy'. But he found it impossible; his sexual urges were too strong. In Berlin he had sex with a woman who came to his room to sell him chocolate; he discovered that she was both married and pregnant, so 'Bless me, I have now committed adultery... Let it go. I'll think no more of it.' And in Siena he spent days making passionate love with the wife of the mayor, who fell in love with him and wrote to him for years afterwards. But Boswell had moved on, and they never met again. He even seduced the long-standing mistress of his mentor, Rousseau, who gave him lessons in the sexual arts after complaining that, although he was a vigorous lover, he had no subtlety.

Boswell alienated his father by marrying his cousin, Margaret, who was not wealthy enough to please the old man. Indeed, his father not only refused to attend the wedding but even announced that he too was to be remarried, and on the same day! Boswell's marriage was, however, a happy one, and his wife seemed to understand his needs. Twice during the marriage she announced that she would no longer be his wife, on both occasions after she had read his diaries – which were always highly explicit and truthful – and discovered dalliances of which she did not approve: feelings of tenderness or love on the part of her husband towards other women were unacceptable, and nor did she approve of passing fondlings with young girls. On both these occasions she forgave her husband, and for the rest of the time she went along with his lustful desires, about which he was mostly honest with her, and accepted his frequent infidelity. He had his standards: he never seduced a virgin, he never slept with his wife when he had the pox, he did commit adultery but either sought to justify it by some form of double-thinking or felt guilty about it. However, he also never thought to protect his wife from repeated pregnancy through any methods of contraception, even though for many years she suffered from tuberculosis and became weaker and more chronically ill.

His diaries throw a great deal of light on eighteenth-century London, with its hierarchies of sexual possibility – from respectable married women who were sometimes willing to indulge in a little extra-marital affair, through actresses and shop girls, to whores who might belong to relatively respectable brothels or, lower down the scale, could be picked up on the street. The less fashionable coffee-houses sometimes carried on a brothel business on the side, and head-dressers' shops were often frequented by harlots who could be had for a guinea. Certain districts of London and other cities were known for the high class of the harlots to be found there, while cheaper prostitutes frequented other areas, and the trade went right down to poor women who would oblige in back streets for a few pence. Parks, in the capital and elsewhere, were places where men and women in search of lovers could parade their offerings, and the piazza outside St Paul's in Covent Garden was also a recognized venue for that sort of assignation.

It is also clear that there were hordes of exploitable young women working in service or in alehouses and inns who were easy prey, and that girls drawn away from rural drudgery to the bright lights of the cities were easily lured. Hogarth's series of engravings, *A Harlot's Progress*, charts the rise and fall of one such young woman. We see her first arriving in London, probably to seek work in service, but almost immediately propositioned by Mother Needham, the notorious brothel-keeper, and offered more lucrative work; she then becomes the mistress of a merchant but entertains other lovers while he is out before being imprisoned in Bridewell for prostitution; out of prison but impoverished and sick with the pox, she finally dies at the age of only twenty-three, her funeral a scene of squabbling prostitutes of whom one is distracting the vicar from his funeral duties with her hand down his breeches. Mother Needham, incidentally, the real-life bawd whose brothel in St James's was much patronized by the gentry, was famous for her tyrannical viciousness towards the girls who came into her clutches, keeping them constantly in debt to herself and abandoning them to debtor's prison or to the streets if they failed to maintain a high workload. She is said to have died after a stint in the pillory, the victim of the pelting she received at the hands of the mob. One of her most notorious clients also features in the Hogarth engraving as the man in the doorway behind Mother Needham. This was the debauched Colonel Francis Charteris, for whom she procured the sort of strong country girls who could stand up to the rough usage he demanded from his whores.

Hogarth's next series, *A Rake's Progress*, is equally illuminating about the perils facing silly young men of the time. After the death of his penny-pinching father, the rake immediately repudiates the young servant, Sarah, whom he has made pregnant, and goes to London to seek the pleasures of society, some of which he finds at the notorious Covent Garden Rose Tavern where the scene is one of sordid dissolution. Having spent all his inheritance and descended into debt he finds himself in the Fleet prison despite the efforts of the faithful Sarah to keep him safe; he is not to be reformed, however, and casts Sarah off yet again in favour of an old, one-eyed but wealthy wife whose money he gambles away. His fate is finally a syphilitic death in Bedlam, laughed at by fashionable young women who go there to stare at the inmates. *Marriage a la Mode* also portrays the descent into poverty and death of a rich, titled young couple who lose everything through their dissolute overindulgence. Amidst piles of unpaid bills, the husband visits a doctor to find out which of the two women with him gave him a venereal disease, and then discovers his wife in bed with her lover, who draws a knife and stabs him. She is left grieving and poverty-stricken, and her father's only response to her suicide by poison is to remove the one valuable item she has left — her wedding ring.

Hogarth's moralistic tales run parallel with Boswell's musings on fidelity and adultery: on the one hand the diarist expected his wife to be faithful and thought it wrong that women might contemplate affairs even if in doing so they were posing no threat to the legitimacy of their offspring; on the other, he frequently took what was offered regardless of the marital position of his partner, guilty though he may have felt. Such standards applied in other ways, too: one Thomas Williams, who died in the middle of the eighteenth century, left an annuity of fifty shillings to his maidservant, Cecilia Philipps, as long as she remained unmarried and lived 'a chaste and virtuous life'. This money was to come from a trust based on one of his properties, the rents and profits from which were to be used mainly for the maintenance and education of John and David, his sons by Cecilia, and he left further money to allow her to build and equip a property for herself and her children. It seems, therefore, that although he was fully prepared to provide for his illegitimate children, he would only look after the woman who had satisfied his needs (he was unmarried) if she remained loyal to his memory: 'in case ... [she] shall either marry or lead a loose, wicked, dissolute and incontinent life after my dowage the said annuity ... shall immediately cease and determine.' Moreover, he was prepared to leave the property she was to live in to her sons at her death, provided again that she kept her virtue. One can perhaps appreciate that he would not have wanted to support her if she used the money to behave badly; but to preclude her from marrying again, not just because she would thereby lose her annuity but also because she would deprive her sons of a valuable inheritance, smacks very much of a dog-in-the-manger attitude.

Women at this time had no independent status in common law, and once married they were regarded as the property of their husbands; religious law, too, which still maintained its authority over marriage, regarded a husband and wife as becoming one flesh, indivisible until death. Nevertheless, there were ways to achieve the break-up of unsatisfactory marriages (even if you were not a king who needed an heir).

The easiest way – particularly where no property was involved – was simple desertion; one or other party would just run off and make a new life elsewhere. Although neither husband nor wife was legally free to marry again, no doubt many did and got away scot-free. Bigamy was, however, illegal and there are several Old Bailey cases of this period which record the trials of those who were discovered and prosecuted, often by the second spouse who had some grievance against the bigamous partner and wanted to be legally free of the marriage.

One bigamist was Jane Watson, who was tried on 29 June 1785 at the Old Bailey. An entry in the parish register of St John's, Wapping, for 1 December 1782 recorded her marriage to Robert Allen, a butcher, and an entry in the register of St Martin in the Fields, Middlesex, for 1 September 1784, had her marrying one Charles Burton. The witness to her first marriage gave evidence that he recognized her and that her first husband was still alive. An attempt by one of the attorneys to mitigate the circumstances was unsuccessful: 'My Lord, may I be permitted to prove that this man, during the short time he lived with the prisoner, treated her in a most brutal manner, and forced her to submit to prostitution to maintain him before he abandoned her.' The court's reply was succinct: 'That might lay her under the necessity of quitting one husband, but could not lay her under the necessity of marrying another.' She was found guilty and sentenced to be branded.

John Trott was also tried for bigamy at the Old Bailey on 3 July 1828: having first married Sarah Stevens on 21 December 1819 in Thorncomb, Devon, he went on to marry Mary Whitten in Speene, Berkshire, on 16 February 1824. She was a widow and he described himself as a widower, but both his legal wife and her mother were at the trial and able to testify that she was still very much alive. He seems to have been a sad specimen as his long and mournful plea for mitigation indicates, ending with: 'if ever pity dwell in your breast towards a poor individual, I trust it dwells there now, for I can truly say "I acknowledge my transgression, and my sin is ever before me."' Perhaps it worked: although he was found guilty, there is no record of the sentence.

It is clear from some of these trials that juries of the time could be inclined to a merciful approach to the offence and its punishment, and to accept mitigating circumstances. Elizabeth Ouston was one of those who benefited, tried on 20 April 1803 after marrying another man while her husband was still alive. Her mother testified that her husband had 'used her very ill… I took one child … he never made any provision or allowance for her, or her [other] child; he would sometimes come and sleep with her…'. She also said that she had frequently noticed the marks of violence on her daughter. The jury found her guilty but with a recommendation to mercy; she was sentenced to a week in Newgate and a fine of one shilling.

In several cases, the evidence shows a couple marrying and living together for only a short while; in the case of John Wheatley, tried on 6 April 1826, it was for a mere six months, at which point his wife left him because of his ill-treatment of her. She went on to live with a Mr Groves, whose name she took, and then died. But before her death Wheatley had married Elizabeth Ann Rogers, who now brought the case against him and testified both that he had not treated her well and that he had told her about a former wife although he did not know whether she was still alive. To his credit, he appears to have gone to some trouble to find out, but went through with the marriage anyway. Again, mercy was recommended and he was sentenced to six months. Different circumstances surrounded the charge of bigamy brought against Charlotte English on 30 June 1831. She had lived with her husband for only a couple of years after their marriage in 1798, and then married William Hands in 1811, after which they lived together for fourteen years before separating. He was now bringing the case against her because 'She troubles me for maintenance', although 'I have no wish to have her punished.' He seems to have sought out the family of the first husband (who was now dead) after discovering that she knew all along during the time they lived together that the first husband was alive and where to find him. They probably both got a good result from the case: he was legally rid of an unlawful wife and she, although found guilty of bigamy, was fined only a shilling and discharged.

Some cases were more reprehensible. John Ward married Anne Huffman on 4 February 1730 and Sarah Woodward on 22 March 1730. Although he claimed he was drunk at the first wedding, he was found guilty and sentenced to be branded. William Johnson was another good-for-nothing: he agreed to marry Sarah Dilbey in order to provide her with a husband since she was pregnant, and then later married Martha Blainey but left her soon afterwards. When she asked him to come home, he kicked her so violently that she had to go to hospital, and then took him to court. His sentence was to be transported for seven years.

It was not just the lower classes who resorted to bigamy. In the case of Lieutenant Colonel John William Speed in the early nineteenth century, physical attraction seems to have been the reason for his short-lived marriage to Ann Thorn while his lawful wife, Sarah Nelson, was still alive. After marrying Sarah in 1785 he lived with her for seven years and had six children with her, of whom three survived. Seven years after that, in 1799, he married Ann Thorn, who was a gardener's daughter, thus using 'the solemnity of marriage as the instrument of seduction'. Ann had no fortune and there was no bastard child to 'legitimize'; the reason for marrying her appears to have been entirely because he wanted to bed her. Five months after the marriage Speed left her, although she was pregnant, to go to Nova Scotia where he started yet another family. Described as 'an elderly and shrewd man', Speed mustered many testimonials at his trial from highly placed members of the military, together with arguments directed against his first wife and his representatives in court (he claimed that his solicitor was a friend of his wife's) and pleas for mercy on the basis of his many sufferings while awaiting trial. To no avail: he was sentenced to seven years' transportation.

A strange case was that of Robert Fielding on 6 December 1706. The account of it is more than a bit rambling: it appears that he sought to marry a woman with a huge fortune, but had to content himself with a widow, Mrs Wadsworth, whom he seems to have forced into marriage on only their second meeting despite her wish to postpone the proceedings. He locked her into his chambers and reappeared with a dubious-sounding priest 'called the Red Father, with a long red gown lined with blue, a long beard, and a fur cap.' Mrs Wadsworth wanted some proof that he was a priest, whereupon he produced 'a paper of the Pope's picture, about the bigness of a crown piece, and said, that none but priests us'd to carry those pictures about 'em.' From the evidence, Mrs Wadsworth was not at all happy about the marriage and was desperately seeking for excuses to stop it, among them objecting when the priest could not read the marriage service in English – whereupon Mr Fielding did it for him and, when she pronounced the words very faintly, required her to say them again more strongly. It is not clear from the indictment whether this was his first marriage, which perhaps he was calling into question after being accused of marrying Barbara, Duchess of Cleveland, while his wife was still alive. He was found guilt of felony, but the sentence is not recorded.

A more unusual way of getting rid of a wife was to sell her – a transaction which usually took place on market day, often with prearranged bidding. This may have been an acceptable form of 'divorce' only when the 'marriage' had been based on informal contracts or perhaps spousals, which were now no longer binding in law. It was a symbolic transfer from one man to another of ownership of the woman and responsibility for her; there could even be a deed of sale, and local newspapers often recorded the transaction. A famous later literary example of wife sale is in the opening chapter of Thomas Hardy's *The Mayor of Casterbridge*, published in 1886, in which Michael Henchard sells his wife in the market, taking her there with a halter round her neck. It seems from entries in his notebooks that Hardy had researched occurrences of wife sale earlier in the century in England: one real case he'd found concerned a man who sold his wife to a shop-mate for a gallon of beer; apparently she seemed quite agreeable to the transaction. Another wife sale in 1827 netted a rather more substantial five pounds for the seller.

A divorce which freed the parties to marry again was extremely difficult to obtain at this time. Divorce was a matter for the ecclesiastical courts, since marriage was regarded as a religious sacrament and so could only be dissolved by a religious authority. Rarely, courts could grant a decree of nullity which rendered the marriage void from the outset – *ab initio* – on grounds such as one party's lack of the ability to enter freely into the relationship, for example through insanity, or consanguinity – including, as with Henry VIII, a family tie through a previous marriage. A decree of nullity had the effect of bastardizing the children and removing from the wife her entitlement to a third of her husband's property on his death (her dower). But it did mean that husband and wife were free to marry again.

More common, though still rare, was an annulment *a mensa et thoro* – from board and hearth – where the rights of both wife and children were preserved, though remarriage was not permitted during the lifetime of the other. This was only granted in cases of proven adultery plus, if a woman brought the action, other iniquitous behaviour such as incest or life-threatening cruelty by her husband. Before such an annulment was granted a man usually brought a case of 'criminal conversation' against his wife's lover, in which he sued for damages on the grounds that the lover had stolen the husband's property by making use of the wife's body. Such cases were also brought after the guilty woman had died, such as when Lord Abergavenny was awarded damages of ten thousand pounds against his friend, Richard Lyddel, who had slept with Lady Abergavenny; she had been driven away from her home and shortly afterwards died, but her lover was still vulnerable to a heavy financial penalty.

Beyond this stage, the only way of achieving a full divorce *a vinculo matrimonii*, i.e. full freedom from the bonds of marriage, was by Act of Parliament. Before 1858, when the law changed, there were fewer than 300 of these full divorces, a statistic that reflects the lengthy, difficult and expensive procedure that had to be followed. Moreover, only four of those divorces were achieved by women, and two of those involved incest. The first ever full divorce under these regulations was in 1670, between John Manners, Lord Roos, and his wife, Lady Anne Pierpont, on the grounds of her adultery. Another, also on the grounds of the wife's adultery, was in the 1790s between the Revd John Thoroton and his wife Elizabeth. The National Archives documents on the case [DEL7/ 1ff.234–58] record the appeal by Elizabeth Thoroton against the action, which came after the original case in the Court of Arches at Canterbury, where the decree *a mensa et thoro* was granted, together with the case of criminal conversation brought by the husband against the lover. The evidence is vivid: 'That John Thoroton, on or about the third day of February 1795, went to London on business; that several times … whilst John Thoroton was absent from home in London, and at Goadby, in the County of Leicester, to attend the funeral of Charlotte Manners, the sister of Elizabeth Thoroton, John Whitchurch came to the house of John Thoroton at Bottesford, and remained there all night, that John Whitchurch on such several occasions, did not sleep in the bed appropriated for him, although the same was prepared for him … but on every of such times they, John Whitchurch and Elizabeth Thoroton slept together naked and alone, in the bed of Elizabeth Thoroton, and that on the next morning, the servants on making the bed ... plainly perceived the marks or impressions of two bodies having lain therein, also certain stains at such times on the sheets of the bed, which convinced those that saw them, that two persons had been in the act of carnal copulation thereon.'

As was common at the time, it was the servants who saw what was going on and told their tales. Dependent as they were on the goodwill of their employers, they must have had to balance the advantage for themselves of coming out with the truth of an illicit affair or conniving at keeping it secret. Listening at doors or peeping through keyholes did not always result in welcome knowledge. In this case, it was Richard Hunt who wrote to his master to tell him what he had witnessed, while at the same time Elizabeth was writing to say that the servants were telling lies about her and that her husband was not to believe them. She contended that John Whitchurch, who was a surgeon and apothecary, had been summoned because she was ill, and she had required him to stay with her all night because she was afraid that she might die. John Thoroton accepted her story and told the servants so; and soon after this he allowed her to go with the children to stay with her parents while repairs were being done on the house – with the proviso that she would not see or summon John Whitchurch while she was there.

Elizabeth Thoroton appears, however, to have been either madly in love or completely reckless, because she did indeed summon Whitchurch to her parents' house on several occasions and spent several hours alone with him in a darkened room. It was when this was reported to him that John Thoroton brought the action which Elizabeth was now contesting. Two loving letters to her from John Whitchurch were presented as evidence, of which the second perhaps betrays the fact that she may have been thinking better of her actions: 'Bettsy, If you loved me half so much as you have given me reason to believe, or could conceive that I loved you half as much as I really do, you would not ... suffer me to remain so long in such a dreadful ignorance of your situation... Should any alteration have taken place in your affection for me, let me know it; let me know the worst; I am miserable, and both prepared and determined for any thing that can happen.'

If she did repent, it was in vain. The divorce was finalized in 1799 by an Act of Parliament, by which time records suggest that Whitchurch had married one Ann Healy. It seems unlikely that Elizabeth Thoroton married again, since she was left an annuity of £100 in her father's will, proved in 1811, under her maiden name, Elizabeth Manners. Since she was eighteen when she married (her husband's age was given simply as 'over twenty-one'), she may have been a foolish young girl who thought, like many before and since, that she would not be found out or that, if she was, her husband would forgive her. That one of her dalliances with her lover took place while her husband was away at the funeral of her own sister argues at the very least for a high degree of recklessness. One can only speculate!

As Lawrence Stone points out, and as is borne out by the records, the high and early death rate that still prevailed often had the effect of freeing husband or wife from an unhappy marriage. The even higher incidence of childhood mortality could also remove the evidence of an adulterous or extramarital fling. And one can only guess that infanticide was not uncommon. A case at the Old Bailey on 16 April 1740 records one such possibility, when Elizabeth Evans was tried for killing her newborn infant. A witness, Sophia Claxton, testified that 'I came home and went to bed, after I had been out all day hard at work; the prisoner in the night got upright upon her knees in the bed; and I asked her, what she was doing? She told me, she was making use of the pot. In the morning ... under her gown I saw a handkerchief; and in the handkerchief I found a baby wrapped up... I did not observe whether the child had received any hurt in its body, nor can I tell whether it was at its full growth. I never heard it cry. Tho' I lay with her, she never informed me of her being with child, and when I found it in the handkerchief, she said nothing to me; she did not own it was hers.'

Another witness was a midwife, Elizabeth Holman, who examined the baby and found that it was dead: 'I can't take upon me to say, whether it was born alive or not. I did not observe any hurt or bruise upon it. After I had seen the child, I asked, how she came to kill it? She said, she did not kill it; she found it dead, and therefore laid it away from her; and before she would have killed it, she would have gone a-begging with it. I desired her to tell me who was the father? She said, she could not tell who it was got it, nor where he was, for one of the men was gone twenty miles, another thirty, and another four miles off.' Evans herself had no witnesses to call and her only defence was her insistence that she had not murdered the baby. The jury acquitted her.

Foundling children were a common sight, left in church porches or just on the street; some were illegitimate while others were born to poor households which did not have the resources to feed another mouth. One such in literature was Tom Jones, in Fielding's novel of that name, who had the good fortune to be left at the door of Mr Allworthy who took him in and brought him up. Had she had her way, his housekeeper, Deborah Wilkins, would have had nothing to do with the baby: 'It goes against me to touch these misbegotten wretches, whom I don't look upon as my fellow creatures. Faugh, how it stinks! It does not smell like a Christian... I would have it put in a basket and set out and laid at the churchwarden's door. It is a good night, only a little rainy and windy; and if it was well wrapped up and put in a warm basket, it is two to one but it lives till it is found in the morning... It is perhaps better for such creatures to die in a state of innocence than to grow up and imitate their mothers, for nothing better can be expected of them.'

It was fortunate for Tom that Mr Allworthy was more charitable, and for other abandoned children in real life that Thomas Coram took a more caring attitude towards them. After a successful career as a merchant seaman, he found himself appalled at the number of dead and dying babies he saw every day on the streets of London. He decided to petition King George II to do something about them, but initially met with indifference, or at least lack of support, partly on the grounds that caring for such children might be seen as encouragement of wantonness and prostitution. It took him years of pressure, but he finally gained the support of Queen Caroline and eventually of much of London society, who were impressed both by his hard-working compassion for the children and by his concern for their education and welfare. Subscriptions for his new institution poured in, and in 1739 the king signed a Royal Charter. The first children were accepted in 1741 and soon afterwards a permanent home was built in Bloomsbury 'for the education and maintenance of exposed and deserted young children'.

The institution became an impressive memorial to the eighteenth century's spirit of benevolence, and it was also London's favourite charity. The childless Hogarth was one of the founding governors, and he and his wife, Jane, fostered some of the children. Handel supported it by giving performances in the chapel, including the oratorio *Messiah* on 1 May 1750 to mark the presentation of the chapel organ; he later left the rights in *Messiah* to the foundation, and his will and his conductor's score of the oratorio are on display in the Foundling Museum. Painters donated their work to the building, so much so that it became the first public gallery of contemporary art in London and led to the foundation of the Royal Academy in 1768. The foundation still exists, still caring for children, and although the original building has been demolished there is still a children's playground on the site, called Coram's Fields.

One institution was not, of course, nearly enough to cope with the scale of the problem, and the hospital soon found itself overwhelmed, with thousands of children arriving each year from all over the country. A new profession of itinerant baby transporters developed who would carry babies in baskets and dump them, dead or alive, at the doors of the hospital. Many others, having received the fee for taking the child, simply abandoned it on the way. It was inevitable that most of the children died, and that those running the hospital had to make poignant decisions about which babies they could accept. But the way was at least opening towards more humanitarian approaches to the problems caused by unwanted childbirth.

The love story of Charles James Fox, Whig grandee, and Elizabeth Armistead, celebrated courtesan, indicates that very occasionally redemption was possible even in those rigid times when a reputation, once lost, was irretrievable. It seems certain that Mrs Armistead started life on the town in a brothel, but she soon graduated to being a woman kept by a succession of high-class lovers. Her shrewd management of both her reputation and her finances meant that she kept her position as a high-class courtesan for many years, acquiring along the way at least two annuities from former lovers and her own houses. Her early relationship with Fox is recorded in his letters to her (hers to him have not survived) and it seems to have been one of mutual friendship and confidence which soon blossomed into love. She tried to break off the liaison at one stage because she was all too aware of the precariousness of her position as the mere mistress; but he was so unhappy that she relented, and even broke all the rules of her profession by selling her assets and throwing in her lot with him. She rented, and later bought, a house near Chertsey in Surrey where they increasingly lived together; but she was not his wife, so she could not move in society as his formal companion or be received herself by respectable women. And even when he decided that he would fly in the face of the mores of the time and make her his legal wife, she had huge doubts. Her 'character' had been lost for ever; marriage would not restore it and there was no guarantee that society would ever accept her. Might not her husband tire of her social ostracism, which would certainly rub off on him? Her class also spoke against her; although she had on the surface moved out of it by her career within cultured society, the rigid structure of the day knew full well how humble her origins were. To quote Katie Hickman in *Courtesans*, 'a married courtesan was a strangely amphibious social creature; no longer fish but not quite fowl either.'

So she hesitated, and insisted that, if they were to marry, they should do so secretly. Fox planned it, and she carried on hesitating, even calling it off at one stage. But it did finally happen, on 28 September 1795. They kept their new status hidden from even their closest family for the next seven years, with Elizabeth maintaining the lowly, pariah-like social position that being an ostensible mistress forced her into. Eventually they announced it publicly, just as they were leaving for three months in Paris where society might accept them more readily. As it did; they were presented to the Bonapartes, and the expatriate English – with some exceptions – were kind to them. And when they returned to England, Fox's family, having had time to get used to the idea, embraced them, too, as did most of his friends. His clear happiness and her intelligent courtesy and good taste won over all but the most rigid of hearts. Their unorthodox but deeply happy marriage lasted until his death in 1806, and she lived on until 1842, surrounded by his supportive family. Just one last wish was denied her: he had been buried in Westminster Abbey and she petitioned William IV to allow her to be buried next to him. But it was not to be; she outlived the king and her petition to him was forgotten.

Elizabeth Armistead had the good fortune to be able to lead a comfortable and 'respectable' life in the years that followed her career as a courtesan. Her exact contemporary, Harriette Wilson, was less lucky. Just as celebrated as Elizabeth at the height of her fame, Harriette resorted towards the end of her life to an extraordinary device to ensure her continued solvency. Between January and April 1825 she published her *Memoirs* in twelve parts, each one ending with a list of the names that would appear in the next one – unless those named chose to buy themselves out. She also sent blackmailing letters to her clientele, and it is said that she amassed a great deal of money from this venture. Society was electrified by the memoirs; the crowds eager to buy them from the publisher had to be held back by barricades, and it was said that the whole of society, including every member of the Cabinet, was reading them.

George IV apparently paid to keep his name out, but the Duke of Wellington refused to do so.

The legal position of women was now beginning to exercise forward-thinking minds. A pioneer of this early feminism, at the end of the eighteenth century, was Mary Wollstonecraft, who found herself rebelling against the attitudes of both women and men towards women's role and status in society and their intellectual capacities. After working as a governess in Ireland for Lord and Lady Kingsborough, she began to hate the way women of that class behaved: coquettish and apparently weakly dependent on the man while also scheming and manipulative. Soon after she left their service she published her polemic *A Vindication of the Rights of Women*, which addressed among other points her abhorrence of Rousseau's view that the education of women should have the aim merely of making them useful to their men.

Mary Wollstonecraft lived her principles as well as writing about them; when her sister went into a deep depression after having a child with a husband she loathed, Mary encouraged her to leave them, suffering a great deal of opprobrium as a result. Horace Walpole called her 'that hyena in petticoats'. And later, when she visited France with other thinkers of the time to observe the French Revolution, she went to live with an American, Gilbert Imlay, with whom she had a child. Although she called herself Mrs Imlay she never married him, and she struggled with her love for the man as against her need for freedom. When she returned to England she embarked on an affair with William Godwin and became pregnant again. This time she preferred to persuade him to marry her, but died soon afterwards, at the age of thirty-eight, from complications after the birth of the child.

That child was Mary Godwin, later to marry Percy Bysshe Shelley and to write *Frankenstein*. She, too, was to live her life among challenging men and ideas, notably – apart from her husband – Lord Byron. It was her sassy intelligence that first attracted Shelley to her when he met her while visiting her father's home and bookshop in London, and – although he was still married at the time – they soon embarked on a relationship.

Shelley had always been unconventional, despite coming from a traditional upper-class background. While at Oxford he wrote a tract on *The Necessity of Atheism* which, because he would not recant, caused him to be sent down. This initiated a rift with his father which got deeper when, just a few months after leaving Oxford and at the age of only nineteen, he eloped to Scotland with a sixteen-year-old schoolgirl, Harriet Westbrook. She was a pretty young girl, daughter of a well-to-do retired coffee-house owner; but it seems that Shelley was less in love with her than sorry for her, and was also targeted as a suitable husband for her by her much older sister, Eliza. Harriet hated being kept at school by her unsympathetic father, and wrote increasingly gloomy letters to Shelley, even threatening suicide in some of them. After their marriage in 1811, she very quickly sent for Eliza to live with them, an arrangement that did not suit Shelley at all; and it was not long before he began to know that his hopes of her as an intellectual companion were not going to be realized. As Leslie Hotson eloquently puts it in his book *Shelley's Lost Letters to Harriet*, 'Their relation could never have survived as a true marriage of minds; never, even if Eliza had not added her weight to their frail matrimonial skiff.'

Harriet's dependence on her sister and Shelley's growing unhappiness caused an estrangement, and they ceased to live together all the time, despite the fact that she was pregnant with their second child; their first, a daughter called Ianthe, had been born just over a year after their marriage. As soon as Shelley met Mary Godwin, he realized that this was the woman who would provide him with 'a true marriage of minds'. His unconventional morals eventually – after much mental turmoil – persuaded him to ask William Godwin for his daughter's hand, a request that the supposedly anarchical Godwin rejected with horror. An increasingly desperate Shelley first proposed a double suicide pact to Mary, and then sought to set up a *ménage à trois*, with Harriet as his 'sister' and Mary as his 'wife'.

It was after he broached this subject with Harriet that he started a correspondence with her which was lost for over a century until copies of it were found in the Public Record Office (now the National Archives). They were part of the documents supporting the later Chancery case about the future of Shelley's children after Harriet's death [Chancery Masters' Papers, Blunt S.13, Shelley v Westbrook] and were published by Leslie Hotson as *Shelley's Lost Letters to Harriet* in 1930. In the first of these letters he thanks her for her apparently kind and understanding reception of the news about his new love, and assures her that he still feels affection for her: 'Our connection was not one of passion and impulse. Friendship was its basis, and on this basis it has enlarged and strengthened.' Then he rather cruelly goes on: 'It is no reproach to me that you have never filled my heart with an all-sufficing passion; perhaps you are even yourself a stranger to these impulses, which one day may be awakened by some nobler and worthier than me; and may you find a lover as passionate and faithful, as I shall ever be a friend affectionate and sincere.'

Soon after this letter he eloped with Mary to Switzerland, accompanied by another young woman, Mary's step-sister Claire Clairmont. It was on this trip that they first met Byron. On their return after only a few weeks, driven back to London by lack of funds, Shelley's letters to Harriet become increasingly concerned with financial matters, together with growing reproaches that she is not treating their dealings in confidence and that she cannot accept his new life. She, it seems, continued to hope that his dalliance with Mary was just an episode and that he would return to her; and when it became clear that this would never happen, she began to complain not just about Mary but about William Godwin, claiming that he had sold Mary to Shelley. In view of Godwin's continued hostility to the new ménage, this is evidence only of Harriet's growing bitterness and unhappiness.

The next few months were miserable for everyone involved in this situation, as the letters show: Shelley and Mary, firmly together but still estranged from her father, plagued by debt, creditors, bailiffs and illness, and deeply anxious about the future; Harriet increasingly unhappy about living back with her parents and sister, and the object of Shelley's growing opprobrium: 'I am united to another; you are no longer my wife. Perhaps I have done you injury, but surely most innocently and unintentionally, in having commenced any connexion with you.' His last letter to her contained a truly desperate plea for some of their joint funds, arrangements for which had not yet been finalized. Shortly afterwards, she gave birth to their son, Charles.

Mary and Shelley returned to the continent, but within the next two years they were faced with two family tragedies. First Mary's older step-sister, Fanny Imlay, committed suicide, and a few months later Harriet drowned herself in the Serpentine in London, leaving a pathetic suicide note for her sister. Shelley was devastated by Harriet's sad end – for which he initially bitterly blamed Eliza – and hastened back to London in order to fight the Westbrooks for his children. In this he failed, though he did succeed in having them placed with foster-parents of his own choice rather than the elderly Warwickshire clergyman and his wife whom Harriet's family had preferred.

The Shelleys, now married, returned to Italy in 1818 and re-established contact with Byron, but also suffered the loss of two of their children in the years that followed. Shelley's early death by drowning in July 1822, just a month short of his thirtieth birthday, devastated his wife, who kept his heart with her until she, too, died in 1851. Unconventional to the last, Shelley was burned on a pyre on the beach near where his body had washed up.

Claire Clairmont's original objective in accompanying the Shelleys to Italy had been to try to meet Byron again; he had been her lover and it soon became apparent that she was pregnant with his child. He had made it very clear that he wanted nothing more to do with her and now refused to see her alone without the Shelleys being present. When she gave birth to their daughter, Allegra, in January 1817 he acknowledged the child and later agreed to take her into his care and provide for her. It was devastating for Claire, therefore, when she discovered that he had consigned Allegra to a convent in Venice where she died, aged five. Claire never forgave him; but Byron's action was typical – he was not a man to depend upon. Later analysis of his magnetism combined with his flamboyant eccentricity suggests that he may have been suffering from bipolar disorder, or manic depression. He was also highly unconventional; forbidden to keep a dog while he was a student at Trinity College, Cambridge, he kept a bear instead.

Byron's lusts and appetites are notorious. 'Mad, bad and dangerous to know' was how his lover, Lady Caroline Lamb, summed him up, and nothing in his history contradicts that view. He was a promiscuous bisexual, embarking on indiscriminate affairs with boys and women of all types. His sexual appetites eventually led him to live abroad; even the lusty London *demi-monde* found him too hot to handle, and the friend to whom he consigned his autobiography burnt it as being far too sensational to publish.

One of his early male liaisons was with a fifteen-year-old choirboy at Trinity called John Edleston, with whom he maintained a relationship until the boy's death; in the series of elegies he wrote to commemorate this love he changed the pronouns to the feminine in order not to cause a scandal. His main aim in going on the Grand Tour, according to correspondence with his Cambridge friends, was to enjoy homosexual encounters, one of which he found with a young Italian boy in Athens. Back home, he embarked on his famous and obsessive liaison with Lady

Caroline Lamb, but he soon broke off the affair, leaving her devastated. Her novel *Glenarvon* painted Byron in a most unflattering light and was read with avidity by the London aristocracy. Byron's furious response in a poem was:

> I read *Glenarvon* too by Caro. Lamb
> God damn!

He is widely believed to have committed incest with his half-sister, Augusta Leigh, and to have been the father of her daughter, Medora; and when he eventually did marry, his wife Annabella – a family connection of Caroline Lamb – left him after just over a year, taking their daughter Augusta Ada with her. It was rumours after this about his amazingly rackety life, including allegations of the capital crime of buggery, that led him finally to leave for Europe, where he lived for the rest of his life before dying of a fever in 1824 after involving himself with the Greek insurgents against the Ottoman Empire. He became something of a typical Englishman abroad, railing against what he saw as the vapidity of his fellow countrymen on the Grand Tour. Rome, he wrote to his friend Thomas Moore, 'is pestilent with English – a parcel of staring boobies, who go about gaping and wishing to be at once cheap and magnificent. A man is a fool who travels now in France or Italy, till this tribe of wretches is swept home again.'

Letters written while he was in Venice are eloquent about his affairs. He talks about Angelina, who was locked away from him by her family after they found out about their liaison, but whom he managed to meet again; on one occasion he fell into the Grand Canal on his way to meet her 'owing to the cursed slippery steps of their palaces', but chose not to miss the appointment by changing his clothes so spent the assignation 'perched in a balcony with my wet clothes on'. Then there was Marianna, who was amiable, tactful, very pretty and with 'great black oriental eyes, and all the qualities which her eyes promise.' Margharita Cogni, La Fornarina, was the baker's wife: 'She said that she had no objection to make love with me, as she was married – and all married women did it – but that her husband was somewhat ferocious and would do her a mischief... For two years, in the course of which I had more women than I can count or recount, she was the only one who preserved over me an ascendancy which was often disputed and never impaired.' Byron's vivid description of Margharita after he had been caught in a storm on the

Grand Canal and she had feared that he had drowned is memorable: 'with her great black eyes flashing through her tears and the long dark hair which was streaming drenched with rain over her brows and breast … and the wind blowing her hair and dress about her tall thin figure – and the lightning flashing round her – with the waves rolling at her feet – made her look like Medea alighted from her chariot – or the Sybil of the tempest…'.

Byron's description of Venetian morals is illuminating: 'a woman is virtuous who limits herself to her husband and one lover; those who have two, three or more are a little wild; but it is only those who are indiscriminately diffuse, and form a low connection, such as the Princess of Wales with her courier … who are considered as overstepping the modesty of marriage.' Meanwhile Byron himself seems to have maintained his feelings for his half-sister Augusta Leigh; a letter written in 1819 from Venice is unsigned and unaddressed, but is widely assumed to have been to her: 'My dearest love … I have never ceased nor can cease to feel for a moment that perfect and boundless attachment which bound and binds me to you – which renders me utterly incapable of real love for any other human being – for what could they be to me after you? My dear xxxx [sic] we may have been very wrong – but I repent of nothing except that cursed marriage – and your refusing to continue to love me as you had loved me – I can never forget nor quite forgive you for that precious piece of reformation.'

Shelley and Byron, their preoccupations and conduct, were very much of the early nineteenth century, characterized by the flamboyant Regency of George IV. After his domesticated father George III, the Prince reverted to the familiar behaviour of lecherous royals. He became Prince Regent in 1811, succeeded to the throne in 1820 and died – after a predictably debauched life – in 1830. He is said to have cut a lock of hair from each of his mistresses and to have kept each one in an envelope with her name on it; by the time of his death there were over 7,000 of these envelopes. George's extravagant lifestyle plunged him into truly massive debt, out of which he had to be bailed several times by Parliament; but the elegance and culture of his court both as regent and as king are proverbial. He also maintained a degree of constancy throughout his life to Mrs Fitzherbert, the twice-widowed Catholic woman for whom he had fallen heavily and whom, when she refused to become his mistress, he secretly married in 1785. The marriage was illegal, both because of her religion and because it was contracted without the permission of the king, his father, who would never have given it. He was therefore technically free to marry Caroline of Brunswick on the orders of his father in 1795. The marriage was doomed from the start. When he first set eyes on her he called for brandy, wiped his brow and said, 'I am not well.' He regarded her as unattractive, unhygienic and not a virgin; she found him ugly and unpleasant. They appear to have had sexual relations only three times during the course of the few months they lived together before he banished her from court, though they did manage to conceive a daughter, Princess Charlotte.

George went to great lengths to repudiate Caroline as his consort. Documents in the National Archives [HO 126/3/71] record depositions made in 1807 at the time when the Princess of Wales was suspected of having had an illegitimate child, possibly by Sir Sidney Smith. These documents include a long statement by Lady Douglas, who had first met the princess in 1801 and had become a confidante in 1802: 'she said that she was pregnant … she never told me who was the father of the child. She said she hoped it would be a boy … and that if it was discovered she would give the Prince of Wales the credit of being the father for she had slept two nights at Carlton House within the year…'. Lady Douglas's no-holds-barred testimony included direct accusations of adultery: 'The Princess of Wales has told me that she got a bedfellow whenever she could, that nothing was more wholesome… She has told me that Sir Sidney Smith has lain with her … that the Prince was the most complaisant man in the world, that she did what she liked, went where she liked and had what bedfellows she liked and the Prince paid for all.' There was further evidence about a child around the place who was said to be an orphan from Deptford whom the princess had taken into her household, but whom many suspected of being the mysterious changeling.

Despite this deposition, George III and his advisers decided not to take action against the princess; there is a long letter from the Prince of Wales to his father protesting against the king's statement that he would continue to receive Caroline at court. The advisers had stated that they believed the accusations of pregnancy and childbirth brought by Lady Douglas to be false, and they felt that the princess should be accorded her rank within the royal family. The Prince of Wales goes on, 'In consequence of which I am left in the unjust predicament … that I was capable of acting from the dictates of an unforgiving spirit, or a severity of judgement, which are wholly foreign to my nature.' George III appears, however, to have had concerns about Caroline's conduct: 'there have appeared circumstances of conduct on the part of the princess which His Majesty could never regard but with serious concern ... His Majesty therefore cannot forebear to express in the conclusion of the business his desire and expectation that such a conduct may in future be observed by the princess as may fully justify those marks of paternal regard and affection which the king always wishes to shew to every part of his royal family.'

Caroline did not stay long in Britain, but spent most of the next few years on the continent, taking lovers and running up debts. When her husband succeeded to the throne she returned, but the new king not only tried to have her stripped of her status as queen by Parliament, but also refused to allow her to attend his coronation. She died only shortly afterwards, some say in suspicious circumstances.

In 1817 George III was still alive and on the throne, though very ill. He had twelve surviving children, but only one legitimate grandchild, the Prince Regent's daughter, Charlotte. She was a feisty creature who had insisted on marrying Prince Leopold of Saxe-Coburg; their marriage was happy and fulfilling, but she endured two miscarriages before carrying a baby to term. She was very unwell during her pregnancy and the treatments prescribed by her doctors did not help; a lengthy labour resulted in a stillborn son and her own death. The royal house was plunged into a succession crisis and the elderly royal dukes were called into action to secure an heir. Edward, Duke of Kent, had lived for twenty years with his mistress, Madame de Saint-Laurent, and William, Duke of Clarence, had produced at least twelve children with his long-term mistress, the celebrated actress Dorothy Jordan, a relationship that had ended in 1811. Now both dukes entered into hasty marriages to more seemly women. William's wife, Adelaide, had two children, but they both died in infancy; Edward's wife, Victoria, managed to produce a living daughter. This princess was now the only legitimate member of the next generation of the royal family.

On George IV's death a piece in *The Times* declared, 'There never was an individual less regretted by his fellow creatures than this deceased king.' The next oldest brother, Frederick – who never had a child – had predeceased him, so his heir was William, Duke of Clarence, who reigned as William IV. It is perhaps ironical that William should have proved so potent with Mrs Jordan and yet have failed to produce a living legitimate child with his wife. He continued to provide for his FitzClarence family, many of whom went on to lead successful lives and to found dynasties whose scions today are still to be discovered among the aristocracy and the wealthy classes – shades of Charles II!

On William's death in 1837, his heir was that one legitimate princess, his niece Victoria, the daughter of the Duke of Kent. Her accession ushered in another extremely long reign which saw more fundamental changes to society in all its forms, along with a moral backlash to the excesses of George IV. The term 'Victorian values', applied more often than anything to the social and sexual realms, heralded new attitudes towards life and love which we can still recognize today.

Four · Fallen angels and moral mazes

Man must be pleased; but him to please
Is woman's pleasure; down the gulf
Of his condoled necessities
She casts her best, she flings herself.

So behaves the 'angel in the house': Coventry Patmore's pure, meek, devoted, submissive wife as expressed in his poem of 1854. She was a Victorian ideal, reflected in the public image of the queen's own relationship with her beloved Albert. Sex was contained within domestic and family concerns and erotic desire channelled into delicate romance. 'How different, how very different from the home life of our own dear queen,' observed one of Victoria's ladies-in-waiting after seeing a performance of *Antony and Cleopatra*. Piano legs decently draped, high-necked dresses, knickers (an innovation unknown to women before the nineteenth century) – all feed the impression of Victorian society as buttoned-up, prurient and often hypocritical. Yet we can identify with the needs and dilemmas of the Victorians perhaps more closely than with those of their predecessors, and recognize ourselves in those who challenged the status quo as well as in the majority obliged, outwardly at least, to conform.

Despite apparent moral certainties, the early Victorians inhabited a time of galvanic exploration and change. It was an era of profound contradiction, which on one hand saw astonishing research into science and redrew the boundaries of the known world; and on the other gave us the word 'bowdlerize' from Dr Thomas Bowdler's reworking of Shakespeare, with the aim of removing 'those words and expressions ... which cannot with propriety be read aloud in a family.' Expanding horizons were complemented by a constraining prudishness with which women, in particular, had to contend. It lasted well beyond the century, too; as Virginia Woolf was to write in 1931, 'Killing the angel in the house is part of the occupation of a woman writer.'

The two sides of the Victorian coin were contradictory indeed. In this era of moral rectitude, prostitution and child labour were endemic, expanding empire – and cultural supremacy – were regarded as natural and inevitable, and dire rural and urban poverty kept death rates high.

Despite growing national prosperity, life for the majority of the population remained short and nasty — and smelly, too! Workers in the new industrial towns lived among factories belching out fumes and smoke, and even the queen and her consort had to endure the stink of the Thames, which left a patina of sewage along its banks every time the tide went out. It was not until Parliament itself had to flee from the rooms overlooking the disgustingly polluted Thames during the hot summer and the consequent 'Great Stink' of 1858 that a new sewerage system for London was begun.

Yet the reverse of the coin reveals an age of massive technological advancement and increasing wealth as well as dramatic discoveries about the natural world and its scientific underpinnings. Darwin's shocking theory of evolution forced open minds to contemplate appallingly fundamental questions about the nature of god and man; Brunel's railways and ships were opening up the country and the world; and the new countries of empire brought exposure not just to material goods, but also to new knowledge, customs and cultures.

These exotic countries gave many opportunities to experience new ways of thinking and living, especially for those serving abroad. The men working for the East India Company or the British government could, if they survived the perils of warfare and virulent new diseases, embrace some of the social freedoms on offer, and it was not uncommon for officers to 'go native' in their brave new worlds. Sexual possibilities were always intriguing, and in the early days of British rule in India the merging of cultural boundaries allowed unprecedented licence in this regard. Sir David Ochterlony, a very successful general, was unusual in being almost penniless when he died in 1825 as he had not bothered to feather his own financial nest. He became famous for his habit of taking the early morning air by the Hooghly river near Calcutta, followed by all thirteen of his Indian wives, each mounted on her own elephant. He is commemorated in Calcutta by a magnificent memorial consisting of an Egyptian base, Syrian column and Turkish dome — a fitting tribute to his enthusiasm for all things Muslim.

William Fraser was another who adopted some of the practices of his adopted land, transforming himself in the process from a shy young scholar to 'a great bear of a man', according to William Dalrymple in *City of Djinns*; Dalrymple traces Fraser's career with fascination; notorious among the British at the time, he kept a huge harem, had a great many children and lived like a potentate. His wives lived all together some distance from Delhi, and passed on to their children both their religion (Hindu or Muslim according to their origins) and the occupations appropriate to the caste of their mothers. A picture of his chief wife – Amiban, a Jat woman of Rania – survives in the 'Fraser Album' that Fraser and his brother compiled, revealing 'a tall and exquisite Indian woman, dressed in a slight, close-fitting bodice and a long pleated Rajasthani skirt.' A young boy stands beside her, his features showing clear signs of his mixed ancestry.

Fraser's embrace of Indian habits extended to growing a thick Rajput beard and to giving up eating pork and beef – traits that deeply shocked the wife of the British Commander-in-Chief on her visit to Delhi. She felt it necessary to remind him that he was a Christian, not a Hindu, and would probably not have been surprised when he came to a sad end. Fraser's mistake was to humiliate a young Mughal nobleman, Shams-ud-Din Khan, both by forcibly ejecting him from his house and by making advances to the young man's sister. Khan shot him dead and then fled on a horse whose shoes had been reversed in order to conceal the direction of his flight. He was caught and publicly executed.

Of course, many British men simply took Indian mistresses and kept their own wives and families at a careful remove. Others entered into monogamous marriages with local women, sometimes in highly romantic, not to say dangerous, circumstances. One such was Captain Robert Warburton, who, aged only twenty-nine, fell in love with the famously beautiful, high-ranking wife of an Afghan courtier. She had an infant son as well as a husband, and was the niece of the Afghan monarch whom the British had recently ousted. In this most perilous of situations, she and Warburton entered into an affair which sparked a scandalous divorce and a risky confrontation with the warlike Afghan lords – especially the bride's vengeful cousin, Akbar Khan. Soon after their wedding (in a Muslim ceremony in 1841), a massive uprising initiated the retreat of the British contingent to India. On the way soldiers and camp followers were attacked and annihilated (the said Akbar having broken a safe-conduct pledge); there was literally only one survivor. Warburton had the good fortune to have been left behind as a hostage, so he escaped the massacre and later managed to escape from Kabul, too. His wife also fled from Kabul dressed as a British officer and eventually, after months in hiding, managed to reach India where she gave birth to their son. Also named Robert, he became one of the Indian Army's most valuable officers, speaking several languages and using his mixed ancestry to good effect in that volatile region. The full story by Mark Bridge, a descendant of the Warburton family, appears in the National Archives' *Ancestors* magazine (issue 46).

New physical frontiers were mirrored by expanding mental horizons as the Victorians sought to advance knowledge in medicine and science. More sophisticated study of anatomy and biology, and the burgeoning new medical schools, probed more deeply into the nature of the human body and its functions, challenging long-established ideas. A popular verse in the early part of the nineteenth century had it that:

> ...though they of different sexes be,
> Yet on the whole they are the same as we,
> For those that have the strictest searchers been,
> Find women are but men outside in.

In other words, women's bodies were just men's bodies in reverse. Now, as medical knowledge began to make it clear that women's anatomy was identifiably different from men's, not just an inferior, topsy-turvy version of it, the first inklings of the possibility that women were physical beings in their own right began to be expressed. But there was still a long way to go before any sort of equality or liberation could be envisaged. The views of Dean Burgon were the norm: 'Inferior to us God made you, and inferior to the end of time you will remain. But you are none the worse off for that.'

Nor were medical discoveries always a benefit. New knowledge was often used to underpin the view that women would find their most complete satisfaction in motherhood, fulfilling the destiny for which their bodies were designed. And when it began to be understood, similarly, that the female orgasm was not an echo of the male emission – that it was not the moment at which an egg was released and therefore an essential element in reproduction – women's enjoyment of sex became unnecessary. Biology now seemed to offer them a destiny as baby machines and instruments to be played for male pleasure.

Male sexual enjoyment, meanwhile, remained essential. Contrary to earlier views, it was now regarded as important for men to ejaculate regularly in order to stay healthy, although masturbation, unsurprisingly, was not considered healthy. So men condemned to live without the company of respectable women – those in the services, for example, who were not permitted to marry, or those extending the far-flung borders of empire – believed themselves justified in resorting to prostitutes. And men remained tolerant of their own tendency towards adultery and could sue for the 'restitution of conjugal rights' when their wives reacted to their infidelity by leaving them.

Advances in scientific knowledge, then, operated almost totally in favour of the dominance of men and the continuing subjection of women, and bolstered the double standard even more; amid growing enlightenment, attitudes towards the sexual role of women remained in the Dark Ages. Even having a female monarch did not help: Victoria wrote in 1870, 'I am most anxious to enlist everyone who can speak or write to join in checking this mad, wicked folly of "Women's Rights", with all its attendant horrors, on which her poor feeble sex is bent, forgetting every sense of womanly feelings and propriety. Feminists ought to get a good whipping. Were woman to "unsex" themselves by claiming equality with men, they would become the most hateful, heathen and disgusting of beings and would surely perish without male protection.'

Despite such views, some controversial thinkers combined ideas on political reform with radical new approaches towards women and sexuality. Mary Wollstonecraft had begun to show the way. A male voice came from Richard Carlile, a polemical atheist, campaigner for electoral reform – including female suffrage – and thoroughgoing thorn in the side of government. A survivor of the Peterloo massacre, he was the first to publish news of the murderous incident in London, and he and his wife both spent time in prison for what the establishment regarded as their seditious publications. *Every Woman's Book*, published in 1826, outlined his radical views on women, sex, contraception and love. The frontispiece alone was controversial, showing Adam and Eve without fig leaves; but it was the book's opinions about the morality of sex that caused the most outrage. In Carlile's view, sexual intercourse was essential for health and happiness whether inside or outside marriage and whether children were the result or not. Far from being sinful, sex was virtuous and both necessary and pleasurable for men and women alike. Women '…who had never had sexual commerce begin to droop when about twenty-five years of age, they become pale and languid, general weakness and irritation, a sort of restlessness, nervous fidgettyness takes possession of them, and an absorbing process goes on, their forms degenerate, their features sink and the peculiar character of the old maid becomes apparent.' Sex was synonymous with love; and love was lust, pure and simple. His atheism influenced his argument, too: why would humans, as animals, deny themselves the activity that nature had made so pleasurable?

Moreover, marriage was in his eyes an authoritarian plot to keep women down, and a couple who had lost affection for each other should part. He dealt for the first time in English with specific methods of contraception, urging its universal adoption to allow continued enjoyment of sex once the family had reached its optimum size. There were economic reasons, too – the poor could limit their families and prevent themselves becoming poorer. Carlile also had a surprisingly modern take on the prevalent view of the time that, free of the burden of pregnancy, women's uncontrollable lusts would overwhelm society: he argued that those who put forward such views were in truth terrified of their own sexuality and were projecting their own fear on to those they both desired and despised.

Stirring stuff, in an age when polite society did indeed regard sex as for procreation alone – 'coaxing an angel-child down from heaven' as one manual put it – and men were increasingly inclined to deny passionate feelings in women. But Carlile was not totally forward-thinking. Although he was a sensualist he decried promiscuity, proposing serial monogamy instead; he had no truck with male homosexuality and no knowledge, it seems, of the possibility of lesbianism. Moreover, although clearly a man happily married to a wife congenial in every way, including in her radicalism, he took his business partner as a lover and made her pregnant.

Most of the laws concerning marital matters were indeed biased towards men. They remained so until the middle of the century, when several campaigns by determined women forced the male legislature to amend the inequity and injustice of the situation. As one of those women, Caroline Norton, said, 'While the laws that women appeal to are administered by men, we need not fear that their appeals will be too carelessly granted.' Even after the laws relating to divorce were rewritten in the middle of the century, it remained true that a man could divorce his wife for adultery, but she still had to prove cruelty as well. This was very difficult to establish in legal terms, as a case in the 1840s brought by the Countess of Dysart demonstrates. She was seeking a judicial separation from her husband, the earl. There seems on either side to have been no adultery involved, and the court was satisfied that, during a marriage that had technically lasted for twenty-five years, they had lived together under one roof for only three of those years. He had now brought a case seeking the restitution of conjugal rights, which she was fighting on the grounds of his cruelty; had she succeeded she would have been entitled to her decree of separation. That she failed appears to be because of the enormous difficulty in proving legal cruelty, particularly in episodes occurring several years before. Moreover, the case underpins one of the givens of the period: that a woman's behaviour had to be irreproachable even in the face of extreme male provocation.

The earl comes across as both unpleasant and deeply eccentric – he was probably clinically mad – as well as impoverished; his wealthy father had disapproved of the marriage so was not prepared to help his son financially. Some of the servants testified that they had heard altercations between the couple and had witnessed some physical violence, but on two of these occasions the violence appeared to be limited to him physically restraining her until she made him a promise of a change in behaviour; one thing he wanted was that she would in future refrain from throwing slops out of the window! It was also clear that he used the foulest of language to her (and that she responded in kind!) and that she had to live in dilapidated and under-furnished accommodation; but none of this could be counted as cruelty.

The judge conceded that the earl was a petty tyrant. He refused the countess access to her bedroom until very late at night, and did not pay due regard to her accommodation needs: 'a very scarce supply even of coal, linen and tea things and, in one particular respect, a disregard for Lady Dysart's health and comfort, which is very disgusting, and this for the almost incredible purpose of obtaining manure for the land; that there was an abundance of provisions, though coarsely cooked, is, I think, beyond doubt.' Further testimony reported that the earl told her 'he mortally hated her, that he had not been before in her room for ever so long, and he would not come again but on business; that if the law allowed him he would give her a damned good thrashing, but he knew that he could not do that, and therefore he would punish her as he did, for he hated her mortally, and he would say so if he had but three minutes to live, and that she had been a torment to him as long as they had been married...'. But none of this was 'cruel' in the legal sense, so her petition failed and his succeeded. The law compelled her to carry on being legally married to a man she hated and who appears to have hated her in return.

But attitudes were slowly changing, and many women neither shared the queen's views on the inferiority of their sex nor accepted the injustice of their legal position. One of these was Caroline Norton, the granddaughter of Richard Brinsley Sheridan, whose deeply unhappy marriage to a vicious man exposed the invidiousness of male-centred laws on sexual matters. Despite a chain of tragic events, she campaigned successfully for new legislation on women's rights, not just once but twice.

Caroline Norton and her two sisters were left in desperate need of making good alliances after their father, the playwright's son, had alienated his wife's family by eloping with her, and then died young. His wife and their seven children were left in very straitened circumstances. Caroline agreed to marry George Norton, brother of Lord Grantley, but he turned out to be a disastrous choice. She was clever; he was not, and disliked cleverness in others, and soon decided to punish her for 'setting herself up' against him by becoming physically violent. They had three children, but when she was pregnant with a fourth he beat her again and caused a miscarriage. Caroline had frequently sought refuge with her own family, but after this Norton sent their three sons away to his cousin, refused to allow his wife back into the house and denied her any access to her children. Moreover, he now brought a suit of 'criminal conversation' against Lord Melbourne, the Prime Minister, who was a close friend of Caroline's and spent a lot of time with her; she had even persuaded him to use his influence to get Norton appointed as a magistrate in order to keep the peace at home. Norton now clearly hoped not only that this would be the first stage in divorcing Caroline for adultery but that he would gain substantial damages from Melbourne. As it happened the trial, in 1836, was a farce and the jury unanimously found for Melbourne without leaving the courtroom. Melbourne's name was cleared, but Caroline's was not, and the scandal would stick to her for the rest of her life. Here was one of the fundamental contradictions of the age: faced with male maltreatment, an intelligent and presentable woman could not hope to enjoy the support of male friends without opening them to the possibility of actions at law.

Norton was still withholding the children, so his wife – discovering to her horror not only that she had no possibility of divorcing him, but also that he had full legal custody of the children – campaigned to change the law on access. She was successful in 1839 when Parliament passed the Infant Custody Bill, allowing mothers to appeal for custody of children under seven and access to children under sixteen. Norton's response was to move with the children to Scotland where the law was different, and it was only after their youngest son contracted tetanus and died that he agreed to limited access. She had not been able to see her son before his death.

Norton now embarked on a new scheme whereby he offered her an annuity as part of what was in effect a deed of separation; she agreed and a legal document was drawn up. But it was all a scam; when later Caroline benefited from both Lord Melbourne's will and her mother's, Norton announced that he would now discontinue the annuity. She protested, but he laughed at her and pointed out that, as she was still his wife and legally a man and his wife were one, they could not enter into a contract with each other and the legal document was meaningless. Since he was still legally obliged to pay her debts she took him to court for one of them, but he used the proceedings to cast doubt once again on her relationship with Melbourne, particularly in the light of the legacy she had received from him. Caroline was enraged enough to stand up and address the court, defending herself against new and old slander to much applause, but she lost the case on a technicality.

She now set out to change the law again and published several pamphlets arguing for new legislation to protect women and their property. One of them was her Letter to the Queen on Lord Chancellor Cranworth's Marriage and Divorce Bill, which includes the telling sentence: 'I desire to point out the grotesque anomaly which ordains that married women shall be "non-existent" in a country governed by a female Sovereign.' The pamphlet goes on to list, in measured yet forceful terms, the injustices heaped on married women in England; it is worth quoting several of them: 'she has no legal existence: her being is absorbed in that of her husband... She has no possessions, unless by special settlement; her property is his property... An English wife may not leave her husband's house. Not only can he sue her for "restitution of conjugal rights", but he has a right to enter the house of any friend or relation with whom she may take refuge ... and carry her away by force... If the wife sue for separation for cruelty, it must be "cruelty that endangers life or limb", and if she has once forgiven, or, in legal phrase, "condoned" his offences, she cannot plead them... If her husband take proceedings for a divorce, she is not, in the first instance, allowed to defend herself... If an English wife be guilty of infidelity, her husband can divorce her so as to marry again; but she cannot divorce the husband *a vinculo*, however profligate he may be.'

The mores of the time found it difficult to cope with women speaking out in public at all, let alone on such inflammatory causes as marriage and divorce. To do so incurred the disapproval of both sexes. But Caroline was undeterred, carrying on to point out the inequalities within a fragmented marriage which the legal system created: 'Her being of spotless character, and without reproach, gives her no advantage in law. She may have withdrawn from his roof knowing that he lives with "his faithful housekeeper": having suffered personal violence at his hands; having "condoned" much, and being able to prove it by unimpeachable testimony: or he may have shut the doors of her house against her: all this is quite immaterial: the law takes no cognisance of which is to blame. As her husband, he has a right to all that is hers: as his wife, she has no right to anything that is his. As her husband, he may divorce her: as his wife, the utmost "divorce" she could obtain is permission to reside alone, married to his name. The marriage ceremony is a civil bond for him, and an indissoluble sacrament for her.'

Her arguments were compelling, and the resulting Divorce and Matrimonial Causes Act of 1857 allowed secular divorce in England for the first time. It also provided that a court could order a husband to pay maintenance to a divorced or estranged wife, that a divorced wife could inherit or bequeath property in her own right and that she could protect her earnings from a husband who had deserted her. She could also now enter into contracts and civil actions on her own behalf. Records held by the National Archives show an immediate increase in divorce cases after the new law came into operation; one example is the petition dated 1 June 1860 by Isabella Mary Adolphus against her husband, Joseph Adolphus, whom she had married on 17 August 1850 and with whom she had two daughters [J77/1]. Sometime in 1859 Joseph had 'formed an adulterous connection with Elizabeth Caroline Bunker' and slept with her several times at his home and elsewhere, including Paris. Isabella's plea was 'that your Lordship will be pleased to decree a judicial separation between your petitioner and her husband, that she may have the custody of her children ... and such further and other relief in the premises as to your Lordship may seem meet.' A second petition on 4

July 1862 repeats the claims of adultery and adds, 'that on the fifth day of May 1860 Joseph Adolphus deserted your petitioner without reasonable excuse and has ever since lived separate and apart ... so she now asks for the marriage to be dissolved.' Sir Cresswell Cresswell [sic] allowed the decree nisi which was made absolute on 24 November that year.

Grounds for divorce were still, however, weighted towards the husband: he had only to prove adultery; she had, in addition, as the case cited above shows, to prove incest, bigamy, cruelty or desertion. Moreover, 'condoning' cruelty by continuing to cohabit would still prevent a divorce; as in the Dysart case in the 1840s, proven cruelty had to have taken place after the couple had separated. As the judge in that case stated: 'as the cohabitation lasted till January 1837, the true question was whether an act of cruelty had been committed since that date, for the cohabitation as husband and wife was a condonation of all past cruelty, which could be revived only by proof of a fresh act of cruelty.' Condoning adultery, too, was a bar to divorce. Mary Ann Evans – aka the author George Eliot – was all too aware of this when she began a relationship with George Henry Lewes. He could not divorce his wife because he had not only condoned her adultery, but had acknowledged as his own all five of the children she had borne with her lover. It took several years before Mary Ann could bring herself to admit her feelings for George Lewes and then to decide that she would defy convention and move in with him as his 'wife'; and before she was prepared to do so she made it very plain to him that he would have to ensure that his legal wife knew about the situation and would not seek to renew her marriage. Mary Ann was all too aware that this was a brave move, and that if George left her she would be disgraced and outcast from society. As she wrote to a friend, 'I do not wish to take the ground of ignoring what is unconventional in my position. I have counted the cost of the step I have taken and am prepared to bear, without irritation or bitterness, renunciation of all my friends. I am not mistaken in the person to whom I have attached myself.'

She was not deceived in the man; they lived together very happily as Mr and Mrs Lewes until his death. But she was equally not deceived in the attitude of society. At first they were ostracized and it was a very few bold friends who risked their reputation by visiting them; and when eventually Mary Ann owned up to her family that she was not legally married they, too, repudiated her, refusing to see her any more. It was characteristic of the era's moral confusion that George Lewes' adulterous wife was regarded as a long-suffering victim whereas the otherwise chaste Mary Ann was a sinner against the sanctity of marriage. And when, after the success of the first few novels written under her pseudonym, the truth came out that the scandalous Mary Ann Lewes was the acclaimed George Eliot, her publisher initially balked at issuing *The Mill on the Floss* in the fear that the censorious public might refuse to buy it. He was proved wrong!

Mary Ann was devastated at Lewes' death, but eventually succumbed to the devotion of their business manager, John Cross, and married him despite the difference in age: he was forty and she was sixty-one. But it was not to be for long; she died a mere seven months after the wedding and was buried in Highgate Cemetery next to her beloved Lewes. Caroline Norton also enjoyed the happiness of a late marriage after her husband's death, to Sir William Stirling-Maxwell, a widower and a long-standing good friend; but sadly she died only three months after the wedding. Despite all her campaigns on behalf of wronged women, she had had to wait until her abusive husband died before she could marry again; her doggedness is all the more remarkable in view of the lifetime of marital violence that she had endured.

Another unorthodox partnership of the mid-nineteenth century was that of Harriet Taylor and the philosopher John Stuart Mill. She was married, though not happily, when she met Mill, who immediately recognized the strength of her intellect and asked her to comment on his work and to collaborate. She was closely associated with him and his work for twenty years before her husband died and they were free to marry. Their relationship scandalized society although they both insisted that, while her husband was alive, they enjoyed a chaste, intellectual companionship only. In his autobiography, Mill claimed that he had wished Harriet to be credited as the joint author of most of the books and articles that were published under his name, but that she had resisted; as he wrote: 'when two persons have their thoughts and speculations completely in common it is of little consequence in respect of the question of originality, which of them holds the pen.' When she died of tuberculosis in 1858 they had been working on his famous book, *On Liberty*, which was published a year later. He was now to collaborate for fifteen years with Harriet's daughter, Helen, whose radical views matched her mother's. Mill gave full credit to both women in his autobiography:

'Whoever, either now or hereafter, may think of me and my work I have done, must never forget that it is the product not of one intellect and conscience but of three, the least considerable of whom, and above all the least original, is the one whose name is attached to it.'

Women living together were much more acceptable to the social conventions of the time, since spinsterhood was common and living alone was not an option for a respectable woman. This could provide a convenient cover for deeper relationships. It is sometimes said that lesbianism failed to become a crime in the Victorian period because Queen Victoria refused to accept that it was possible. In truth, it has never been illegal in Britain, and it usually failed to attract the opprobrium that male homosexuality did. The only criminal charges that may have involved lesbians before the nineteenth century related to acts of fraud perpetrated by women posing as men. The Ladies of Llangollen (page 75) attracted gossip, but also visits from highly placed members of political and literary society. The diary of Anne Lister, a prosperous Yorkshire landowner who died in 1840, reveals her intriguing romantic involvements, but also acknowledges the importance of her financial position in allowing her to live as she wished.

Anne Lister never married, conducted several affairs with women and wrote explicitly about her sexual feelings and her identity as a woman with what she regarded as male longings. She wrote in a secret code using Greek letters and algebraic symbols, and although she did not use the word 'lesbian' of herself she referred to 'Saffic regard' and was quite clear about her preferences: 'I love and only love the fairer sex and thus beloved by them in turn, my heart revolts from any love but theirs.' She was subtle in her approaches to other women, often seeking to establish whether they might be amenable to her advances by questioning them about books, mainly volumes of the classics, which had overt homosexual content. One woman passed her a note saying '*Etes vous Achilles?*', a reference to the incident in Achilles' life when he dressed as a woman at the court of Lycomedes; and she enjoyed the exchange of coy cultural banter during her seduction of Mrs Barlow, an older woman who became her lover.

Anne Lister's code in the diary for female homosexuality is 'connection with the ladies' and her euphemism for full female sexual congress is 'going to Italy'. She also often uses the word 'kiss' for 'orgasm' and is explicit in her description of her sexual congress with Mrs Barlow and

other women. The main love interest for most of her life was Marianna
Lawton whose marriage (to Charles Lawton) was a severe blow; though
she was delighted to discover that Charles' incompetence as a husband
meant that Marianna was still a virgin. The marriage on Marianna's side
was clearly one of financial convenience, even though it was not until
some time after the wedding that he made provision for her in his will;
she, of course, had had to turn all her property over to him on marriage.
He attempted to break off all relations with Anne when it became clear
to him that she and Marianna were hoping that he would die an early
death and free them to live together; but a year or so after the marriage
they restarted their relationship and he became reconciled to it, even
turning a blind eye when they slept together under his roof. Anne wore
rings given her by Marianna together with a locket containing snips of
her lover's hair; and they went through a form of marriage service,
declaring their love for each other. But Charles inconveniently failed to
die and the relationship came to an end. Anne was to live out most of the
rest of her life with Ann Walker, a rich heiress who became her companion and proved her devotion through the lengthy process of bringing
her lover's body back from America after she died there. Anne Lister
now lies buried in the local parish church close to her home at Shibden
Hall, near Halifax in Yorkshire.

For Marianna Lawton, the status of wife together with the financial
security it would bring was clearly an important issue; the story of her
marriage, even when seen through the eyes of a biased recorder, indicates a match of convenience. She and Anne were not blatant about their
relationship, however; nor was Anne open with her uncle and aunt, or
her servants, about her proclivities. As she recounts in her diary, her
aunt considered her 'the oddest person she ever knew' and Anne herself, when asked what her servants thought about her way of life, said
that her maidservant thought that she had 'her own peculiar ways'.
When pressed as to whether these close connections knew about her
sexuality, her reply was that they are 'all in a mist about it'.

Male homosexuality, and the blackmail that often went along with it,
had a higher profile as law court records continue to show. In one case, in
1833, sixteen-year-old William Jones was charged with threatening to
expose Robert Colley as a sodomite unless he 'received recompense for
what had been done to him'; he was charged in addition for delivering a
letter which he claimed came from someone else with the same demand.

The letter, with its original grammar, is cited in full: 'Sir, I am veary sorry to trouble you a gain, but you know your situation is that, and I expect you wilt give me some recompence for wat you have don, you recollect you intised me in this house for your own purposes, I consider you acted a unnatural crime, sodomy, and therefore I shal expect you will lend me the sum of two pounds, and if you do refuse it, I will rite a letter to your master, for I am determined to have the money. I remain, with much respect, yours, &c &c — I want an answer, and will not go with out it. I have somebody close at and, that has got another letter for your master relating wat you have done.'

Robert Colley's evidence was that the boy had come up to him in the street asking for money or something to eat as he was starving, and that he had taken him to the house where he was a servant and given him some food. After that the boy had pestered him several times, and when he received the letter he had finally decided to go to the authorities. William Jones was robust in his defence: 'Can you deny that I never stopped in the house all night one Friday last January, until Saturday morning? I was going along, the young man came up to me ... he asked me to drink; he walked down Blackfriars-bridge to Bankside, and there he committed what was highly improper; he put my hand into his trousers, and said, he thought it was not safe in the street, but he would let me in for the night if I chose...'.

He also claimed that he could prove that he had been into Colley's room by describing it. Colley was adamant that, because he never closed the shutters, anyone standing outside could see into it well enough to describe it, and he called a witness to that effect. Jones insisted at length that it was impossible, and the jury even intervened to ask the policeman for his view about whether or not the room could be seen from outside the building. Jones further insisted both that there were drawers under the bed that could not be seen from the window and that there was an old Dutch clock in the kitchen that he could not have known about unless he had been in the house. Rightly or wrongly, he was not believed, and was sentenced to transportation for life.

The archives of *The Times* yield a number of cases of men demanding money from other men with menaces, though these are trial reports which do not record the verdict. One of them, in 1846, has a man threatening his victim in a public urinal that he would commit an indecent assault upon him unless he handed over his cash. Urinals, then as now, were clearly places of assignation as well as danger. As *The Times* of 16 February 1863 reported, 'John Darnton, a porter employed by the Brighton Railway Company, proved seeing the prisoners grossly misconducting themselves in a urinal in Tooley Street about half-past three o'clock in the afternoon. With the assistance of Mr Arthur Casey, a builder, of Camberwell, and Police-constable 191 M, the prisoners were secured... The Magistrate committed both prisoners for trial.'

Another report of a trial taking place at Marlborough Street must have proved very embarrassing for one of the defendants. He had initially sought to conceal his real name, but had inadvertently admitted that he was 'Sir F...' before correcting himself and claiming to be Richard Simpson. It turned out that he was one of two men charged with indecent exposure in Hyde Park and that the other was the butler to Sir Frederick Roe, a wealthy baronet. *The Times* of 15 February 1843 had no compunction about exposing him in their pages, adding that he was 'a respectably-dressed gray-haired elderly person'. Two policemen had observed the two defendants walking towards a woody clump of trees near the gravel-pits and had hidden behind a tree to observe and intercept them.

If nineteenth-century laws on sexuality could prove damaging to men, they were also often harmful to women. Florence Nightingale was one of the middle-class ladies who, together with Josephine Butler and others, defied the disapproval of their peers to form campaigning associations. They challenged such controversial laws as the Contagious Diseases Acts, passed in the 1860s with the aim of combating venereal disease. The perhaps unlikely beneficiaries of this particular campaign were prostitutes.

The rules forbidding members of the armed forces to marry had two consequences that were unacceptable to the authorities: one was that the men contracted venereal diseases; and the other that they were liable to resort to homosexuality. Rather than allowing the men to marry or taking the realistic line of licensing brothels or providing condoms – or even turning a blind eye to homosexual practices – Victorian morality turned on the women from whom the men were catching the diseases. Policeman were now empowered to arrest prostitutes in ports and army towns and bring them in for compulsory physical examinations. If they refused to accept this degrading process they could be imprisoned, while if they were found to have a disease they were locked up in hospital for months until cured.

The logic of these laws should have required men to be similarly subject to health checks, but it was felt that such intrusion would demoralize them. The feelings of the women were not consulted; they were, after all, already so depraved and corrupt that further humiliations could not possibly affect them. The priority was to protect men, not to fight venereal disease; the use made by needy men of these 'fallen women' was implicitly condoned while the women were punished.

Protest against this legislation came from women across the social spectrum, mainly because it enabled the police to detain and inspect any woman about whom they had even the slightest suspicion. 'Respectable' working-class women, therefore, were particularly vulnerable, as prostitutes who serviced members of the armed forces invariably came from that class. There were claims that innocent women were forced to submit to degrading inspections and that they could even lose their livelihoods simply through suspicion falling on them; there was, indeed, at least one suicide. Josephine Butler, in particular, understood the contradictions of the laws, even though, as a devout Christian, she abhorred prostitution and men's recourse to it. As an intelligent woman she hated even more the double standard which allowed men to satisfy their needs with prostitutes while reviling and humiliating the women with whom they consorted. She saw them as victims of male oppression, and she stood up against it. The Acts were finally repealed in the 1880s, and the campaigns against them still resound as magnificent examples of women of all classes taking to the public platform to defend their rights.

Women as intelligent and independent beings, with judicial and marital rights to boot, were beginning to assert themselves. The Married Women's Property Acts of 1870 and 1882 finally allowed women to retain property acquired during the course of a marriage and, later, to keep also whatever they had owned before marriage. The long-standing surrender of a woman's body and possessions to the ownership of her husband on marriage was beginning to be eroded; but it was not until 1923 that a woman could achieve a divorce from the man on the grounds of his adultery alone. And as ever, a woman's reputation – her armour against scandal and rumour – was easily lost while a man's was hard to tarnish: he was a gay dog if he played around; she was a slut! He was judged on factors such as his profession and his wealth; she relied on her purity for the good opinion of society.

And that purity was especially vulnerable for working women who often had to rely on the good nature of their male employers. Even young middle-class governesses could be compromised, and from one perspective Charlotte Bronte could consider herself fortunate that her infatuation with the married Constantin Heger never led to a disastrous affair. She stayed with the Heger family while teaching in Brussels and developed a close friendship with her mentor from a mutual interest in poetry and literature. On her return to Haworth, she struggled to free herself from what she now acknowledged to be a hopeless, adulterous love, restricting herself to passionate letters every six months or so – to which he was increasingly loath to reply. The last surviving letter she wrote is dated November 1845, and is a moving testimony to her desolation at his silence: 'I have tried meanwhile to forget you, for the remembrance of a person whom one thinks never to see again, and whom nevertheless, one greatly esteems, frets too much the mind... I have denied myself absolutely the pleasure of speaking about you ... but I have been able to conquer neither my regrets nor my impatience... To forbid me to write to you, to refuse to answer would be to tear from me my only joy on earth.'

For women and girls who fell into the clutches of more unscrupulous types, the predicament was complex. The men had power over them – whether they were the bosses in factories or, for those in domestic service, the men of the house – and there often seemed little option other than to succumb. Yet this, too, was a dangerous strategy. Any female servant who got 'into trouble', or whose liaison was discovered in another way, would be likely to lose her position, and dismissal without a positive character reference could lead to penury and the workhouse. Henry Mayhew's *London Labour and the London Poor* quotes a serving girl who was defiled in this way: 'Of course I was drugged, and so heavily I did not regain consciousness until the next morning. I was horrified to discover that I had been ruined, and for some days I was inconsolable, and cried like a child to be killed or sent back to my aunt.' The story later inspired a powerful poem by Philip Larkin, 'Deceptions', which ends:

> For you would hardly care
> That you were less deceived, out on that bed,
> Than he was, stumbling up the breathless stair
> To burst into fulfilment's desolate attic.

For the upper and middle classes sex before marriage was unthinkable;

even flirtatious behaviour on the part of the woman was frowned on, and it was not done to appear too keen. Status and fortune were important elements in the choice of a mate, and the influence of family was still very strong, although marriages arranged against the wishes of either party in the transaction were becoming rare. The lower middle and working classes, on the other hand, enjoyed what might in some ways appear a greater degree of freedom: an ever-increasing need for workers of both sexes in the new factories and in the households of the newly wealthy industrial owners resulted in more people moving around the country, especially into the growing towns. It was no longer the case that people spent all their lives in one place; and this meant that there was a greater choice of partners available to both men and women, and the possibility of courting several potential partners before settling down. But, as breach of promise cases throughout the nineteenth century show, this 'freedom' could be a double-edged sword; entering into a sexual relationship with a fiancé after a proposal of marriage, and sometimes bearing his child, did not always lead to the respectability of marriage and wifehood. And losing one's chastity in this way, though not perhaps as devastating as the fate that awaited women who slept with men without the prospect of marriage, could still lead to life as a ruined and derided spinster and an unmarried mother to boot.

Children born out of wedlock were legally bastards even if they were born to couples who subsequently married and went on to set up a stable family environment. Such children might still endure the opprobrium of being illegitimate, but they did not have to suffer the hardships of children born to women – almost inevitably lower-class women – who were either deserted before marriage or had never been in a position to marry. Single motherhood at this level of society was financially and socially disastrous, and many women went on to marry men who were not the biological fathers of their children just in order to regain a measure of social respectability. But on those who did not, or could not, Victorian morality now imposed ever harsher sanctions.

Previous Poor Laws had placed the responsibility for the maintenance of illegitimate children on both parents. If the father failed to support his child the mother had access to a judicial warrant which could result in him being imprisoned, and the parish funds available to help the mother and child were, theoretically at least, recoverable from the father. In some cases the man was required to marry the woman. However, in 1833, when a commission was set up to look into reforming the Poor Laws, it was felt that the ready availability of parish relief was simply encouraging licentiousness and that forcing the putative father to marry the mother was undesirable. Moreover, more public money appeared to be available to support illegitimate children than those who were poor but legitimate. Society was insistent that poor relief was for the destitute, not the immoral, and that it was the 'vicious mother' who should be called to account for her role in this 'great offence against the sacrament of marriage.' The Lord Chancellor in the House of Lords denounced 'the lazy, worthless and ignominious class who pursue their self-gratification at the expense of the earnings of the industrious part of the community'. The Bastardy Clause in the 1834 Poor Law decreed that from now on all illegitimate children were to be the sole responsibility of their mothers until the age of sixteen. Fathers were absolved of any responsibility for them.

The sanctimonious cynicism behind this measure is reflected in sentiments expressed at the time: 'We trust that as soon as it has become as burdensome and disgraceful, it will soon become as rare as it is among those classes in this country who are above parish relief'; and 'making the victims of the seducer's art maintain their own bastard children is a "boon to the female population"' on the grounds that women suffering in this way would be a lesson to others. The hypocrisy cries out loud: 'victims of the seducer's art' they might be, but they alone would bear the guilt and the humiliation as well as the financial burden. Women carrying bastard children could not hide the fact; the men who made them pregnant could deny their involvement, and it was simply too costly and too difficult to pursue such men. Promiscuity had to be punished, and the easiest and cheapest way was to punish those who could neither deny the sin nor flee from it.

The principles underpinning the 1834 Poor Law accepted responsibility for the poor who could not avoid their poverty while seeking to deny help to the undeserving; though Victorian fiscal parsimony meant that, in both cases, poor relief was so difficult and unpleasant to obtain that people needing it would resort to almost any other possibility. Poverty in itself was a disgrace and the workhouse was universally dreaded, with reason. Single mothers, in particular, were to be forced to work to support their infants; yet most employment for women required them to be unmarried and without children, and a pregnant woman working in service or a factory would be promptly dismissed when her condition was discovered. Nor could she easily gain employment after childbirth with a baby or young child in tow.

Unmarried mothers and their children were, moreover, subject to the opprobrium of the rest of society; they were an affront to Victorian morality, often thrown out by their own families and forced to leave their villages or neighbourhoods, segregated in the workhouse from respectable young women, spurned even by charities set up to help the indigent. Many orphanages refused to take illegitimate children on the grounds that they had been conceived in sin and would certainly therefore both inherit their parents' immorality and corrupt the legitimate children with whom they would have to associate. No wonder that single mothers often killed their babies or abandoned them. No wonder, too, that these new harsh laws led to another new profession involved with unwanted children: the baby-farmer.

These were unscrupulous women who put adverts in newspapers offering to look after a child for a monthly or one-off fee; often posing as childless widows, they would offer 'a parent's care' to children whose mothers needed to work. Few survived this 'care' for long: they were kept drugged and fed on watered-down, adulterated milk, and given no medical care when they inevitably became sick. Young babies of only a few months were preferable because they were vulnerable anyway, and their deaths could be put down to natural causes if questions were ever asked. Moreover, burying them or otherwise disposing of their bodies was easier; wrapping them in newspaper and throwing them in the Thames was one method in London. Yet older, more robust babies – perhaps children whose mothers had tried and failed to raise them while holding down a job and wished to continue to maintain them and to visit them – had their advantages, too, in that the weekly fees could continue to be extorted while the babies gradually sickened and died.

Many mothers knew the fate to which they were consigning their children when they put them in the care of these women, yet they often had little choice in the matter. Others were deceived by the promises made in the adverts and continued to pay for and visit their children in the belief that they were receiving at least the minimum of care. One such was the mother whom circumstances forced to hand over her four-teen-month-old son, Frederick Wood, to a Mrs Savill of Bow in east London; when he died, ten months later, he was found to have malformed bones, fluid on the brain and a hip that had been broken for several weeks. Mrs Savill was charged, but the jury had no choice other than to listen to the doctor who testified that the child had died of natural causes. She had to be acquitted, but the jurors asked that the verdict should include a motion of censure against her; the coroner refused, and she went free without a visible stain on her character. She was found to have had fourteen children in her care, of whom five had recently died.

Victorian moral condemnation of illegitimate children and their mothers made it difficult for reformers to amass support for laws to combat these practices. Laissez-faire attitudes were another obstacle; the rights of the individual, the sanctity of the family, hatred of government interference in social reform all militated against the efforts of the few who sought to enact regulations with teeth that would prevent this wholesale child murder. Occasional high-profile horrors, such as the sixteen infants starved to death and discarded on the streets of Brixton by Margaret Waters – who was hanged for the crimes – outraged society and galvanized support, but only in the short term. Even the case of a Mrs Hall, owner of a lying-in house also in Brixton, failed to have the desired effect: neighbours reported steady streams of young pregnant women going into the house, but little evidence of emerging babies. It may have been an over-active imagination that reported the sight of Mr Hall feeding bloody lumps believed to be aborted foetuses to his cats; when Mrs Hall was eventually arrested she was found to be a wealthy woman – evidence of the profitability of her profession as an abortionist and baby-farmer. Reform still appeared to be out of the question, however: children had no legal status, particularly if they were bastards, and Parliament always had more pressing business on its collective mind. There was a toothless Act passed in 1872 seeking to regulate child nurses, but it was not until 1897 that proper, effective legislation was enacted.

It is tempting to suspect a link between the increased repressiveness of Victorian society in the matter of morals and social behaviour and the rapidly broadening world that Victorians were experiencing. Technology was transforming daily life within the home and the workplace, and making it possible for more people to enjoy a wider range of leisure activities. Education was, slowly but surely, opening minds to new possibilities; in 1859, only some two hundred years after Archbishop Ussher had declared that the world was created in 4004 BC (a date refined even further by Sir John Lightfoot, Vice-Chancellor of Cambridge University, to 23 October 4004 BC at nine o'clock in the morning), Charles Darwin published *On the Origin of Species* proposing his theory of evolution and adding at a stroke – at least to those prepared to listen – millions of years to the history of the world. Hunkering down and defending the status quo, the tried and tested, the known and the unchallenging are responses perhaps to be expected. And having a woman as the monarch, a role model happily married and many times a mother, must have reinforced the view that values needed to be reasserted after the excesses of previous incumbents. It is perhaps ironic that Victoria is said to have been very keen on sex with her husband and to have pursued Albert round their apartments in Buckingham Palace and Osborne House; he is even thought to have contemplated separating from the queen towards the end of his life, worn out both by her demands and by his hard work for the country as her consort. It is telling that her bedroom at Osborne House had a remote control device for locking the door – on her side of the bed.

Women had begun, in the previous century, to explore their bodies and their sexuality, and to question some of the myths surrounding the sexual act and responses to it. The semi-pornographic *Aristotle's Masterpiece*, published in 1684 and in continuous circulation after that (though banned in Britain until 1961), had at least promoted sex as both purposeful and enjoyable, and as pleasurable for women as for men. But by the middle of the nineteenth century this approach was frowned upon. The publication in 1857 of *The Functions and Disorders of the Reproductive Organs in the Youth, Adult Age, and Advanced Life* took a different line. Women were generally passionless – 'the majority of women ... are not very much troubled with sexual feeling of any kind' – and the only respectable purpose of sex was once again reproduction. 'Ladies don't move' was the view of many men of the time about their wives' enjoyment of the sex act; and 'Lie back and think of England' was the mantra taught to (some) brides by (some) mothers. And it was still the fault of women if their men strayed. The predominant view was that men were different; husbands could not be refused sex because they might go on to commit sin – sin caused directly by their wives' obduracy. There were 'New Women' and their male counterparts who were beginning to insist that men were responsible for their own sins; but they were few.

At this time, scientific disciples were beginning to recognize that sex was itself a subject for serious study in both scientific and sociological terms. 'Sexology' sought to impose elements of rational research on the subject: sexologist Edward Carpenter, for example, declared that this new discipline was 'instrumental in changing perceptions of homosexuality from sin to perversion'. Some saw this new science as oppressive to women since it failed to argue against the pervading view that men were biologically and constitutionally superior, while others thought that its advent as a respectable area of research was, at least potentially, liberating. Yet as late as 1888, John Cowan could write, in *The Science of a New Life*, 'Constricting the waist by corsets prevents the return of blood to the heart, overloads sexual organs and causes unnatural excitement of the sexual system. The majority of women ... also wear their hair in a heavy knot. This great pressure on their small brains produces great heat and chronic inflammation of their sexual organs. It is almost impossible that such women should lead other than a life of sexual excess.' And it continued to be a given that masturbation was both evil and debilitating. Henry Guernsey in *Plain Talks on Avoided Subjects* described the 'habitual masturbator' thus in 1882: 'See how thin, pale and haggard he appears; how his eyes are sunken; how long and cadaverous is his cast of countenance; how irritable he is and how sluggish, mentally and physically; how afraid he is to meet the eye of his fellow; feel his damp and chilling hand, so characteristic of great vital exhaustion.'

Despite apparent advances in sexual knowledge (and recurring examples of continued delusion), young women in polite society were largely brought up ignorant about sex, and many of them were totally unaware of what they might expect on their wedding night. Evidence of this comes from a bundle of exhibits held by the National Archives which were placed before the court in a Chancery case in the early 1870s [J90/1266]. The outcome of the case itself is unknown; it seems to have been related to the financial arrangements made by their ailing father on behalf of Elizabeth Ann Henry and her sister, both of whom were described as 'infants' since they were under twenty-one, and both of whom had been made wards of court. Among the documents is a set of folded sheets of paper on which Elizabeth has written, elegantly and clearly, her own account of what had passed between herself and one Theodore Fitzwalter Butler, younger son of Lord Dunboyne.

The implication is that her family was wealthy and his was not; or it may be that, as a younger son, he had few financial expectations. Marriage to an heiress must have been an attractive prospect for him. At all events, he proposed to Elizabeth only a few days after meeting her while she was staying with his family in Scotland and, though she initially refused, her family seems to have been favourable to the match so she eventually accepted him. However, there must have been doubt on his side as to whether the marriage would go ahead because very soon after the engagement, and egged on by his uncle, he attempted to have intercourse with her. In her own words, 'On the night of Tuesday January 3/4 1871 I was sleeping in a small room which opened off from the room occupied by Mr Butler's uncle (the Honourable Henry Butler Johnstone) … which Mr Butler observed "was most providential". Mr Butler came through his uncle's door. I was half asleep and he roused me by a kiss. He got over me persuading me that "it was the best thing to do", "most people did so" and that he was sure his brother and his wife had done it before their marriage, that it was "sanctioned by the laws of God and Man" and it was the "greatest proof I could possibly give him of affection and confidence as after our marriage it would not be the same."' Theodore Butler proceeded to announce that they were now married and insisted that she call herself his wife and him her husband. When she remonstrated with him that they had not been legally married in church, he told her that this was a 'Scotch marriage'. In her statement, opposite the page where she describes what had happened on that night, there is a comment written in another hand: 'Mr Butler alleges that the proposed connection was for the express purpose of rendering the supposed marriage valid and binding.' But Elizabeth had written next to it: 'This allegation is perfectly and utterly false.' There are other documents in the bundle that indicate that the engagement went on for a short while, with her going along with his wishes as to how they addressed each other; but at some point it came to an end and the issue as to whether or not they were legally married went before the court.

She clearly had no idea what ought to have taken place on that first night if he had succeeded in full intercourse. But it seems that he had not, since also in evidence are affidavits from two doctors who had been called in to examine her and testified that she was still a virgin: 'This is to certify that we the undersigned have on this the 18th day of February 1871 personally examined Miss Elizabeth Anne Henry and we found the hymen perfect in every respect – there was no evidence whatever of any act of copulation – we are of the opinion that there has never been any penetration and that she is *virgo intacta*.' Theodore Butler had been committed to prison pending the outcome of the case, presumably because he had violated a ward of court, and he now wrote to the court to repent of his actions; Elizabeth also wrote to say that she did not consider herself legally married and that she would have nothing to do with Butler ever again. One hopes that the so-called 'Scotch wedding' was declared illegal and that she was free of the young man; but it is more than possible that her reputation was tarnished, despite the doctors' opinions and the fact that she had been duped.

One sad case where we do know the outcome was also the result of sexual ignorance, exacerbated by the harsh morals of the time. It was also, unusually for the latter part of the nineteenth century, the result of a marriage where the pretty but rather vacuous young girl, Lady Constance de Burgh, was made to marry Lord Ward, a man she did not love, by her domineering parents. He had peculiar sexual tastes which she found distasteful: he liked nothing more than to strip her naked, load her with jewels and beautiful objects and admire her for hours. When she complained to her parents they regarded his predilections as strange but excusable, and insisted she stay with him. The crunch came when she went to a ball and was escorted back home by another man whom her husband met as he was leaving the house. He went straight up to his wife's bedroom, accused her of committing adultery and then and there – though she was pregnant – threw her out of the house. Her unsympathetic parents refused to take her in and she took refuge for the night with her old singing master before taking the boat to Belgium the next day. Her child died in premature birth, followed soon after by its miserable mother.

Literature, as ever, was a medium through which advances in understanding could be expressed and iniquities in life and in the law could be held up for scrutiny. An extraordinary example was the action for breach of promise brought by Mrs Bardell against Samuel Pickwick in Charles Dickens' *The Pickwick Papers*. This fictional case was frequently cited in actual cases in the law courts, with barristers using the names of its characters to refer to their opponents in breach of promise suits. The novel was also used to bolster arguments for legislative change, was quoted in books on legal issues and appeared in the opening statement in the House of Commons in 1970 when the Bill which would abolish breach of promise was introduced.

The story hinges on Pickwick's ambiguous approach to his widowed landlady, Mrs Bardell, when he was thinking of hiring a manservant. He asked her, 'Do you think it a much greater expense to keep two people than to keep one?' at which she believed he was proposing, threw herself into his arms and fainted. When she realized that he did not mean to keep what she thought was his promise, she went to the law and hired a firm of lawyers who, at the trial, used every trick in the book to sway the jury. Pickwick's lawyer was inept and the judge slept all the way through, so the jury found for her. Pickwick refused to pay and was consigned to the Fleet prison for debt, but eventually agreed to pay the lawyers' bill in order to stop them pursuing Mrs Bardell for the money, which she could not afford. She then waived the damages and the case was at an end.

There were other fictional accounts of breach of promises cases, notably Gilbert and Sullivan's *Trial by Jury*, and it seems that most of these dramatizations were aimed at challenging the law, which was seen as damaging to men – perhaps the only law relating to marital affairs at this time which was. Moreover, the law was not one to which the more wealthy classes tended to resort: with a few exceptions, breach of promise cases were brought by women of the lower middle and upper working classes – those from respectable families of moderate income where marriage was the only aim for the daughters and the loss of marriage prospects a disaster. And the courts tended to agree: men were expected to keep their word to the weaker vessels to whom they had offered the status and security of marriage. One man who had set a wedding date four times and failed each time to show up found himself having to pay a massive £3,000 to his jilted fiancée in 1824.

It was a remarkably egalitarian piece of legislation for the nineteenth century, and breach of promise cases offer fascinating – and elusive – windows onto ordinary people's sexual and marital affairs. (They represent, too, the tip of the iceberg when one considers the many instances where cases did not come to court.) Suing for breach of promise to marry was the only way in which a woman who had been deserted could gain some level of financial compensation from the man whom she had expected to be her support through life. One of the more interesting revelations from the case histories is the surprisingly large number of women who succumbed to male sexual blandishments before marriage. Interestingly, provided these women had otherwise been chaste and there had been a definite promise of marriage, and even when the pre-marital sex resulted in an illegitimate child or two, they were not tarred with the same brush as their sisters who simply slept with men and had bastards. Jilted women could, and did, retain at least an element of respectability and they could usually rely on family support, even though if the man reneged on the arrangement their marriage prospects were almost always damaged beyond repair. And if their cases came to court, they could also hope for the sympathy of judge and jury and a substantial financial award against the man.

The double standard had not, of course, gone away, though in some ways in these cases it operated in favour of the woman. The different behaviour expected of men and women reflected prevalent attitudes: men were strong and women were weak; men were aggressive while women were passive; men had to behave as independent individuals whereas women could be forgiven for submitting to family pressure; women could be emotional and hysterical while men had to be brave and stand by their actions; and, as ever, men were forgiven their sexual peccadilloes while women could not be allowed any sort of sexual 'past' except sometimes with their fiancés. The reasons for broken engagements were various, but often came down to financial problems or differences in class and status. In those pre-contraception days men worked and supported the family while women ran the household and brought up the children; it followed that the man had to have sufficient resources to keep them all afloat, and so engagements tended to last years while the man worked to build up a career or a trade. It often therefore also followed that affections changed, one or other of the parties met someone more congenial (or richer) or family pressures became impossible to resist. In one case in the late 1860s a woman schoolteacher became engaged to a medical student and her family helped him financially while he pursued his studies. For ten years the engagement persisted while he worked his way through medical school and began to develop his career. When he finally got a position with a doctor his fiancée gave up her job and began to prepare for the wedding – only to be jilted at the last moment in favour of his employer's daughter, who was clearly a much better long-term prospect.

Differences in status or wealth could also imperil engagements. One fourteen-year-old went to work as a servant and became secretly engaged to the son of the household, who promised to marry her when his father died; after ten years and two children with the girl, he promptly married someone else when he came into his estate. In another case a woman became engaged to a young man who had come to live with her family as an apprentice carpenter; she also had two children with him, and stayed at home after he was fully trained while he set off to a neighbouring town to set himself up in his trade. It was only after several years of apparent continued engagement and his protestations that he could not yet afford to marry that she became suspicious and went to confront him – only to find that he had not only established himself in a flourishing business, but had married another woman a good while before.

At this level of society it was the norm for a man to accept responsibility for his fiancée's child and to support mother and child even when he finally baulked at marriage. The 'tip of the iceberg' assumption from breach of promise cases would indicate that, in the majority of instances where an engaged couple conceived a child, the man did the decent thing and married the girl. The condemnation of both society and judiciary might be his lot if he failed to do so and she went as far as suing him. In the case brought by Emily Kitteridge against Thomas Crowe, the judge was highly incensed when it was reported that Crowe's response to the news of her pregnancy was 'she has got into trouble, and she must get out of it': 'in my long experience, I never recollected a more unmanly or cowardly expression' was the castigation from the bench.

Despite the evidence that women were frequently induced to yield their chastity to men who had promised marriage, they were still highly vulnerable to society's disapproval if things then went wrong. John Lloyd jilted Alice Spink after he made her pregnant and, though she begged him to marry her, refused unless a larger dowry was forthcoming and went on to ignore several offers of money from her family; she miscarried the baby but was still disgraced in the eyes of her family and the world. In the worst cases, the seducer himself would cast a woman aside on the grounds that she was now unchaste and therefore not a suitable wife; and some men were not above repudiating women they had made pregnant on the grounds that they were trying to entrap them. Even in cases of rape, the attitude of the woman was almost always that the rapist was now the only man she could possibly marry since he had irretrievably tarnished her virtue and no other man would have her. A woman with a sexual past was also at risk, and even more so if she was part of a profession regarded as of dubious morality – a barmaid, say, or an actress. Maria Foote, who was a well-known actress in the early years of the nineteenth century, lost her fiancé because he could not cope

the lady whose union with me you may excusably regard as the cause of
your sister's ruin should permit you to mention her with the honor with which
Ianthe must be accustomed to regard the wife of her father's heart.
To deal frankly with you, I cannot believe that you will refrain from
inculcating prepossessions on her infant mind the most adverse to my views,
I do not think the worse of you for this: perhaps you would have the
generosity to curb the feelings that would lead to this effect — but I cannot
consent that days & weeks should pass, & that what I consider my duty
& the happiness of my child should depend on your forbearance

I had the strongest wish to consult your feelings in this affair.
And I cannot but think that they would be best consulted by immediate
compliance. Nothing can shake my resolution. The lapse of a few weeks
would only render the execution of it more distressing to you. As to Ianthe,
a child's sorrows are over in a few hours.

Mr Hunt will attend any appointment you may be pleased to make
for delivering the children to his care in my behalf — I should feel
most happy in complying with any request which you might make that
is consistent with that agonising & impatient sense of duty which
will not endure the absence of my child. I can most sincerely say, that
I should eagerly seize any occasion of convincing you that I bear
no malice

I purposely omit adverting to the event from which the occasion of
this letter springs. All parties I imagine suffer too deeply to find any
consolation in the unnecessary display of their sensations.
                              I remain, Dear Eliza,
                                Yours very truly
                                  P. B. Shelley
I may as well say — tho' I dare say Mrs B has told you as much
— that my applying to my Attorney on this occasion was founded entirely
in error

This is the paper writing marked 10 referred to in the Affidavit of
Elizabeth Westbrook sworn before me this 10th day of January 1817
                                Wm Alexander

(12)

Left | 14 | SHELLEY'S
LETTERS to his wife, Harriet
Westbrook, were lost for
decades, until copies of
them were found in a
bundle of Chancery papers
relating to the action he
brought against his wife's
family, after her suicide, for
custody of their children.
This one was written to
Harriet's sister, Eliza, about
his concerns for the care
of his daughter Ianthe
[C124/874/1]. **Below** [15]
CARICATURISTS made hay
with drawings lampooning
the Duke of Clarence,
later King William IV, with
his mistress, the actress
Dorothy Jordan. This
etching of 1797, by James
Gillray, depicts the family
on their way to Bushey
where they were to live a
happy, if illicit, rural life for
a further fourteen years.

Left [16] AT A TIME when married women's rights in relation to their husbands and children were non-existent, Caroline Norton defied her vicious husband by campaigning – and achieving – important changes to the laws on divorce and access to children afterwards. This photograph, taken later in her life, is on a visiting card.

Below [17] SIR DAVID Ochterlony, a distinguished and successful general, also enjoyed the freedom of a British man to 'go native' in India. He kept a harem and adopted local dress and habits. Ochterlony is probably the central figure here, smoking a hookah and watching an Indian entertainment in this scene from 1820.

On the night of Tuesday - January 3=4 - 1871 - I was sleeping in a small room which opened off from the room occupied by Mr. Butler's uncle - Col: the Hon'ble Henry Butler-Clinton. (I had changed my room a few days previously on account of a smoky chimney, which Mr. Butler observed "was most Providential.")

Mr. Butler came through his uncle - the Colonel's door. - I was half asleep & he roused me by a kiss. - There was still firelight. I should think it must have been between one and two o'clock. He got over me - persuading me that "it was the best thing to do:" "most people did so - "also that "he was sure his brother Bob & Maude had done it before their marriage." - That it was "sanctioned by the laws of God and man." It was the "greatest proof I could possibly give him of affection & confidence. as after our

This allegation is perfectly & utterly false.

Above [18] ELIZABETH Ann Henry's articulate account of what passed between herself and her fiancé is part of a bundle of National Archives documents relating to an appeal against an alleged marriage under Scottish law [J90/1266]. Theodore Butler had tried to seduce her before their church marriage in order to make it impossible for her to change her mind. The annotation scratched out opposite her account records the comment that his action had been for that purpose; she has written next to it, 'This allegation is perfectly and utterly false.'

Right [19] THE CELEBRATED actress Lillie Langtry was one of King Edward VII's many mistresses. This photograph, taken c. 1885, shows her as Lady Ormonde in *Peril*.

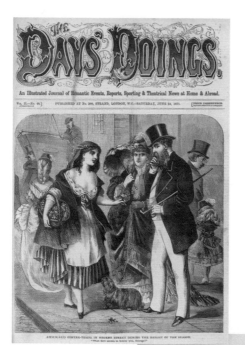

Left [20] 'AN AWKWARD encounter in Regent Street', from *The Days' Doings*, June 1871. The cartoon seems to sum up the prevalence of prostitution in Victorian London, as the suspicious wife seizes upon signs of familiarity: 'That girl seems to know you, George!' **Below** [21] CATHERINE WALTERS, known as 'Skittles', was a Victorian courtesan celebrated for her beauty and her brilliance as a horsewoman. This photograph of *c.* 1870 shows her in her much-admired riding habit. **Right** [22] THE ELDEST son of the Prince of Wales and second in line to the throne, Prince Albert Victor, Duke of Clarence, was embroiled in the homosexual Cleveland Street Conspiracy. His death soon afterwards was regarded as fortuitous, and letters published many years later have revealed the full extent of his involvement.

Clara Walters, (Skittles).

Left [23] OSCAR WILDE and Lord Alfred Douglas, 'Bosie', photographed in 1894. The determined campaign by Bosie's father, the Marquess of Queensberry, to have Wilde convicted of sodomy led to his imprisonment and disgrace. **Below** [24] THE EDWARDIANS, led by their king, took up the new idea of seaside holidays with enthusiasm, particularly since they offered opportunities for illicit goings on away from home. This couple and their dog, pictured on a postcard of 1903, are finding it 'quiet but – hem – bracing' [COPY/1/204]. **Right** [25] WOMEN doing men's work during the First World War were praised for their patriotism but also suspected of loose morals. The 'munitionettes' had a particular reputation, and it is possible to see in this poster a subtle depiction of both views.

~IT IS VERY QUIET HERE BUT~HEM~BRACING

Top [26] FASHIONABLE flappers of the 1920s reacted against the privations of the war years by indulging in new freedoms. This advertisement for the Morris Oxford Six shows an elegantly dressed girl about town smoking, driving a fast car. **Above** [27] AN ILLUSTRATION from *The Sphere*, Christmas 1920, captures the festive mood of Bright Young Things. Note the black musicians – symbols of the new jazz age, with faster, louder music and wilder dance crazes.

with the disapproval of his friends, not only about her profession but also because she had been the mistress of another man and had two children with him. May Gore lost her breach of promise case because she had been the mistress of another man as well as the man who she claimed had offered her marriage.

Women who could have been expected to know better were also subject to less sympathetic treatment in the courts and within society than young girls who were, it was believed, easily led through the innate weakness of their gender. Widows and older women were vulnerable in this way if they had been bamboozled by a charming rogue; and a woman who was a few years older than the man could be charged with being a 'husband-hunter' and a predator on inexperienced young men. Even though such women would often win their cases, the damages tended to decrease with the number of years of age discrepancy.

Woe betide, too, women seen as assertive or flirtatious. The indulgence of the courts and the level of damages were highly dependent on a woman's supposed devastation at her desertion. Sarah Chedzoy lost her action against Harry Woodberry not only because she had become engaged to him almost immediately after the funeral of her previous fiancé, but also because the engagement had only lasted a short time; she was judged not to show evidence of deep feelings or anguish. Another woman who won her action received an award of only forty shillings as she had refused her former fiancé's willingness to make up with her before and during the trial. Women had to be seen to be victims.

Men, meanwhile, could continue on the whole to enjoy the tolerance afforded by the double standard towards two-timing behaviour, or even courting and bedding a previously chaste young girl while married to someone else. Making advances to one woman for sexual favours while offering marriage to someone else was not uncommon, and the response of the wronged women in these cases was frequently the same as in instances of rape: they desperately wanted to get married and were all too ready to forgive errant lovers as long as they kept their word and married them. This didn't work, of course, when the man was actually married. Carlotta Hutley, an actress, agreed to marry Sidney Master, a club owner, and promptly became pregnant by him; it was only when he deserted her before the birth of the child that she discovered that he was already married and had four children. However, breach of promise cases do throw light on the other side of the coin of Victorian double standards;

the success of the majority of women bringing such cases and the obvious indignation of judge and jury when men were shown to be perfidi-
ous and deceitful indicate that wronged women had some rights in law
and men did not have it all their own way. And certain commentators on
the legal system at the time, despite being opposed to the law as it stood,
recognized that poorer women had to resort to it, since society placed
women in the invidious position of needing marriage in order to survive.

Although women were the plaintiffs in the vast majority of breach of
promise cases, there were some instances when men sued. George Hole
was one. He was one of a family of farmers with land near the farm
owned by Minnie Harding's father. She had first been engaged to George's
brother, but broke it off because of her father's disapproval. When she
became engaged to George they initially kept it secret but eventually
both families were reconciled to the match – until it appeared that the
Hole farm was losing money. Minnie again claimed parental disapproval
in the new circumstances and broke off the engagement. George then
went to law, and his solicitor used language in the claim that was more
usual for female plaintiffs: that he had been cruelly treated, that his
whole life had been blighted, that his social position had been injured.
He did eventually win the case, but was awarded derisory damages; a mere
farthing! It seems that the court could not understand a man who could
so weakly complain about wounded feelings or who could bring a case
against a woman; while the fact that she had jilted two men and was still
– although she was in her early thirties – in need of her father's approval
did not go against her. The statistics of these cases indicate generally that
male plaintiffs lost a far great proportion of their cases and received
much lower damages if they did win: complaining about a broken heart
was clearly not proper behaviour for a Victorian man.

Despite the prejudices and preconceptions surrounding sex and marriage, the nineteenth century was a time of real social change. It took
time, but the early Victorian campaigners for more equal rights for
women and the legislative changes in response gathered more momen-
tum in the later years of Victoria's reign. Falling in love could still be a
risky venture, and unorthodox affairs a social minefield, but manners
and morals were in flux as prosperity impacted on all classes, offering
different perspectives from even the recent past. The final decades of the
nineteenth century were to be a time of decadence and flamboyance, as
well as establishing the need for a more equitable social conscience.

Five · New Women and old Adam

A RADIO SERIES seeking to decide on the most important invention in history once made a strong case for the bicycle. It did not win, but the arguments were compelling: the safety bicycle, developed towards the end of the nineteenth century, provided an easy, effective mode of transport for both men and women, and was moreover much more accessible to the less well off than horses and carriages. It was a true liberation; and for women particularly it offered freedom both of mobility and of dress that became symptomatic of a changing age. Billowing skirts and tight corsets were unsuitable clothes for a bicycling woman, so dress became less encumbering and simpler. Trousers for women were still in the future, but the shocking wearing of bloomers – baggy divided skirts fastened below the knee – offered new possibilities for 'New' Women who increasingly wanted to explore the opportunities offered by new horizons, both physical and in the mind. It is telling that when Cambridge University male undergraduates protested against the admission of women as full members of the university in 1897, they hung an effigy of a woman on a bicycle in the town square.

Women's colleges at both Oxford and Cambridge had been founded in the late 1860s and early 1870s, to be greeted with much opprobrium among those who took a traditional view of the female place in society. Girton College, the first Oxbridge women's college, was called 'that infidel place' because it was seen as distracting women from their duties at home; the daughters of the headmaster of Marlborough were prevented from attending for that reason. But education for women had arrived in schools and universities, and would not now go away; New Women were challenging the status quo and were prepared to act and to use their brains without deferring to men. Such women had to be made of stern stuff; many of their counterparts – including some of the mothers and sisters of the early Oxbridge women pioneers – regarded them with pity and horror. As the first principal of Lady Margaret Hall, Oxford, said to the mother of one of her first potential students: 'I feel it my duty to warn you that our girls do not marry well.' Progressive thoughts and robust intellect were far from being sexual assets.

Yet Britain was moving on despite itself, as education, travel, better communication and increased prosperity led to the merging of worlds which had previously hardly met. Progress was fed by the riches of empire and the technological advances of industry, but hampered, too, by the paradoxes and convulsions that lay at its heart. The decades following the publication of Darwin's *On the Origin of Species*, which had struck at the roots of traditional religious belief, saw a gradual increase in secularity paralleled by continuing deep Christian faith. Many of the women who fought like tigers against the legal and social restrictions and inequities that faced them did so because of – and supported by – their religion; but at the same time new moral structures were emerging, buoyed up by the new climate which challenged unquestioning assumptions. And the opportunities and possibilities opened up by the widening world and growing knowledge led on one hand to eyes wide open to the future, and on the other to hankerings for a safer and more certain past.

It was a glamorous and exotic age – a time to celebrate the splendours of the present. Terms such as 'the Naughty Nineties' and '*La Belle Epoque*' evoke opulence and decadence, and combine with the anticipation of a new century to describe an age of both pleasure and radical change. It was a time which not only tolerated but celebrated the novels of Elinor Glyn, which by modern standards are pretty standard fare but were then regarded almost as softcore pornography. Glyn coined the term 'it' for sex appeal, and went to Hollywood to help promote the idea of the 'vamp' and Clara Bow as the 'it girl'. She had a long affair with Lord Curzon, sometime Viceroy of India and later Foreign Secretary, and is also remembered for the verse:

> Would you sin
> With Elinor Glyn
> On a tiger skin
> Or would you prefer
> To err with her
> On some other fur?

Indeed, with the advantage of hindsight, and the knowledge of the war that was to come, the turn of this particular century encapsulates a sort of high-kicking, crazy splendour that was never to recur. And the death of the old queen just as the new century was starting heralded the glories of the Edwardian decade named after the new king.

The beginning and end of the nineteenth century might be defined as the ages of the two Princes of Wales — both well-known womanizers and men-about-town, both the despair of their respective parents, both castigated in the press for their lurid lifestyles. Both also gave their names to eras renowned for a certain decadent pleasure: the Regency, led by the prince himself as a time of foppish splendour; the Edwardian years the last hurrah of a generation which was soon to lose its children, and with them its happy insouciance, to the horrors of the Great War. Both, too, introduced an element of farce to their coronations. George IV refused to allow his long-estranged queen admittance to the ceremony and barricaded Westminster Abbey against her importunate demands to enter; Edward VII was happy to invite several of his mistresses, including Sarah Bernhardt and Alice Keppel. They and his other ladies were ensconced in what racegoing wits of the time called 'The King's Loose Box'.

Edward's life of pleasurable frivolity had started when he was young. His mother, Queen Victoria, never much liked her oldest son, regarding him as irresponsible and indiscreet, and their relationship plumbed further depths when she blamed him for the loss of her beloved Albert; he died only two weeks after visiting his son at Cambridge to reprimand him about an affair with an actress. The queen, who never reconciled herself to her husband's early death and wore mourning for the rest of her life, believed that Albert's distress over Edward's dissolute lifestyle had contributed to his vulnerability to the typhoid that killed him.

Edward did not respond to his father's death by reforming. He dutifully married Alexandra and had children, but carried on taking mistress after mistress, among them some of the most celebrated women of the age: the actresses Lillie Langtry and Sarah Bernhardt; Jenny Jerome, wife of Lord Randolph Churchill and mother of Winston; and the Countess of Warwick — Daisy 'Babbling' Brook — among many others. Edward was even summoned as a witness in a notorious divorce case in 1870, when Sir Charles Mordaunt was suing his wife for divorce on the grounds of her adultery with several prominent men, including two of the prince's close friends. Edward was warned that cross-examination would be bound to reveal a connection between himself and Lady Mordaunt, and that he could well be damaged by guilt by association; however, he declined to invoke the royal prerogative by which he could refuse the subpoena and to shrink from 'answering these imputations'. He acquitted himself in the witness box with dignity, but inevitably became the subject of lewd broadsheets and hissings on the street after the end of the trial. *The Times* weighed in, too, calling on him to behave: 'if royalty has many privileges, it must suffer not a few privations, and the charm of personal intimacy is one that must be almost denied to the inheritors of crowns.'

Edward had to wait a long time to come into his inheritance: a pun of the era joked, 'she reigns and reigns, and never gives the poor son a chance.' And when he did become king on Victoria's death in January 1901, he proved a surprising success at it. Despite his mother's misgivings, he established himself as a wise and much-loved monarch, though it was not to be for long; he died in 1910. And on his accession it was noticeable to those around him that he quickly established himself as his own man; in small ways, such as smoking in places where his mother had forbidden it, and with the major statement he made by denying his mother's wish that he should become King Albert Edward, he showed that he had finally stepped out from under the shadow of his parents.

Edward was far too wise to deny his enjoyment of physical pleasures, from rich foods and smoking to feminine allure. Two of the best known of his mistresses were with him until the end of his life: Agnes Keyser and Alice Keppel who, in truth, became more like a constant wife than a mistress. Queen Alexandra tolerated this situation and allowed Alice Keppel to be present at her husband's deathbed as he had requested, though she did not like her. Agnes Keyser was more to her taste: a wealthy, unmarried woman who supported humanitarian causes including a hospital for wounded officers, to which she devoted the rest of her life after Edward's death.

Alice Keppel had established a reputation for adultery early in her life, and took many lovers during her marriage, seemingly with the compliance of her husband, George; even her eldest daughter was rumoured not to have been her husband's child. After she met Edward in 1898, and despite the twenty-eight-year age gap between them, he became a constant visitor at her house, with George obligingly making himself scarce. Vita Sackville-West, in the early days of her friendship with Alice's daughter Violet, recorded sometimes seeing 'a discreet little one-horse brougham waiting outside', and being slipped into a dark corner of the hall by the butler 'with a murmured "One minute, miss, a gentleman is coming downstairs."' Coming as she did from an upper-class background, without the social disadvantages felt by courtesans whose humble origins usually counted against them, Alice's dalliance with the heir to the throne served to enhance her own social standing and the career of her husband. Adultery was not condoned but it was tolerated, and Alice's background rendered her presence unexceptional, though discretion was still essential. Alexandra was often irritated when Alice turned up at social events at which she was present with her husband. The mistress was, however, of great help to the wife; Alice was one of the few in the king's circle who could temper Edward's infamous mood swings, and a contemporary is on record as believing that she deserved the grateful thanks of the nation: 'I would like to pay a tribute to her wonderful discretion and to the wonderful influence she always exerted upon the king. She never utilized her knowledge to her advantage or to that of her friends and I never heard her repeat an unkind word of anybody.'

One of Edward's mistresses was to transcend the old century and the new, and was also to provide a telling example – in some cases at least – of rather more tolerant attitudes towards women. With the honourable exception of Elizabeth Armistead (p. 89) and one or two others, few courtesans, however beautiful and famous, had been able to make the transition to respectability from the pariah-like status that went with their calling. But Catherine Walters achieved it. Known as Skittles because she is said to have started her career as a prostitute in a skittle alley behind a London pub, she became famous in the 1860s, when crowds flocked to see her riding out in Rotten Row in London's Hyde Park. She was not only a beautiful woman but also a brilliant horsewoman, and the cut of her simple yet elegant riding outfit was widely copied. Rumours placed some of the highest in the land among her clientele, but she remained the soul of discretion, and her success allowed her to retire as a wealthy woman. Yet her presumption in intruding into the high society of Rotten Row was decried in scandalized letters to *The Times*, and even her horses had to be stabled secretly lest their ownership bring down opprobrium on others who used the stables. She was, however, fortunate in her lovers: the Prince of Wales both corresponded with her and supported her financially until his death, and the poet and traveller Wilfrid Scawen Blunt was similarly attentive until her death in the early 1920s. He had fallen violently in love with her when they were both young, and although he could never expect to marry her, he pursued a lifelong relationship with her which started passionately but ended in sincere friendship.

Courtesans were at the top of the 'oldest profession'. Lower down the scale earnings were smaller and life was more insecure; but here, too, the rewards could be valuable for the wise, especially for women working independently. One who did manage to better herself was Sarah Tanner, whom the diarist Arthur Munby met in his quest to find out more about the working women of London. He took a robust view of prostitutes and seemed to have no particular moral revulsion against them or their trade, 'provided they be sober, well-dressed and not too importunate.' He noted that, particularly for those who worked in the West End where they could command higher prices, their lives could be successful and prosperous. He first met Sarah when she was a maid-of-all-work but then came across her again, 'arrayed in gorgeous apparel. "How is this?" said I. Why, she had got tired of service, wanted to see life and be independent; and so she had become a prostitute, of her own accord and without being seduced. She saw no harm in it: enjoyed it very much, thought it might raise her and perhaps be profitable. She had taken it up as a profession, and that with much energy: she had read books, and was taking lessons in writing and other accomplishments, in order to fit herself to be a companion of gentlemen.'

During the next two or three years Munby saw her around and about pursuing her profession, and usually stopped to talk to her. Then, one evening in early 1859, he met her again in the Strand – walking with another woman, looking better than ever and dressed 'quietly and well, like a respectable upper servant'. She had saved money during her three years on the streets and had taken over the Hampshire Coffeehouse, over Waterloo Bridge. He visited her there five days later and found it to be a respectable, well-run place – something confirmed by a local policeman who told Munby that it was not frequented by women of ill repute.

However, Sarah Tanner's sensible and pragmatic approach to her life as a prostitute – and her clear determination to use her earnings to change her circumstances – was not a course that many prostitutes were able to adopt. Life for women in the grimmer parts of cities and towns was much harsher, especially for those subject to a pimp or brothel-keeper. The probability of catching venereal disease was an ever-present adjunct to their work, and they were also at serious risk of violence and even murder, as Jack the Ripper demonstrated. He killed at least four East End prostitutes and possibly as many as eight between August and November 1888, strangling them and then mutilating their bodies. He was never caught and his identity is a matter of keen speculation to this day, perhaps particularly because the anatomical skills he displayed led to the conjecture that he may have been a doctor, or at least a member of the educated classes.

'The oldest profession', as ever, embraced all classes and all levels of society, from the dregs of the slums who were the Ripper's prey to high-class courtesans and women such as Sarah Tanner who moved beyond their lower-class status to enjoy some of the finer things in life. Yet the insecurities remained. Courtesans were inhabitants of a shadowy world – *the demi-monde* – on the one hand invisible to polite society, yet on the other celebrated and followed with eager interest. Their very notoriety was their fortune, just so long as they could retain their allure. Once their looks began to fade and their value as high-class mistresses began to decline, they were highly vulnerable. Respectable women never received or acknowledged them, despite their close connection with men of the same class; those very men, too, only sometimes continued to look after their former mistresses. It took forethought and wisdom – or sometimes, as in Harriette Wilson's case, blackmail – to ensure that they did not sink into a penurious old age.

In truth, prostitutes and the brothels that housed them were a necessary and inescapable part of urban life. Christopher Hibbert estimates in *London: The Biography of a City* that there were at least 80,000 professional prostitutes in the city in the 1860s, along with nearly 3,000 brothels. And this was not counting the thousands of women who worked in the seedy backstreets – or, at the other extreme, those who were classy enough to be 'kept women' in apartments paid for by their keepers. Other prostitutes also used their own apartments, in places such as Soho, Pimlico and Chelsea. And there were many places which would let rooms for an hour to those men who preferred not to go to a brothel or an apartment – the seedier coffee houses in Covent Garden, for example, or dedicated houses of accommodation with notices outside announcing 'Beds to be had within'.

The centre of London, as well as all other cities, was full of places of assignation where men would go to pick up women of easy virtue. Large dance halls known as 'casinos', cafés, fashionable shops – some of which even had rooms on the premises which could be hired – all offered venues where men and women could meet. At some of the most luxurious places there were dress codes for both men and women, and only high-class prostitutes were allowed in. Mott's was one of them, frequented, according to Donald Shaw's *London in the Sixties* (published in 1908), by 'girls of education and refinement who had succumbed to the blandishments of youthful lordlings, fair women here and there who had not yet developed into peeresses and progenitors of future legislators.' Another was the Café Royal, in Princess Street near Leicester Square, known as Kate Hamilton's after the woman who ran it. She was an enormous woman, whom Shaw describes as 'shaking with laughter like a giant blancmange' as she held court. These establishments made their money by charging outlandishly high prices for food and drink, and by only allowing in men who could afford to spend large quantities of cash.

Prostitutes and the madams who controlled them were a threat to society not just because of the scandal they could cause; they were also visibly independent of male control, and often rich. Many of them had several establishments catering to all sorts of sexual tastes, and were both prosperous and protected. Within the stultifying morality of the time – Victorian values at their height – they were an affront to the norm, in terms not just of sexual propriety but also of women's perceived natural role in society. Some of those who supported purity organizations were concerned for the safety and health of young women; others were anxious to keep women in their place. And in some cases moral values concealed more disturbing realities. It seems likely that inner turmoils were the motivation that led William Ewart Gladstone to seek a purer society. His endeavours took the form of engaging with prostitutes and trying to persuade them to a better way of life.

Gladstone's diaries make it clear that his reforming initiatives with prostitutes were motivated partly by his own disturbed sexuality. His work as an MP and later Prime Minister kept him away from his wife for long periods, and also caused him much stress. By his own confession a man of intense sexual urges, he sought relief from the pressures of his life first in pornography and later in work with 'fallen women'. His activities were, initially at least, conventionally charitable, and they were encouraged by the lay Tractarian brotherhood to which he belonged. His wife was well aware of this work and participated in it; the couple often invited the women they were trying to save to their home. But, as the diaries show, Gladstone became increasingly aware that his interest in these women went further than their rehabilitation; he felt a Christian justification in undertaking the work, but perceived that it was becoming a craving. He was, in his own words, 'courting evil'.

Moreover, it was not very successful; by early 1854 Gladstone had attempted to redeem nearly a hundred women 'but among these there is but one of whom I know that the miserable life has been abandoned *and* that I can fairly join that fact with influence of mine.' This is perhaps not surprising in view of the fact that the Houses of Mercy into which he tried to tempt the women were places of extremely strict discipline. As one Jane Bywater wrote to him in 1854 after a short spell in one of them, 'I have no doubt that you wished to do me some service, but I did not fancy being shut up in such a place as that for perhaps twelve months. I should have committed suicide.'

Gladstone's intense temptations are recounted in his diaries, but in language that followed the conventions of the day by being anything but explicit. He used codes and foreign words as well as hints and innuendoes, all of which make it impossible to know for sure whether he ever yielded to the urges that he felt so strongly. Shortly before his death, he told his son that he had 'never been guilty of the act which is known as that of infidelity to the marriage bed', which might be read as a highly qualified admission. But what is painfully clear is that he felt enormous guilt – which he dealt with by self-flagellation with a scourge. He started doing this in the 1840s and continued for much of his life, as we now know from his diaries where he recorded each episode with the Greek letter lambda.

Gladstone's activities were not publicly questioned during his lifetime. Even if they had been, protecting the great and the good from scandal appears to have been a major preoccupation of the police and the authorities in the later nineteenth century. The prosecution of Mary Jeffries is indicative. She was one of the chief brothel-keepers of the time, whose clients were among the highest in the land including, she once boasted, the king of Belgium. Described by a journalist as 'the wickedest woman of the century', she was also suspected of procuring girls for the 'white slave trade'. This led to her becoming the target, in the mid-1880s, of both the new Salvation Army and the splendidly named London Committee for the Exposure and Suppression of the Traffic of English Girls for the Purposes of Continental Prostitution. An ex-police officer called Jeremiah Minahan started to watch her premises on behalf of the Committee, and when she tried to bribe him to go away he helped them to prepare a case against her for keeping a disorderly house.

The preliminary hearing in the police court was attended by observers from the Home Office, clearly worried that revelations about vice in high places might be about to hit the headlines – just what her prosecutors wanted. They were foiled, however, when she evaded the publicity that would have attended the full court case by pleading guilty. Fined £200 and bound over for a further £400, she went free for the time being, but was later prosecuted again and this time imprisoned. It was outrage at the apparent connivance of the authorities in concealing the guilty men's identities that led very shortly afterwards to furious campaigns for better safeguards for vulnerable women and children. In *Madams, Bawds and Brothel Keepers*, Fergus Linnane quotes the contemporary thunderings of *The Sentinel*, a pro-purity journal: 'The inferences point to a state of moral corruption, heartless cruelty and prostitution of authority almost sufficient, even in this country, to goad the industrial classes into revolution.' The final outcome of the campaigns was the Criminal Law Amendment Act of 1885.

The main purpose of this Act was to tighten up the laws protecting women and children from sexual predators. The 1861 Offences Against the Person Act had set the age of consent for a girl at twelve years old (raised to thirteen in 1875); the aim was to protect the very young and also to prevent men making off with rich young heiresses and marrying them for their money. The 1861 law also imposed a penalty of two years' imprisonment on men who assaulted or raped girls below the minimum age; but anyone above the age of thirteen remained vulnerable. Although public opinion was heavily in favour of harsher legislation for sexual offenders, Parliament was more than a little apathetic about changing the laws and several attempts to enact new statutes failed.

One of the many people and organizations determined to campaign for the cause was W.T. Stead, the editor of the *Pall Mall Gazette*. He set out to prove how easy it was to 'buy' a young girl for prostitution and for export into the white slave trade. With the help of Rebecca Jarrett, a reformed prostitute and procurer, and Bramwell Booth of the Salvation Army, he bought thirteen-year-old Eliza Armstrong from her parents and went about the usual procedure for preparing her for export. She was placed in a brothel, examined to ensure that she was a virgin, drugged and left to wait for her 'purchaser'. W.T. Stead turned up at the brothel, turned Eliza over to the Salvation Army and wrote the story up. It caused an uproar, and Parliament was forced to give further consideration to the campaigners' demands. It also earned Stead a three months' prison sentence for indecent assault arising from the girl's physical examination; a lesser consequence was the Prince of Wales' cancelled subscription to the *Pall Mall Gazette*.

The final Act contained several clauses which gave increased protection to girls and young women, among them raising the age of consent to sixteen, making it a criminal offence to procure girls for prostitution by drugging or intimidating them, allowing children under the age of twelve to testify in court against molesters, empowering the courts to remove a girl from her guardians if they connived at her seduction and punishing householders who permitted under-age sex on their premises. After its passage the number of reported sexual offences rocketed, including child molestation cases.

But the Act had another effect, not originally intended by those who introduced it. It included a clause introduced late at night during the debate by Henry Labouchere, a rabid homophobe, which effectively criminalized homosexuality. The death penalty for sodomy had been removed in 1861 and replaced with life imprisonment; but in order to be convicted men had to have been caught committing buggery – full carnal relations with other men. This new clause would allow the prosecution and the imprisonment for up to a year of any man found guilty of 'gross indecency' with another man 'whether in public or in private' – a much wider catch-all. There were protests that this clause had nothing to do with the main focus of the Bill, but it was ruled that, if Parliament agreed, any amendment was permissible. The only suggestion was that a one-year prison term was too lenient, so it was increased to two years and the amendment was passed. From now on, homosexuality as an activity was in itself criminal. There were public worries on the basis of the 'in public or in private' wording, which protesters argued could be a 'blackmailer's charter' as a man could be accused simply on the word of another. But the public were in full support of the Act as a whole, so such worries were ignored.

It was not to be long before the homosexual clause in this new law was tested in a very high-profile case: that of Oscar Wilde. But before that, outrage at male homosexuality – perceived as an aristocratic vice that corrupted working-class youths – erupted in what became known as the Cleveland Street Conspiracy.

It started in 1889 when the police were investigating thefts of cash at the London Central Telegraph Office and a telegraph boy called Thomas

Swinscow was found to have eighteen shillings in his pocket – the equiv-
alent of several weeks' wages. He insisted that he had not stolen the
money, but had earned it working for a man called Charles Hammond –
and he eventually admitted that it was payment for 'going to bed with
gentlemen' at Hammond's house and that he had been introduced to
Hammond by one Henry Newlove. Moreover, he knew of two other
telegraph boys who also worked for Hammond.

The police raided Hammond's house at 19 Cleveland Street, but
found that he had fled. They did, however, manage to pick up Henry
Newlove hiding at his mother's house, and when he and the telegraph
boys were further questioned they divulged the names of some of their
clients. One name given was that of the Earl of Euston and another was
Lord Arthur Somerset, a major in the Royal Horse Guards and an
equerry to the Prince of Wales, of whose stables he was in charge. They
also hinted that someone even more illustrious was involved – Prince
Albert Victor, the Duke of Clarence, known as 'Prince Eddy', grandson
of Queen Victoria, eldest son of the Prince of Wales and second in line to
the throne.

Charges were duly brought against Newlove and the telegraph boys
and they were sentenced to several months' imprisonment with hard
labour. But meanwhile no action was taken against the more prominent
figures involved in the scandal, and it was found that Somerset had
escaped arrest and fled abroad. (He eventually settled in the south of
France and lived there for the rest of his life with a male companion.)
The press began to sniff a high-level cover-up.

It was Ernest Parke, editor of a radical weekly, *The North London Press*,
who took it up. He published two articles alleging that several aristocratic men were involved, but that charges had never been brought and,
moreover, they had been tipped off and allowed to flee the country. He
even suggested that a gentleman 'more distinguished and more highly
placed' was being protected; his readership had no difficulty in identifying this gentleman as Prince Eddy. He had gone too far, however, in
naming names including that of the Earl of Euston, who had not fled,
had no intention of doing so and now brought a libel action against
Parke. He was unable to name his sources and so was found guilty and
imprisoned for twelve months.

It was another lawsuit, however, that kept the case on the boil:
Newlove's defence lawyer was convicted of warning Charles Hammond

about his imminent arrest, thus allowing him to escape the police and avoid having to testify against his clientele. Henry Labouchere now once again involved himself in the issue and took up the case in Parliament, thundering that it must have been a prominent member of the government – perhaps even the Prime Minister himself – who had warned Lord Somerset to flee and was now protecting other guilty men. His speech was so confrontational that he was suspended from Parliament for a week and his motion to have a committee formed to investigate the cover-up was defeated.

The aftermath for Prince Eddy is unclear. He was officially said to have died in January 1892, three years after the scandal. But rumours surrounded his death; maybe the cause was syphilis, or possibly a deliberately administered overdose of morphine. He is even said to have survived until the 1920s shut up in an asylum. Since documents now released and published, including the private letters of Lord Somerset, implicate him very clearly in the Cleveland Street scandal, he would certainly have had to be removed from the line of succession. His legacy as a rake and a womanizer, however, lived on in the form of an alleged illegitimate son born to a Margery Haddon who, she claimed, had had an affair with him during a royal tour of India in the late 1880s. She was apparently paid off and letters written to her by the prince were bought up by the authorities; but the son, Clarence Haddon, turned up in England in the 1920s and made a fuss, demanding to be recognized as the prince's child. Documents in the National Archives indicate that the authorities took him seriously enough to do some high-level investigation, in the worried belief that he might have some sort of proof. But as it turned out, all evidence had long since disappeared and his claims came to nothing.

It is perhaps fair to say that male homosexuality was, if not condoned, at least tolerated among the upper classes and the literati at this time. The circle within which Oscar Wilde moved was well known for its decadence. The artist Aubrey Beardsley was perhaps one of its most outrageous characters: he said of himself, 'If I am not grotesque, I am nothing,' and his erotic drawings on themes taken from history and mythology included illustrations for *Lysistrata* and Wilde's play *Salomé*. Described by Wilde as having 'a face like a silver hatchet, and grass green hair', he seems to have been of ambiguous sexuality: while a prominent member of the homosexual London coterie, he was also suspected of having an incestuous relationship with his sister, who may have miscarried his child. He was to die of tuberculosis at the age of only twenty-five.

Oscar Wilde – an Irish poet and playwright who was enjoying a great deal of success on the London stage – could almost certainly have saved himself from deep humiliation in court, two harsh years in prison and an early death if he had taken the advice of friends such as George Bernard Shaw and Frank Harris, dropped his libel case against the Marquess of Queensberry and continued his writing while living abroad. It has also been suggested that, when he had lost the libel case and a warrant for his arrest had been issued, the authorities delayed serving it in order to allow him to catch the boat train for France. He was reluctant to flee in disgrace, and lost his chance to escape.

Wilde first met Queensberry's son, Lord Alfred Douglas (known as 'Bosie'), in 1891 when he was thirty-eight and Bosie was twenty-two. They immediately embarked on a close relationship which was initially accepted as an innocent friendship by both Wilde's wife and Bosie's father. But Wilde's outrageousness and his homosexual adventures were beginning to arouse gossip, and Queensberry threatened his son with the withdrawal of all financial support unless he ceased to consort with the man whom he considered to be endangering Bosie's reputation and health. Queensberry's antipathy must have been considerably strengthened by the death of his older son, Lord Drumlanrig, in an apparent hunting accident in October 1894. Rumour had it that this was no accident but suicide, occasioned by the threat of blackmail which now hung over the young man because of his sexual relationship with Lord Rosebery, who had just become Prime Minister. And Queensberry's impassioned anger can only have been deepened by the annulment that same year of his second marriage; his new wife had left him almost immediately after the wedding in 1893, and had sought an annulment on the grounds of 'malformation of the parts of generation' combined with frigidity and impotence.

Whatever his motivation, Queensberry now began to pursue Wilde with frenzy, determined not to lose another son to what he saw as 'the evils of sexuality'. In February 1895 *The Importance of Being Earnest* opened in London to great acclaim – but Wilde had to arrange for a police presence on the opening night because he had heard that Queensberry was intending to disrupt the performance. Shortly afterwards the Marquess delivered a card to the Albemarle Club, to which both Wilde and his wife belonged. It contained the poisonous, socially damning message 'For

Oscar Wilde, posing somdomite [*sic*]'. Against the advice of many of his friends, but egged on by Bosie, Wilde decided to sue for libel.

Both the solicitor he consulted and, later, his barrister, the famous Sir Edward Clarke, asked Wilde whether there was any truth in the accusation. Clarke pressed him eloquently on this point: 'I can only accept this brief, Mr Wilde, if you assure me on your honour as an English gentleman that there is not and never has been any foundation for the charges that are made against you.' Wilde's answer – that the charges were 'absolutely false and groundless' – was disingenuous. He had already had to pay blackmail to an indigent young friend of Bosie's who had found some extremely incriminating letters from Wilde to his lover in the pocket of a suit Bosie had given him. And when the trial began in April at the Old Bailey, Wilde's demeanour in the witness box did not help his cause. He began by lying about his age and became flippant and foppish in his answers. When Queensberry's barrister – another celebrated lawyer, Edward Carson – asked him whether he had kissed Walter Grainger, a young man aged sixteen years, Wilde's reply was, 'Oh dear, no! He was a peculiarly plain boy.'

Much of the defence testimony related to the apparent immorality and homosexuality of Wilde's work, which he defended as beautiful and artistic. But when it became clear that Carson was about to introduce into the court a string of young men with whom Wilde had consorted – many of them not of a class with whom he might have mixed in the ordinary way – Clarke urged him to drop the case. He told him that it was 'almost impossible in view of all the circumstances to induce a jury to convict of a criminal offence a father who was endeavouring to save his son from what he believed to be an evil companionship.' Wilde was forced to agree.

Immediately after the libel case ended, a warrant was issued for Wilde's arrest on charges of gross indecency under Section 11 of the 1885 Act, and the trial opened on 26 April 1895. His co-accused was Alfred Taylor, who had been his procurer. A parade of young men testified to the sexual fantasies that they had acted out with Wilde, and they almost all expressed remorse and shame over their involvement. But it became clear, both from what was said in court and from what Wilde admitted later, that he had relished the danger and the excitement of these encounters: 'feasting with panthers' was how he described them. The judge evidently found the witnesses unlikely companions for a man of

Wilde's status; as he put it to the jury, 'Are these the kind of young men with whom you yourself would care to sit down and dine?'

A memorable moment was when Wilde was asked the meaning of an expression in one of Bosie's poems: 'the love that dare not speak its name'. His answer drew loud applause mixed with hisses: '"The love that dare not speak its name" in this century is such a great affection of an elder for a younger man as there was between David and Jonathan, such as Plato made the very basis of his philosophy and such as you find in the sonnets of Michelangelo and Shakespeare. It is that deep, spiritual affection that is as pure as it is perfect. It dictates and pervades great works of art like those of Shakespeare and Michelangelo... It is beautiful, it is fine, it is the noblest form of affection. There is nothing unnatural about it. It is intellectual, and it repeatedly exists between an elder and a younger man, when the elder man has intellect and the younger man has all the joy, hope and glamour of life before him. That it should be so the world does not understand. The world mocks it and sometimes puts one in the pillory for it.' Moving as they were, Wilde's words were not without cunning, hiding the physicality of his affairs behind professions of pure, spiritual love.

Clarke's closing speech was masterly. He urged the jury to 'clear from this fearful imputation one of our most renowned and accomplished men of letters of today and, in clearing him, clear society from a stain.' It worked, up to a point; the jury failed to come to a verdict and Wilde was released on bail for three weeks before his retrial.

At this stage even Edward Carson was urging 'Can you not let up on this fellow now?' But Queensberry was determined to pursue Wilde to the end, and there is much speculation that he put great pressure on the vulnerable Lord Rosebery to throw the government's weight behind the continued prosecution. This time the verdict was guilty, and Wilde was sentenced to two years' hard labour in prison. He served most of the time in Reading Gaol, and on his release went immediately to France where he died, aged forty-six, on 30 November 1900. His wife and children had moved abroad after the guilty verdict and he never saw them again.

There is little doubt that Oscar Wilde's downfall lay partly in his defiant desire to fight his own corner and partly in the stupidity and vanity of Bosie, who urged him to carry on down a path of clear self-destruction. He was certainly unlucky in his choice of a lover whose father had already lost one son to what he saw as 'unnatural' vice and who was determined to pursue the man whom he believed to be the corrupter of another. What the trials make clear is that society of the time was not anxious to prosecute men such as Wilde, and he received much overt support from friends and literary connections. But he was also clearly a scapegoat for the sexual and moral insecurities and ambiguities of the time, and his conviction would result in a backlash against what was seen as moral laxity on high.

Wilde's conviction took place in a context of perennial disgust and disapproval of homosexuality among the majority offset by tolerance towards it from the more sophisticated elements of society. Those who wished to expose it, however, did not always find it easy. Behaviour such as cross-dressing could be ambiguous, as is shown by a celebrated case in 1870, reported by *The Times*. Hugh Alexander Mundell was initially indicted with two other men, Ernest Boulton and Frederick William Park, but after the court agreed that he had been duped the charge against him was withdrawn and he gave evidence against the others. The defendants' dress in court is described in detail: Boulton wore 'a cherry-coloured evening silk dress trimmed with white lace; his arms were bare, and he had on bracelets; he wore a wig and plaited chignon.' Park – who was described as a law student – had on 'a dark green satin dress, low necked and trimmed with black lace, of which material he also had a shawl round his shoulders; his hair was flaxen and in curls, and he was wearing a pair of white kid gloves.' When Mundell had first seen them at the theatre they were in male dress, but he was assured that they were actually women dressed as men. His interest was aroused and he made their acquaintance, even 'chaffing them about their being women, and telling them that they ought to swing their arms a little more to look like men.' The next time he met them they were dressed as women and told him their names were Stella and Jane. Other witnesses had seen them in various places around London, sometimes dressed as women but also often dressed as men: 'Their faces were painted. They had low shirt collars, and open. They walked about in an effeminate way, and people gathered round them, saying they were two women dressed in men's clothes. They had been walking about looking at men offensively, and had excited indignation.' On another occasion they were both in a private box at the Alhambra 'dressed as men, but their faces were painted up and powdered, and they were got up effeminately as before. They hung their hands and pink gloves over the box. I could never quite make up my mind about them. Sometimes I thought they were men and some-times that they were women. Whenever they appeared in male costume their faces were painted.'

The case aroused a great deal of interest. *The Times* reported that even the bench was 'inconveniently crowded' and the courtroom was besieged by people hoping to get in to watch the case, 'including many persons of rank, besides many literary and theatrical celebrities, who were probably admitted by special application to the authorities.' On the second day 'the prisoners appeared in male apparel, much to the disappointment of the crowds assembled to see them.' Their defence was that the whole thing was 'a lark', and their barristers pointed out that no money had been solicited or extracted from Mundell or any other person. They were acquitted.

Women cross-dressing as men were the target of much prurient pub-lic interest when exposed in court, and the reasons behind their decep-tions were also varied. Crowds would flock into court to see a woman accused in this way, and she often had to be protected from being mobbed. One case in Manchester, reported in *The Penny Illustrated Paper* of 5 April 1862, concerned a woman who gave her name as Ann McGaul, alias Ann Hughes, alias John Jones. She claimed that she had passed as a man for the previous six years in order 'to earn 2s 6d a day at man's work instead of 1s a day at woman's'. She was up before the court because of a distur-bance she had caused at her landlady's by threatening to beat another woman, Sarah Jones, with whom she was living as her husband. She had once, because of a shortage of space, shared a bed with her landlady's son for four nights without her sex being discovered, and she had clearly successfully concealed it at work; her jobs had been quite rough manual ones, including employment in the hard environment of a colliery. The magistrate discharged her on her promise not to repeat her behaviour; but she had to be kept in the building after the case to protect her from the crowd milling around outside.

Another woman who dressed as a man in order to earn a man's money was Sarah Geals. Her story is known because of her trial at the Old Bailey in the 1860s for trying to shoot her employer, James Giles, for which she was convicted and sentenced to five years' penal servitude. It seems that she had begun to dress as a man at some point in the 1840s, calling herself William Smith. Her transformation was not entirely out of the ordinary: many cross-dressers of the time were women who had reached the age where they were expected to support themselves economically, but found it hard in a male-dominated society. In Sarah's case she appears to have been quite open about her change of role, at least to her mother and brother, and she also lived with a woman called Caroline who behaved as her wife. There is some evidence that they enjoyed a happy relationship – though it is not known whether it was sexual – from a surviving letter that demonstrated a real attachment between them.

In her years as a man, Sarah worked as a shoemaker in Shoreditch for James Giles, who did not suspect her real status as a woman; during the trial, indeed, he stated that, had he known that she was a woman, he would not have paid her as much – an apt demonstration of why she had changed her identity in the first place. In January 1863, when his wife fell sick, James asked Caroline, as William's wife, to go to his house as nurse and housekeeper. After three days James's wife died, but Caroline continued to look after the man and his house over the next several months. At some point she let the truth about William's gender slip out. In court James said that he did not know how she revealed it to him; one wonders whether it was an accident, or a whim, or maybe they were having an affair.

James's response was to dismiss Sarah, demand that she return to dressing as a woman and also demand that Caroline, who was clearly not legally Sarah's wife, should marry him. Caroline agreed on condition that James would get Sarah a woman's job, and that they could still spend their traditional Sunday together, which he accepted. However, two years after the marriage, he decided to close the shop in which Sarah worked and arranged for her to live in what he called a 'respectable' house but was in reality a place where many prostitutes lived. She, perhaps understandably, blamed him for her change of circumstances and, after trying to persuade him to treat her more equitably, went to his shop and pulled a gun at him. She had not loaded it properly, despite her experience with firearms when she worked in the colliery as a man, and so failed to shoot him. James contacted the police and she was arrested and sent for trial. Her five years' sentence appears to have been disproportionately severe: on that same day a man found guilty of murdering another man was sentenced to twelve months, a man found guilty of killing a child received nine months and a man accused of rape was acquitted.

The language used in the report of a case heard before a magistrate at Hatton Garden concerning another woman cross-dresser indicates the bewilderment such people evoked, as well as the contempt in which they were held. The report was headed 'Extraordinary case – a man-woman', and the policeman who had brought the case that she was a common cheat and impostor and had created a disturbance testified that 'though the thing before them, that called itself Bill Chapman, was attired in man's apparel, he had ascertained that it was a woman.' He had known her for about ten years without suspecting her true sex, 'and moreover, Chapman smokes; and whenever Watson gives her any offence, she beats her and blackens her eyes, though Watson is so much taller and apparently stronger.' Isabella Watson, who was also in court, had apparently been Chapman's companion for many years and they had travelled all over the country together as man and wife. The magistrate was reported as being 'puzzled'. 'She may be a disorderly and disreputable character, which, in fact, her dressing as a man clearly shows, but I know of no law to punish her for wearing male attire.' He had no option other than to discharge her. The report goes on: 'The prisoner, who was chewing tobacco, then bowed his head, and walked out of the office with Isabella, who exclaimed, "Never mind, my lad, if we live a hundred years it will be in this manner."'

It is clear from another case that some women cross-dressed simply because of the extra freedom they enjoyed as men in a man's world: one Mary Newell, for example, had robbed her employer, dressed up as a man and gone to Yarmouth, where she smoked cigars and propositioned her landlady. The initial case in the police court was observed by Arthur Munby, who recorded in his diary, 'After she had been committed for trial at the Sessions, I walked away with her master – a surveyor – and his pupil, the young man whose name and garments she assumed. She was a dirty and untidy servant, they said; was in the habit (they now found) of stealing out to low theatres alone, hiring cabs to go in and smoking cigars with the cabmen…'.

Arthur Munby was a curious character: the son of a solicitor, he was well educated and read for the bar though he did not practise; instead he worked as a civil servant in a job which gave him a lot of time off to pursue his lifelong obsession: meeting, talking to and recording the lives of working-class women, particularly those who did hard, dirty, physical jobs. He eventually filled sixty-plus volumes of diaries, made many drawings and collected hundreds of photographs. Like Henry Mayhew's survey, Munby's archives are an invaluable social record of the time.

This middle-class civil servant mixed with a wide circle of literary and cultured contacts; his diaries mention meetings with Darwin, Thackeray and Dickens, among many others, and he himself published several volumes of poetry. But it is likely that his obsession with women of lower class than himself had a sublimated sexual element: unable to see women of his own class as sexual objects, he turned instead to his social inferiors. Indeed, he married one of them: Hannah Cullwick, a Shropshire-born maid-of-all-work whom he had met in London in 1854 when she was twenty-one and he was twenty-five. They formed a relationship, married secretly in 1873 and remained married and together for the rest of their lives, though they did not share a home after the late 1870s. Her presence in his ostensibly bachelor household in London became more difficult to sustain, and he arranged for her to return to Shropshire where he frequently visited her.

The marriage was clearly a happy one, although Hannah resisted all his attempts to 'ladify' her and insisted on calling him 'Massa' even after they were married; she tried 'Arthur' once, but never again. Moreover, the marriage remained secret from all save a very few close friends, and was never revealed to Munby's parents. During all the time they lived together in London Hannah acted as Munby's servant when guests called. Once, when his brother George arrived unexpectedly, she had to hastily put on her maid's outfit and wait on him. He had no idea that the servant whom he hardly noticed was actually his sister-in-law, and when, shortly before his death in 1910, Munby told him that Hannah was not just his servant but also his wife, George was sad but determined still to keep it secret. Hannah died in 1909, a few months before her husband, and her gravestone reveals the truth, giving her the name Hannah Munby and naming her as the wife of Arthur. Munby seems, at the end of his life, to have been able to drop the pretence: his final volume of poems contains one titled 'Hannah' with the line 'But the best of all my servants is my faithful servantwife.'

For most of his life Munby had to conceal his socially disgraceful marriage by a secrecy that his wife, fortunately for him, went along with. And in an age where parental consent was certainly desirable, if not essential, for a respectable marriage, there were many instances of couples entering into relationships regarded as illicit by their families, even if technically legal and above board. Despite the success of many of these alliances, some parents never accepted the situation. One example was the happy marriage of the poets Robert Browning and Elizabeth Barrett, opposed and never forgiven by her eccentric and domineering father; after a secret ceremony they eloped to Italy where they lived more or less for the rest of their lives. She died in 1861 in Florence and he in 1889 in Venice, while staying in the magnificent Ca' Rezzonico which their only son had acquired after marrying a rich American wife.

Retreat abroad was typical of the wealthier and more educated English during the nineteenth century and the beginning of the twentieth, particularly where there were reasons to flee from home. D.H. Lawrence eloped abroad with Frieda von Richtoven, the wife of one of his university professors, at about the same time as he was finding his distinctive voice as a novelist. He was travelling in Europe with Frieda when *Sons and Lovers* was published in 1913, and their unconventional liaison fuelled the belief that his novels were scandalous. It was to Italy that many others went – the country with which expatriate English people had long enjoyed a love affair. Homosexuals in particular often gravitated to Venice. John Addington Symons was one of the gay Englishmen who found the city a refuge, engaging in a long affair with a gondolier, Angelo Fusato. Another was the eccentric Frederick Rolfe, whose only success during a life of serial failures was the novel *Hadrian VII*. He lived in Venice for the last five years of his life, fascinated by the boats that plied the canals and the half-naked, sweaty men who worked on them. This conjunction of mysterious sexiness with doom-laden unease is the essence of the Venice celebrated by so many writers. The gondola encapsulated it, particularly during the years when sumptuary laws forbade decoration: for many at that time it resembled nothing so much as a coffin. Thus did it strike Gustav von Aschenbach in Thomas Mann's deeply homoerotic novel *Death in Venice*. Ageing and ill, the distinguished writer follows the beautiful boy Tadzio round the city, full of regrets about a life during which he had never allowed himself to succumb to such emotions.

It was in Italy that E.M. Forster found the inspiration for his great Edwardian novels, and memories of his stay there are to be found in the places and the buildings he portrays: the pension with a view over the Arno in *A Room with a View* is easily identifiable as the one where he stayed with his mother at around the turn of the century. The freedom from stuffy convention that Forster, along with many other writers, found in Italy is the underpinning of his plots. Lilia finds the strength and conviction in *Where Angels Fear to Tread* to defy her stultifying and controlling in-laws in an Italian small town with a new – and ultimately disastrous – Italian husband. And the Schlegel sisters, heroines of *Howard's End*, were 'New Women' who 'walked over the Apennines with [their] luggage on their back' and were independent enough to make their own way in life. When Helen Schlegel has an illegitimate child she does indeed go abroad, but not in shame nor stricken by Victorian notions of morality.

Travelling abroad was one of the pastimes of the rich during the Edwardian era, including Edward VII himself. Paris and Biarritz were his playgrounds in the late spring, and in the autumn he went to take the waters at Marienbad in Bohemia. The rest of the year was divided between cruising on the royal yacht, attending the high-society events of the London season, going racing and shooting and generally enjoying himself. At a time when holidays were beginning to catch the popular mood at all levels of society, Edward's ostentatious pleasure-seeking was not something that his subjects begrudged him, as Roy Hattersley notes in *The Edwardians*. Enjoyment was in fashion, and they relished a king who was out and about in public, in contrast to his mother's years of seclusion.

Even for the poorer members of society, a day or two at the seaside was becoming an achievable ambition. The press might thunder that Blackpool, Bournemouth and Scarborough were corrupting the morals of the young by offering them too much unsupervised freedom, but they were not about to deny themselves the pleasures of 'kiss-me-quick' hats, 'what the butler saw' in the end-of-pier amusement arcades and naughty postcards with fat ladies, weedy husbands and captions thick with *doubles entendres*. Meanwhile, their 'betters' attended house parties – the epitome of the opulent Edwardian age. Led again by the king, who frequently descended on his hosts with only a day or so's warning, the upper classes travelled the country to visit each other and relish the var-ied delights of grand houses with access to shooting, racing, sailing and other sport. The gratification of entertaining the king as a house guest was tempered to some extent by his demands for particular foods (some houses kept stores of provisions from ginger biscuits to bath salts to anticipate the royal requirements) and the size of his entourage, which could number a dozen or more. If the queen was with him there would be even more servants to accommodate; but frequently his companion, certainly in later years, was Alice Keppel.

By this time she was his main companion, recognized widely as an excellent influence on him and a sensible advisor. Her own aristocratic background (she was the daughter of an admiral and sister-in-law of a peer), coupled with her relationship with the king, ensured that she was welcomed almost everywhere – though two great houses, Welbeck and Hatfield, refused to receive her. House party hostesses knew how to allocate bedrooms appropriately, not just when Edward and Alice were of the party but on other occasions, too. Vita Sackville-West sums up the dilemmas they had to resolve: 'It was necessary to be tactful and, at the same time, discreet. The professional Lothario would be furious if he found himself [allocated a room] by ladies who were all accompanied by their husbands.' And yet it was a typical characteristic of the age that double standards could be, and were, applied. Edward was well known for his dalliances; yet he found it not at all hypocritical that he should warn a duke and duchess considering a divorce that they would not be welcome afterwards at any party or entertainment at which he or the queen were present.

A satirical take on Edwardian house parties is to be found in a short story by Saki, the writer H.H. Munro; his suppressed homosexuality contributed to the sense, very apparent in his writing, of being an observer looking in on social events. *Tobermory* features a cat that has been taught to speak, causing serious alarm among the fashionable house guests. Not only does he regale the party as a whole with the private conversations of some of those present about the brainlessness or cupidity of others who were there, but they all suddenly realize with fear that there is much else that he might have observed and could reveal, exposing them to gossip in the servants' hall and beyond: 'The panic had indeed become general. A narrow ornamental balustrade ran in front of most of the bedroom windows at the Towers, and it was recalled with dismay that this had formed a favourite promenade for Tobermory at all hours, whence he could watch the pigeons – and heaven knew what else besides. If he intended to become reminiscent in his present outspoken strain, the effect would be something more than disconcerting.' Small wonder that he meets an untimely end, or that the party is brought to a swift conclusion.

If with hindsight the decade of Edward's reign is regarded as the last long, hot summer of innocence, when God was in his heaven and all was right with the world, L.P. Hartley's novel *The Go-Between* encapsulates the moment. Literally set in a long, hot summer, it traces the nostalgic musings of a solitary man, looking back over half a century to one golden year in his youth. Invited by a wealthier schoolmate to spend the summer at his country home, he falls gently in love with his friend's sister and becomes increasingly embroiled in her illicit affair with a local tenant farmer. Leo, the young boy, is the go-between of the title, delivering letters from one to the other and witnessing a situation that inevitably spins out of control. The escapade ends with the suicide of the farmer and the birth of an illegitimate child; but the novel also exposes the life-long, debilitating guilt Leo carries for his part in the outcome. The story describes love across the classes, doomed and scandalous; tensions are embodied in a dramatic cricket match between house and village, where both the daughter of the house and her messenger secretly and guiltily want the village team to win. Even during a magical golden summer, affairs eventually have a price, as social class and loyalty are overturned by the realities of love and desire.

The Edwardian world proved ephemeral, the legacy of its glamour dying in the trenches. Yet many of the people who inhabited that period cast a long shadow. Alice Keppel's great-granddaughter was also to be the long-standing mistress of a Prince of Wales; Alice's daughter Violet became famous as the lover of Vita Sackville-West; and Alice herself made the noted remark, on the abdication of Edward VIII so that he could marry his mistress, that 'things were managed better in my day'. But the country had first to endure the horrors of the First World War, a conflict that transformed the society that those living under Victoria and Edward had known, and which they probably believed would go on for ever. And the century that had seen an accelerating pace of exploration and change, with new ideas and attitudes spreading through society and around the world, was about to give way to one that would see ever-faster change in manners and morals.

Six · The Great War and the Roaring Twenties

THE EDWARDIAN YEARS had seemed at first just a continuation of prosperity and progress. The arrival of a new century, followed almost immediately by the death of the queen who had reigned for most of it, must have passed as a couple of major but ultimately unimportant staging posts that did not alter the greater scheme of things. Edward succeeded his mother, and his stolid second son succeeded him as George V. People knew their place and they generally lived within it. Life went on.

But prophetic bubbles were beginning to pop up to disturb the seemingly tranquil surface, impacting on both public and private lives. Women were becoming increasingly vociferous in their calls for the vote; the Labour Party and the trades unions were finding their own voice in their campaigns for better rights for the workers; crusading politicians were legislating to shift the balance of power from the unelected Lords to the elected Commons; and all the while the biggest bubble of all was fermenting away beneath the surface, gathering strength to unleash a war that outdid all wars in death and horror.

The assassination of Archduke Franz Ferdinand in Sarajevo on 28 June 1914 provided the catalyst for a series of events that resulted in war being declared over most of Europe in September. The underlying reasons were complex, and it must have seemed incomprehensible to ordinary people to find themselves, almost out of the blue, in the midst of a war with their neighbours. But this did not stop them joining up in their thousands, urged on by Kitchener's pointing finger and the white feathers later handed out to young men out of uniform on the streets of Britain, mainly by young and ignorant women. 'It'll all be over by Christmas,' was the received wisdom in September 1914; but it was not. It dragged on for four long years, killing over nine million young men in its course and casting its lengthy shadow over the new century. Nearly a hundred years later its horrors may have faded, but they emphatically refuse to die.

The war, and the influenza pandemic that followed it, killed millions of people world-wide and also finished off a way of life. Women were rewarded for their war efforts by male politicians who finally – and grudgingly in some cases – realized that they could no longer deny them the vote and a (small) place in the legislature; the poverty and depression that followed the war caused a cataclysm among the working classes leading, slowly but inexorably, to better wages and working conditions; and both these revolutions unleashed on society new sets of people with tongues in their heads to speak out and change the way things were done. It would still take decades; but society's morals and mores were under siege.

Private lives, especially women's, were to be transformed by reliable contraception and legal abortion, but for many decades of the new century they were still far out of reach. When Victoria died, the former was possible though chancy and the latter was illegal. Inducing a miscarriage was prohibited in 1803, but women carried on, as they had always done, trying to 'manage things' when a surprise pregnancy manifested itself. In 1847 Lord Alderley had been horrified when his wife told him that she was pregnant yet again: 'I am afraid, however, that it is too late to mend, and you must make the best of it.' She, however, was more resourceful: as she wrote to him the same day, 'A hot bath, a tremendous walk and a great dose have succeeded.' Other traditional methods were jumping off tables and galloping on horseback, and women of all classes appear to have seen nothing at all wrong in ridding themselves in these ways of unwanted babies. There were murkier methods, too. The broadsheets were full of advertisements for vile-sounding potions hiding their purpose behind cloudy language, and the truly desperate turned to backstreet abortionists whose brutal interventions could often lead to death.

The insertion of poisons or sharp instruments into the uterus was done without any knowledge of medicine or hygiene, with no anaesthetic and without any sort of aftercare. Rich women could go to illicit doctors, who at least had some medical training and might be expected to be cleaner; it was a very profitable trade, commanding high fees. The poor and desperate would resort to do-it-yourself methods, sticking knitting needles or knives up themselves. Medical complications frequently followed, and it was all extremely painful and dangerous. It was to remain so broadly until 1967, although new legislation in 1929 and again in the late 1930s introduced circumstances in which abortions could be performed, initially when it was essential to save the mother's life, and subsequently when a pregnancy was considered damaging to psychological health.

Contraception, however, had an advocate earlier in the twentieth century in Marie Stopes. There had always been some recognition that preventing pregnancy was possible, mainly through the withdrawal method known as *coitus interruptus*, and condoms had been available since the late seventeenth century, though they were regarded mostly as protection against venereal disease. There had been previous advocates, too: Richard Carlile had been imprisoned in the 1820s for publishing a book advocating contraception (p. 104), and Annie Besant and Charles Bradlaugh were prosecuted in 1877 when they published *The Fruits of Philosophy* by Charles Knowlton which promoted birth control. The charge against them was that the material was 'likely to deprave or corrupt those whose minds are open to immoral influences' and the public prosecutor set out his reasons for bringing the case: 'I say that this is a dirty, filthy book, and the test of it is that no human being would allow that book on his table, no decently educated English husband would allow even his wife to have it… The object of it is to enable a person to have sexual intercourse, and not to have that which in the order of providence is the natural result of that sexual intercourse. That is the only purpose of the book and all the instruction in the other parts of the book leads up to that proposition.' The defence in court was that they thought it 'more moral to prevent conception of children than, after they are born, to murder them by want of food, air and clothing.' They were found guilty and sentenced to a £200 fine and six months' imprisonment, but the sentence was quashed on appeal.

Marie Stopes had been born in 1880 to a well-educated family. Her mother was the first woman in Scotland to obtain a university certificate – awarded instead of a degree because she was a woman. This turned her into a passionate feminist who made sure that her daughter grew up to share her convictions. Henry Stopes was a distinguished scientist, and his daughter went on to win a science scholarship to University College, London, and to gain a double first in botany in 1901 and then a doctorate in 1905; she was at that point Britain's youngest doctor of science. She was also a suffragette and a campaigner for women's rights.

Her marriage in 1911 to Reginald Gates was unconsummated; as she told the divorce court which granted her an annulment, he had failed ever to become 'effectively rigid'. So when in 1916 she began to write *Married Love*, her controversial book about marriage and sex, she was still, in her late thirties, a virgin. She had great difficulty in finding anyone to take the book on. The male publishing world was repelled by her argument that marriage should be an equal partnership between the man and the woman, and by sentiments like 'Far too often, marriage puts an end to women's intellectual life. Marriage can never reach its full stature until women possess as much intellectual freedom and freedom of opportunity within it as do their partners.' Walter Blackie, of Blackie & Son, rejected the book with the words: 'The theme does not please me. I think there is far too much talking and writing about these things already... There will be few enough men for the girls to marry [after the war]; and a book like this would frighten off the few.' It took her until March 1918 to find a small company willing to take the risk; it was an instant success, selling 2,000 copies within two weeks and reprinting six times in the first year (including four before the Armistice).

The book caused outrage in some quarters: one Sidney Cliff wrote to her, 'Do you really think that my wife and I and our poverty-stricken friends (though none of us can afford to have more than two or three children) are sadly in need of such dirty advice as you offer? Is it a desire to put bank notes in your pocket that you wrote such stuff as *Married Love?*' And a Catholic priest, Father Zulueta, also protested: 'Madam ... I consider it most useful to pray God that your writings may not do as much injury to morals – to the ignorant poor especially – which they are calculated to do... It appears to me that a pagan might have written as you do... I had hopes no women would write such books.' It was published in America, too, but was promptly banned after the courts ruled it obscene.

At around this time, Marie Stopes met an American nurse called Margaret Sanger, who had fled to Britain after starting a newsletter which argued for contraception and abortion and was consequently charged with publishing an 'obscene and lewd article'. She had decided several years before to take her courage in both hands on this subject after the sad case of a New York woman called Sadie Sachs. She had been summoned to attend to Sadie in the aftermath of a self-induced abortion, and with the help of a doctor managed to save her life. The sick woman was only twenty-eight and had three children whom she and her husband, Jake, could barely afford to keep; but when she told them that she realized the next time would be the end of her and asked for their help in preventing pregnancy, they had no answers for her. All the doctor could say was, 'Any more such capers, young woman, and there'll be no need to send for me. Tell Jake to sleep on the roof.' Nurse Sanger could not help either, despite their pleas, and it was not long before she was summoned yet again, this time to a miserable deathbed in the presence of a distraught husband and three small children. She made a resolve that 'no matter what it might cost, I was finished with palliatives and superficial cures; I was resolved to seek out the root of evil, to do something to change the destiny of mothers whose miseries were vast as the sky.'

When Marie Stopes and Margaret Sanger met, Marie had decided to embark on a book on birth control, despite the limitations of her own experience. Margaret therefore furnished her with all the information in her possession, and the resulting book, *Wise Parenthood*, caused a predictable furore. Church dignitaries, both Anglican and Catholic, were particularly incensed: a pamphlet published by the Catholic Truth Society reaffirmed the pope's condemnation of all forms of contraception and went on to laud faithful Catholic mothers who were 'doing wonderful work for God. In time, if methods of birth control continue to prevail among the non-Catholics, their race will die out and the Catholic race will prevail and thus England will become again what it once was, a Catholic country.' Although Marie was not prosecuted, other campaigners for birth control, Guy and Rose Aldred, were found guilty of selling an obscene publication after publishing one of Margaret Sanger's pamphlets, and newspaper articles called for Marie likewise to be sent to prison. She sued one of those authors, Halide Sutherland, for libel after he had accused her of writing obscene books, and she won her case, though the ruling was later overturned in the House of Lords.

However, the times were changing, and contraception was gaining ground. As a diplomat returning after the war reported, 'When I left England in 1911 contraceptives were hard to buy outside London or other large cities. By 1919 every village chemist was selling them.' As for Marie Stopes, now married to a rich husband, Humphrey Roe, her next step was to found the Society for Constructive Birth Control and to open the first of her birth control clinics in north London in 1921. Letters such as the one from the twenty-seven-year-old wife of a farm labourer, which she received in 1924, kept her going. This woman was expecting her fourth child on an income of £1/7 a week (£1.35 in today's currency) and wanted to know how she could prevent any more children: 'I wrote and told my mother but she cannot help me because my father has died and left her with three children still going to school. She says I must stop having children… Do you think it would be best if I leave my husband and go into the workhouse … so we don't have any more children? I have gone without food and have tried to win money but everything I try fails. If you can kindly advise me I would be very grateful.' Marie Stopes carried on campaigning for the rest of her life, managing her clinics and writing articles for her newsletter, *Birth Control News*. She died in 1958.

Her books and the practices they advocated were described by many of her contemporaries as obscene; but they addressed real concerns. Fears about illegitimacy were high throughout the First World War, and there was great anxiety in 1914 about the supposed 'khaki fever' exhibited by young women for men in uniform. Upper- and middle-class women became members of the Women's Police Service and the Women's Patrols Committee of the National Union of Women Workers, and undertook 'morality patrols' to curb the 'uncontrolled excitement' that was rumoured to surround places of temptation such as army camps. The morality of the wives of those who had departed for the front was also a worry to the authorities, and initially the police were instructed to keep an eye on them to ensure that they remained on the straight and narrow and did not indulge in drunkenness, promiscuity, child neglect or crime. Yet again, women away from their menfolk were considered to be prone to lust and depravity, and easily tempted. As Sylvia Pankhurst said after the war, 'Alarmist morality mongers conceived most monstrous visions of girls and women, freed from the control of fathers and husbands who had hitherto compelled them to industry, chastity and sobriety, now neglecting their homes, plunging into excesses and burdening the country with swarms of illegitimate children.' In fact, there were more marriages and fewer illegitimate children in 1915 than in most years, despite press alarm over 'war babies'; and although illegitimacy rates rose by thirty per cent during the war, the overall birth rate declined, so fewer women were actually having illegitimate children. Nonetheless, there were undoubtedly opportunities for affairs. As one Mary Agnes Hamilton later put it, 'How and why refuse appeals, backed up by the hot beating of your own heart, which were put with passion and even pathos by a hero here today and gone tomorrow?'

In addition, the novelty of regiments of women in work – particularly those doing 'men's work' – was the cause of much unease and suspicion. Members of the Women's Land Army were exhorted to remember that, although they were 'doing a man's work and so you're dressed rather like a man' they should conduct themselves with female propriety; '. . . just because you wear a smock and breeches you should take care to behave like a British girl who expects chivalry and respect from everyone she meets.' The male establishment fretted about women's worrying new freedoms, as they cut their hair shorter, took up drinking and smoking, wore shorter skirts that shockingly revealed not just ankles but even stockinged lower legs and, in the factories, dared to wear trousers. Moreover, they ate out by themselves or with a female friend, and dispensed with chaperones. As the *Daily Mail* observed in 1916, 'The wartime business girl is to be seen any night dining out alone or with a friend in the moderate-priced restaurants in London. Formerly, she would never have had her evening meal in town unless in the company of a man friend. But now with money and without men she is more and more beginning to dine out.' As the war dragged on, and casualty figures rose ever higher, it was becoming clear that it was not going to be over soon and that death for young men and spinsterhood or widowhood for women were all too likely. A *'carpe diem'* attitude took hold, but – if the marriage figures are a reliable guide – often within the constraints of accepted morality.

Those serving in the Women's Army Auxiliary Corps were particularly prone to allegations of promiscuity. An official enquiry was set up in 1918 to investigate allegations of massive immorality in the Corps, but it could find no evidence. Also viewed with suspicion were the 'munitionettes' – the women and girls who worked in munitions factories and other essential industries. Munitionettes were especially dangerous to the pre-war status quo; their working-class origins, increased economic spending power and growing independence were all worrying straws in the wind to male authorities. Moreover, these were women who had formerly worked overwhelmingly in service; their previous employers, upper- and middle-class women, were now finding themselves having to do the work in the house that had never before concerned them.

Even socially acceptable war work, such as nursing, was viewed with concern as the war progressed. This was in part due to the intimate physical nature of the work that young women nursing desperately ill men had to undertake; as Vera Brittain, who gave up her Oxford studies to serve as a VAD, explained, 'short of actually going to bed with them, there was hardly an intimate service that I did not perform for one or another in the course of four years.' She appreciated the men's unembarrassed acceptance of her care, and the liberating effect of this simple physical exposure; but stories were rife about immorality among the VADs and she found herself viewed with suspicion on her post-war return to Oxford – 'who knew in what cesspools of iniquity I had not wallowed? Who could calculate the awful extent to which I might corrupt the morals of my innocent juniors?'

For women working under stress and far from home, there were undoubtedly temptations, despite the authorities' attempts at segregation and control. In her autobiographical *Testament of Youth*, Brittain describes her experience as part of a large medical contingent sailing to Malta, in which a rope across the main deck divided 'the VAD sheep from the RAMC goats; by this expedient they hoped automatically to terminate the age-long predilection of men and women for each other's society.' The consequences were unsurprising: being denied the opportunity of normal conversation on deck, 'the guardians of our virtue were astonished and pained beyond measure when one or two couples ... were found in compromising positions beneath the gangways.'

Vera was herself not tempted, deeply in love as she was with the memory of her fiancé, Roland, killed in 1915. She is amusing, however, about the adventures of others, including having to decamp with a friend to a different hotel for lunch when an officer turned up with a nursing sister 'sidling in beside him' and was clearly furious that they were witnesses to his illicit romance. Then there was the nursing sister 'who was not young and very far from beautiful' and an ill-mannered medical officer with whom she was 'hopelessly and inexplicably enamoured'; having been part of a foursome at an opera, Vera found herself abandoned by the two of them to the tender clutches of a whisky-sozzled, middle-aged Scotsman whom she had to fend off. And on another occasion she, together with all her VAD colleagues, had to swear on her honour to the matron that she was not the nurse who had managed to evade recognition after being surprised with a naval officer in a disused tent. As she mused at the time, she would not have owned up even if she had been guilty, because it seemed such a pity that all her experience and staying power should have been wasted by being sent home from Malta under a cloud.

Conditions for nurses in the field were bad, but those in the trenches were horrendous, and often had to be endured for months at a time. Men were placed under the continual fear of bombardment and gas attacks, living with lice and vermin as well as cold and damp, with nerves stretched to – and beyond – breaking point. Psychological understanding of behaviour under stress was in its infancy at this time, as the numbers of soldiers shot for 'cowardice' (which today would be recognized as post-traumatic stress disorder) indicate. In the same way, the military authorities did not consider that they ought to cater for sexual needs. Condoms were not official issue; instead the men received a message from Lord Kitchener which urged them to look after their health and abstain: 'Your duty cannot be done unless your health is sound. So keep constantly on your guard against any excesses. In this new experience you may find temptations, both in wine and women. You must entirely resist both temptations, and while treating all women with perfect courtesy, you should avoid any intimacy. Do your duty bravely. Fear God, honour the king.' Naturally they ignored such pious injunctions; and sexual extravagance, accompanied by venereal disease, ran riot, both during the war and when they returned home after it. Even far from the front, war caused raised passions; a New Orleans brothel-keeper reported considerably increased business once America had joined in: 'I've noticed it before, the way the idea of war and dying makes a man raunchy... It wasn't really pleasure at times, but a kind of nervous breakdown that could only be treated with a girl and a set to.' When tomorrow might never come, today was there to be enjoyed to the hilt.

Sexual frustration was heightened even more in the trenches by the close proximity within which everyone lived, and which made even the relief of sexual tension by masturbation difficult. But still, for many men, it was their only outlet; as one Austrian soldier remarked, 'Formerly my wife was my right hand; now my right hand is my wife.' There are reports that bestiality, too, was not uncommon, usually with horses! And at the same time, brothels behind the lines flourished, and women both at home and in the occupied territories became the prey, willing or not, of sex-starved men. Edward Brittain wrote to his sister about one example of 'the old, old story, as old as the hills' which was taking up his time. An eighteen-year-old corporal in his company had got the ward of a local innkeeper pregnant. His parents had forbidden him to marry her, at least till after the war, though the boy himself was willing to do so and knew where his duty lay. Edward was now having to write to the parents on the boy's behalf. As he said in his letter, dealing with such incidents was a constant and time-consuming part of a company commander's role.

The cavalier attitudes of fighting men towards sex and women were hardly surprising. Casualty figures in the First World War were appalling – the overall numbers of dead were higher in the first war than in the second, despite the large numbers of civilians killed in the latter, and its much broader reach. Moreover, many of those who survived the first war were permanently damaged, either physically or mentally. And – unlike most other wars before or since – the officer class suffered as much as the men. The death rate for middle-rank officers, who came from the middle and upper classes, was horrendously high: Vera Brittain lost her only brother, her fiancé and two close male friends, and such losses were not uncommon. Moreover, as year followed year of seemingly endless stalemate, frustration and anger took over. Heightened tension and nervous aggression, combined with a woman-free environment, had an inevitable impact on fighting men, many of whom, when released on leave either behind the lines or at home, went wild. An officer is reported as saying, 'Most soldiers are ready to have sexual intercourse with almost any woman whenever they can.'

Brothels and prostitutes flourished in cities such as London, awash with servicemen seeking pleasure and forgetfulness. Cinemas were regarded as particularly problematic, first because they might exert a bad influence, showing films depicting violence and immorality, and later because it was thought that prostitutes had taken to plying their trade in the darkness. A proposal in 1917 that increased lighting might deter them was vigorously resisted by cinema authorities, who claimed that more light would aid rather than hinder any loose women soliciting in their establishments. The authorities also noted that deterring prostitutes was now even harder, as they had taken to dressing more soberly, and so were more difficult to distinguish from respectable cinema-goers. The demand for their services was not in doubt, however, the cinema authorities themselves commenting that fines were no longer a deterrent as 'the calling for these women is so lucrative that any fine inflicted is paid with ease.'

The war did eventually drag to its end, although for many it must have seemed to come too late. For other survivors, the heavy privations and massive death toll saw an almost orgiastic outbreak of pleasure-seeking once it was over. And it was not just the young men who reacted to the relief of the armistice by deciding to celebrate as loudly as they could. Women, too, who had seen fathers, brothers, sons and neighbours killed, and had joined the workforce in their thousands to replace the absent men, were not about to return meekly to the traditional female roles that their mothers had espoused. There was a shortage of marriageable men after the war and an excess of widows and unmarried women at all social levels. So with husbands in short supply, girls were not prepared to sit around waiting for a sad spinsterhood. They shouted their rebellion aloud by smoking, drinking and wearing make-up; they went to dances where the decorous waltzes and foxtrots of previous generations were replaced by the wild extravagance of the Charleston and other jazzy crazes; they attended 'petting parties' where physical intimacy — up to a point — was the norm. Some of them drove cars, and some also installed the new telephone in their homes.

These were the flappers, immediately distinguishable by their outrageous clothes and hairstyles as much as their behaviour. Before the war, women's fashion had followed much the same trajectory as ever: long hair, piled on top of the head; long skirts and high-necked blouses or dresses, designed to show the beauties of a curvy figure through pinched-in waists accentuated by the still essential corset. Now, in the 1920s, young women decided to be freer in all ways: they cut their hair into the short bob, a style followed soon afterwards by the even shorter shingle; they threw away their corsets, preferring a much looser undergarment, and flattened their breasts with strips of cloth — 'boyish' was the preferred look; skirts rose to just below the knee and waists descended to the hip.

For rich youth who had survived the carnage, there were opportunities to live dangerously in all sorts of ways. The darker side of extravagant parties involved drink, gambling and sexual abandon, fuelled by drugs such as heroin and cocaine. The novelist Dorothy L. Sayers, creator of Lord Peter Wimsey, depicts this affluent loucheness in her detective story *Murder Must Advertise*, particularly through the pathetic yet unscrupulous Dion de Momerie and 'her tame dope-merchant', Milligan. The shadowy world of criminal dealers eventually overwhelms the glamour of illicit revels, with Dion herself ending up with her throat cut in the appropriately suburban setting of Maidenhead.

The post-war decade was a volatile one, with revolution of all sorts on the cards. The conflict had disrupted social conventions and long-standing social taboos regarding class and gender. Fundamental changes were taking place in how men and women interacted, both privately and publicly. Legislation which came into effect in 1918 had given some women the vote – though only those over thirty who were either householders or married to householders; the male legislature was still not quite ready to enfranchise women on the same terms as men. Many women rejoiced in their new economic independence and resented having to give up their jobs to men returning from the war. But society overall still disapproved of daredevil young women who challenged the perennial female inferiority to man – a startling and dangerous concept. Feminism was still in its infancy. Illicit pregnancy was still ruinous and spinsterhood a state to pity.

Women who flouted the social norms of the time were, nonetheless, becoming more visible – and not just through sexual misbehaviour. Mata Hari was a Dutchwoman whose abusive marriage ended in separation from both husband and daughter, and who then supported herself as a dancer on the Parisian stage and as a courtesan. Pictures of her as a dancer always show her in her trademark bejewelled metal breast cups, which she wore even when in bed with her lovers because she was ashamed of her small breasts; she used to tell those who asked that she wore them because her husband, in a drunken rage, had bitten off her nipples. Mata Hari was suspected by all sides in the First World War of being a spy: on a brief visit to England she was taken into custody in the belief that she was a German spy called Clara Benedix who looked a bit like her, and she was later imprisoned by the French, who accused her of being a double agent. At her trial she announced that she was certainly a harlot but was not a traitoress; she was nevertheless condemned to death and met her executioners with courage.

Isadora Duncan was another unconventional woman. An American who came to live in Europe, she developed and taught a new kind of free-flowing dance, very different from the formality of ballet. She set up several schools in France and Germany to teach her dance techniques and enjoyed considerable success. She was open about her disdain for marriage and her socialist principles – she once bared her breast on stage in Boston, waved a red scarf and proclaimed, 'This is red. So am I.' She had one child with her lover, the theatre designer Gordon Craig, who was Ellen Terry's illegitimate son, and another with Isaac Singer of the sewing machine family; tragically, both children drowned when the car in which they were travelling plunged into the Seine. She also had affairs with women, including the poet Mercedes de Acosta to whom she wrote long, revealing letters and poems: 'Mercedes, lead me with your little strong hands and I will follow you – to the top of a mountain. To the end of the world. Wherever you wish.' Isadora's sudden death in 1927 is the stuff of legend: one of the trailing scarves she habitually wore caught in the wheel spokes of the open-topped car in which she was being driven, breaking her neck.

Female dancers and performers, as ever, were controversial figures. Maud Allen, a dancer and actress well known for her performance as Salome, hit the headlines in 1918, when she brought a libel case against Noel Pemberton Billing. He was an Independent MP who had asserted that the Germans had a list of 47,000 British men and women who would be open to blackmail for sexual depravity, and who had allegedly des-cribed her as 'a lesbian and a sexual pervert'. She took him to court – where he was acquitted.

Relationships between women were gaining a higher profile, how-ever, particularly through the life and work of the writer Radclyffe Hall. Born Marguerite Radclyffe-Hall in 1880, she was known by her family first as Peter and then as John, and seems to have had obvious lesbian inclinations from a young age. She was quite open about her sexual pref-erences and refused to hide behind social convention: 'Let them criti-cize. Everyone has a right to think and say exactly what they like in this world. If no one took any notice of them, slanders would injure no one.' Her most famous work is *The Well of Loneliness*, a classic of lesbian litera-ture, but it was her poetry that initially drew the attention of the first woman with whom she set up home. This was Mabel Batten, who was over twenty years older and married with a daughter; they lived together after Mabel's husband died until Mabel's own death, by which time Hall had fallen for Mabel's cousin, Una Troubridge. She, too, was married, but that did not deter them from beginning an affair, and they stayed together – despite several other dalliances – until Hall's death. *The Well of Loneliness* was the subject of an obscenity trial in 1928 after which all copies of it were ordered to be destroyed. It remained out of print until a less censorious age allowed it to be republished.

When Nigel Nicolson discovered his mother's account of her own lesbian affairs after her death in 1962, he felt constrained by the nature of the material from publishing it until over ten years later. By that time the other major players in the drama were also dead, and attitudes towards homosexuality were beginning to lighten. Although lesbianism had never been illegal, the decriminalization of adult male homosexuality in 1967 indicated a society more open to same-sex relationships, and he felt able to reveal to the world the nature of his parents' marriage and their other inclinations. *Portrait of a Marriage* is the story of Harold Nicolson and Vita Sackville-West, told partly by Vita in the words she wrote in the early 1920s and partly by her son. Although the book is mainly about Vita's tempestuous affair with Violet Trefusis, the 'marriage' in the title is that of Harold and Vita, a relationship that supremely suited them both although their physical attraction began to fade very soon after they married; both subsequently preferred affairs with their own sex.

Vita's forebears also indulged in exotic relationships. Her grandfather, Lionel Sackville-West, never married but had a Spanish mistress known as Pepita who bore him seven children, of whom five survived. Their liaison lasted until her death, and he acknowledged all the children, bringing the three girls to live with him at Knole after he inherited the title of second Baron Sackville and the grand house that went with it; the two boys were sent to South Africa to become farmers. He even made the scandalous suggestion that he should take the youngest daughter, Victoria, as his official hostess to Washington, where he had been appointed to the British Legation; Queen Victoria gave her consent to this unusual request provided no objection was raised in America, and there a ladies' committee, headed by the president's wife, was raised to discuss the matter. They agreed to accept Victoria, and during their seven years there she took the city by storm, becoming the belle of the ball and the star of the diplomatic circuit. She is even said to have received a proposal of marriage from the elderly widowed president; at any rate, his family were concerned enough to deny it formally.

Her story is the unusual one of an illegitimate child becoming not just accepted but celebrated in polite society. She then consolidated her position further by marrying her first cousin, also Lionel, who as her father's nephew was the heir to Knole. Their only child, Vita, was born there in 1892, and they inherited the title and the estate on the death of Lord Sackville in 1908. Two years later they had to fight a legitimacy case which gripped the general public, when Lionel and Pepita's second son, Henry, claimed that his parents had been formally married and that he was therefore the legitimate heir; his older brother, Maximilien, could make no such claim because the names on his birth certificate were those of Pepita and her husband, Juan de la Oliva. Henry's claim was ludicrous, and he made it worse by clumsily fabricating documents to 'prove' both that Pepita and Juan were not legally married and that Pepita and Lionel were. His case collapsed and once again Victoria's strange heredity was held up to public scrutiny; this dignified and elegant ornament of Edwardian high society had to stand up in open court and agree that she and her brothers and sisters were all illegitimate.

Moreover, she found herself in court again three years later when she had to defend herself against the claim brought by his family that she had exerted undue influence over her long-standing friend and benefactor, Sir John Murray Scott — known as 'Seery' — in the matter of his will. The unmarried Seery had inherited enormous wealth from Sir Richard Wallace, founder of the Wallace Collection, whose secretary and adopted son he had been, and he had spent a great deal of it on Knole and Lady Sackville, to whom he was devoted. He now left her large amounts of money and property in his will, which his brothers and sisters disputed despite the fact that they too had been well provided for. Victoria defended herself with unfaltering spirit against the vicious cross-examination of the famous barrister F.E. Smith, and again won her case. Vita had had to appear, too, to refute the suggestion that she and her mother had made away with a later codicil to the will that was injurious to their claim.

A photograph in *Portrait of a Marriage* shows Vita arriving at court to give evidence flanked by Harold Nicolson, whom she had recently met, and Rosamund Grosvenor. As her autobiographical account much later revealed to her son, Rosamund was Vita's first lesbian lover, and at this stage they were in a passionate relationship, which continued after Vita and Harold became engaged; Rosamund was one of her bridesmaids, despite feeling hurtfully betrayed, at their wedding in 1913. But Vita's ardour was cooling, and for the first few years of her marriage she remained faithful to Harold and had three sons, of whom one was stillborn. But an old attachment was about to burst into passionate flames, coming within a whisker of destroying her marriage.

This was her hot-blooded affair with Violet Keppel, daughter of Alice Keppel, Edward VII's mistress. They had known each other in childhood and become firm friends, both recognizing an undercurrent of stronger feelings, and in April 1918 they became lovers. Vita had always known about what she called the 'duality' of her sexual nature, and now she abandoned herself to a passionate love affair. She wrote with prescience in her account of the affair, 'I hold the conviction that such connections will ... cease to be regarded as merely unnatural, and will be understood far better ... and it will be recognized that many more people of my type do exist than under the present-day system of hypocrisy is generally admitted.' She also revealed that she had dressed as a boy, browning her face and hands and winding a khaki bandage around her head, and in that disguise had strolled through the streets of London and Paris, smoking a cigarette, to meet Violet and escort her as if she were her husband. On these occasions Violet called her Julian.

They took trips abroad, once for over four months, refusing to return despite the pleas of their families and the growing scandal about their increasingly blatant behaviour. Harold mostly accepted the situation – by this time he and Vita were no longer enjoying marital relations and he had turned to casual affairs with men. Violet had allowed herself to become engaged to Denys Trefusis, though with the proviso that there were to be no sexual relations of any sort between them. She and Vita then plotted to elope before the wedding and their plan was only stopped when Harold got wind of it and intervened; he was relaxed about an affair, but he was not prepared to risk losing his much-loved wife for good. It all came to a head when Violet and Vita did after all elope to Amiens, chased by Harold and Denys, and there was a great scene when Vita accused Violet of allowing Denys into her bed after all. That was the beginning of the end, although high passions and betrayed feelings were to resonate for many months more.

It was an extraordinary story. Open lesbianism was scandalous although not illegal, and the positions within society of the people involved only heightened prurient gossip. Vita later had a short fling with Virginia Woolf, though in the long run their friendship became more important to them. Woolf's novel *Orlando*, the story of a sex-changing time-traveller, published in 1928, was based on Vita. Vita also had a heterosexual liaison with Geoffrey Scott, but her relationship with her husband was to remain platonic for the rest of their lives. Despite this, they maintained a thoroughly happy and mutually supportive marriage until Vita's death in 1962; Harold gently faded away afterwards, dying in 1968.

Male homosexuality had largely gone underground after the Oscar Wilde trial, though it is clear from accounts such as *Portrait of a Marriage* that – as ever, of course – it went on. Harold Nicolson was a senior diplomat, yet his career was not threatened by his homosexual affairs, discreet as he was. Evelyn Waugh's diary for 1924 includes an intriguing exchange between two High Court judges, one of whom was seeking advice from the other on the right level of sentence to hand out to a man found guilty in a sodomy case: 'What do you think one ought to give a man who allows himself to be buggered?' 'Oh, thirty shillings or two pounds, whatever you happen to have on you.' And the uproarious novel *The Girls of Radclyffe Hall*, by Gerald Berners, depicting himself and his friends as lesbian schoolgirls, caused much gossip and scandal. One of those included, Cecil Beaton, is said to have bought up all the copies and destroyed them.

Yet at the same time, Siegfried Sassoon was struggling to come to terms both with his memories of the horrors of the war and with his homosexuality. He had become a mentor and an object of romantic love to Wilfred Owen when they met towards the end of the war shortly before Owen's death, but had maintained a certain distance; he later burned some of the letters he had received from Owen, which presumably contained personal material. It seems unlikely that they had developed a relationship, not least because Sassoon was deeply torn by his sexual preferences. It was to be some years before he was able to acknowledge his homosexuality, though he wrote about his first male crush in a very guarded way in *Memoirs of a Fox-Hunting Man*, giving the object of his affection the pseudonym Denis Milden. He then embarked on a series of short-lived affairs with men like the artist Gabriel Atkin, who probably provided Sassoon with his first sexual encounter, the actors Ivor Novello and Glen Byam Shaw, the writer Beverley Nichols and aristocrats such as Stephen Tennant and Prince Philip of Hesse. He surprised society and his friends in 1933 by marrying and having a son, but the marriage broke up after the Second World War and he lived the rest of his life in seclusion, though maintaining contact with a few gay writer friends such as E.M. Forster and J.R. Ackerley.

The Bloomsbury Group stood largely outside the conventional morals of the first quarter of the twentieth century. This set of artists and writers has been categorized as a group of men and women in love with Duncan Grant; and it started its existence in the Gordon Square home of the Stephen family when Thoby Stephen introduced his lover, Grant, to his brother Adrian and his sisters Virginia (later Woolf) and Vanessa. Vanessa was married to the critic Clive Bell, but nevertheless went on to have Grant's daughter, Angelica. The tangle of relationships became ever wider and more intricate, including as it did people of every sexual persuasion, and it survived well into the later lives of everyone involved.

Lytton Strachey was one of the most flamboyant members of this set. Openly homosexual, he wrote a semi-pornographic novel, *Ermyntrude and Esmeralda*, which sent up the middle classes and their attitudes towards sodomy. Written in 1912 as an exchange of letters between two innocent young girls, it was not published until 1969. Strachey was both loved and loathed. Vita Sackville-West hated him, as did Rupert Brooke, and Duncan Grant found him too overwhelming when they conducted an affair. But he was the lifelong emotional prop, confidante and muse of the painter Dora Carrington, who idolized him for nearly twenty years, despite her affair with the Russian-Jewish painter Mark Gertler; she committed suicide when Strachey died, claiming that she could not carry on living without him.

John Maynard Keynes was another member of the group, initially regarded as indubitably one of the 'Bloomsbuggers' but later surprising them when he married the Russian ballerina Lydia Lopokova, a member of Diaghilev's Ballets Russes. By now Duncan Grant and the Bells were living at Charleston in Sussex, the house which they decorated in their own flamboyant style. Keynes, painter Roger Fry and novelist and bookseller David Garnett lived there for long periods too; and when Keynes turned up there with his new wife, they were somewhat shocked at her penchant for dancing naked in the dewy fields around the house in the early morning. Strachey, Virginia and Leonard Woolf and E.M. Forster were frequent visitors, and Charleston became the centre of the group's life. Bloomsbury can perhaps be best summed up by the strange story of one of its less notorious members, David Garnett. Although in his youth he had affairs with Francis Birrell and Duncan Grant, he married Rachel Marshall, sister of Frances Partridge, who was to be the last surviving member of the group; after Rachel's early death, and to the horror of his new wife's parents, he then married Angelica Bell. He had been present at her birth, and even then thought of marrying her in the future although he would be twenty-six years her senior.

Ottoline Morrell's house, Garsington, was, along with Charleston, a centre of their activities. Both Ottoline and her husband, Philip Morrell, conducted many affairs during their married life together. She was bisexual – Dora Carrington was one of her lovers – but she also had affairs with, among others, Roger Fry, Augustus John and the philosopher Bertrand Russell. That liaison ended after she refused to leave her husband and son for him, upon which he immediately moved on to Lady Constance Malleson, wife of the actor Miles Malleson. Meanwhile, Russell's wife Alys Pearsall Smith, whom he had met when he was only seventeen and soon tired of, pined for him for the rest of her life. Ottoline Morrell was also a friend of Siegfried Sassoon, and was one of those who encouraged him to take a stand against the war by refusing to return to the front after a spell of convalescent leave; he prepared a statement setting out his reasons for doing this, which was published in the press and read out in Parliament. He hoped to be court martialled so that his protest would achieve a higher profile, but the military authorities preferred to keep the matter quiet and he was instead diagnosed with shell-shock and committed to hospital. It was while he was at this hospital that he first met Wilfred Owen.

Ottoline Morrell is said to have been one of the models for the women in D.H. Lawrence's novel *Women in Love*. She was Hermione Roddice, mistress of Rupert Birkin who leaves her for one of the two women of the title, Gudrun Brangwen. Gudrun in her turn was modelled on Katherine Mansfield, and Birkin on Mansfield's husband, John Middleton Murry, while the other woman, Ursula Brangwen, was Lawrence's wife, Frieda, and he himself was her lover and later husband, Gerald. The free-loving Frieda was Lawrence's lifelong wife and partner; when they met, she was married to one of his tutors at Nottingham University and the mother of three children, but despite a six-year age gap they were to remain together until his death.

Emancipation and unconventional living seemed for many to go hand in hand with private incomes, and it was certainly much easier for those with financial freedom not to conform. However, the 1920s saw one small step taken towards sexual 'equality' that had consequences across the social spectrum. A new law in 1923 decreed that wives could finally divorce their husbands for adultery alone, without having to prove cruelty or desertion as well.

Previously, cases such as that of Mabel Blanche Shewell had been the norm; married in 1902 to George de Coeurdoux Shewell and mother of three daughters, she had to testify not only to his frequent adultery with Guliealma Ethel Anderson, but also to his viciousness towards her — rushing at her with clenched fists in front of their twelve-year-old daughter, who had had to intervene between them, and forcibly preventing her from tending a younger daughter who had chickenpox. The court granted her a decree nisi in July 1918 and it became absolute in October. Shewell seems to have belied his middle name in almost every way: orders made against him for costs remained unpaid and creeping upwards until just before the decree absolute, when they totalled a substantial £48/18/11.

That case is one of many held in the National Archives [J77/1310, 1330, 1360]; others indicate growing numbers of men suing for divorce after returning from the war to find that their wives had taken lovers and often had children by them. One such is an example not just of this increasingly frequent occurrence, but also of the rigid rules surrounding divorce at this time. Mortlock v. Mortlock details the case of a man — officially labelled a 'poor man', presumably in relation to costs — who had returned from service in the navy to find that his wife had been unfaithful. A decree nisi was granted, but was rescinded at the order of the King's Proctor when it was found not only that he, too, had committed adultery, but that he had also condoned his wife's sin by resuming relations with her. One hopes that they managed to retrieve something from their marriage through being forced to remain man and wife.

At this time, as had always been the case and would remain so until the laws changed later in the century, the concept of 'fault' in a divorce was fundamental. The documents recording the cases usually bear the name of a co-respondent — the man or woman whose adultery with the guilty party was the justification for the action. Now that women, too, could get out of a failed marriage through adultery alone, hotels began to benefit from a new kind of business: men agreeing to be caught apparently in flagrante in a hotel room with women who were not their wives. It was still not the done thing for a woman to be cited as the guilty party in a divorce case, and where marriages had broken down husbands would often agree to this sort of arrangement. Brighton speedily acquired a reputation for it.

Despite the disapproval with which the majority still viewed divorce, society had not broken out in a rash of morality. Several prominent people of this period are known for their illicit liaisons as well as for their professional achievements. David Lloyd George, for example, was a brilliantly reforming Chancellor of the Exchequer, introducing old age pensions, unemployment benefit and state support for the sick and infirm in the teeth of rabid opposition by the old guard. He became Prime Minister during the later war years and the first years of peace —

and was a determined and notorious womanizer. His wife, Margaret, preferred to stay at home in Wales with their five children while he pursued his political career in London; as a consequence they lived most of their lives apart, though they remained married until she died in 1941. His best-known lover was Frances Stevenson, to whom he offered the job as his secretary in 1911 with the proviso that 'he could only work with her if he made her his mistress as well.' They were together for the rest of his life, and he married her two years after Margaret's death despite the bitter opposition of his legitimate children. He was not faithful to Frances, but then nor was she entirely to him; she had two abortions on his insistence, but then bore a daughter in 1929 who is believed to be Lloyd George's though she was pursuing a passionate affair at the time with Thomas Frederic Tweed. Her loyalty, however, remained with Lloyd George, despite his compulsive womanizing and his selfishness; he responded to the news of her brother's death in the First World War by reminding her that he and the future of the nation depended on her to remain stalwart and supportive – she was not, in other words, to waste time feeling sorry for herself. Intelligent and personable she may have been; but she remained true to the notion that it was important for a woman to have a proper alliance with a man.

H.G. Wells was another man who pursued many affairs: having married his cousin, Isabel, in 1891, he left her for one of his students, Amy, whom he married in 1895 after Isabel had divorced him. Amy bore him two sons, and they remained married until she died in 1927, despite his dalliances elsewhere and his two illegitimate children. Both of these were with fellow writers: a daughter with Amber Reeves and a son with Rebecca West. He also had a fling with Margaret Sanger, the American woman who had helped Marie Stopes with her birth control work. Wells proclaimed 'free love' as a liberating way of life, epitomized by his 'New Woman' heroine Ann Veronica, who insisted on making all her own choices in life and refused to conform to a woman's traditional role. Real life for Wells proved more complex, and a story – denied by Wells – circulated that he had been pursued to Paddington station by an angry father wielding a horsewhip. It is also said that he went back to see his first wife, Isabel, after several years and his strong physical feelings for her, which had been his initial reason for wishing to marry her, reignited. The news that she had married again made him fly into a jealous rage. But nevertheless he said of himself in his autobiography, 'I was never a great amorist, though I have loved several people very deeply.'

People who led their lives out of the public eye could also be found out in illicit liaisons. Clarence Tomlinson, a solicitor whose strange life was chronicled by his son, the actor David Tomlinson, was discovered, by a bizarre chance, to have been maintaining two complete but quite separate households since before the First World War. As David Tomlinson recounts it, his brother was travelling to Heathrow in the 1950s on an airport bus which was held up by traffic in Chiswick. Glancing out of the window, he was amazed to see his father sitting up in bed in a strange house drinking a cup of tea. It transpired that he had started a relationship when he was very young with his landlady's daughter, and had had two children with her. However, a more suitable wife had turned up, whom he had married; but he had kept up his first family and even had several more children. It turned out that his legal wife had known about the other woman for most of her life, after Clarence had posted a letter meant for one to the other when he was serving in the First World War. For decades thereafter, with the connivance of both women, who were keen to keep up appearances, he had spent the working week in London with his first family and the weekends in Folkestone with the others — and none of the children were any the wiser.

Women, too, had their dalliances. Rebecca West had affairs with Charlie Chaplin and Max Beaverbrook among many others. And the letters of Dorothy L. Sayers, who in fiction had denounced the wild ways of decadent youth, reveal a secret that she managed to keep from her elderly, strait-laced parents — that she was pregnant with an illegitimate child. She had fallen very much in love with John Cournos, an American writer who professed to be against marriage as an institution and wanted to live with her without marrying and to use contraceptives to prevent children. She wanted a conventional marriage and family so she left him, only to fall in with another man, Bill White, who made her pregnant. Sayers dealt with the situation skilfully, managing to conceal her condition at work and leaving for an extended rest, claiming exhaustion, shortly before the birth. She arranged for the child to go to her cousin, Ivy Shrimpton, who, along with her mother, was fostering other children: 'There's an infant I'm very anxious you should have the charge of... It won't have any legal father, poor little soul... The parents want to do the very best for it, and will be ready and willing to pay whatever your usual terms are.'

[177]

Sayers also managed to keep away from her parents at the crucial time by claiming pressures of work: 'Don't come up till the Spring... Don't expect me at Xmas... At present you'd hardly see me.' She went away when the child was due, arranging for her letters to be sent on so that her family had no idea that she was not at home. Her son, John Anthony, was born on 3 January 1924, and she looked after him for the next three weeks before delivering him to her cousin. The letter that revealed the boy's true parentage was enclosed in another letter making arrangements for the handover. Marked 'Strictly confidential', it said, 'My dear – everything I told you about the boy is absolutely true – only I didn't tell you that he was my own!' She urged Ivy to conceal the child's parentage from her mother, Dorothy's Aunt Amy, and also to ensure that no word ever reached Dorothy's own parents: 'It would grieve them quite unnecessarily. You know it's not the kind of ill-doing Mother has any sympathy for.' Dorothy later married 'Mac' Fleming, a divorced father of two, and they eventually also adopted her son, though he never lived with them. After Ivy Shrimpton's death Dorothy asked John to destroy all the letters concerning his birth, but he did not do so.

Dorothy L. Sayers' honesty about her predicament and her skilful management of its outcome make fascinating reading less than a century later, when social attitudes have radically changed. Even fifty years ago, just before her death in 1957, she dreaded what would come out in her obituaries about her son. She was, however, robust about what had happened in her letters to John Cournos, who came back into her life shortly afterwards. 'Look here, John – when I see men callously and cheerfully denying women the full use of their bodies, while insisting with sobs and howls on the satisfaction of their own, I simply can't find it heroic, or kind, or anything but pretty rotten and feeble.' As ever! The sentiments were ahead of their time, although many of her contemporaries would have sympathized. Despite the changes wrought by the war, and the uncertain, complex world emerging from it, the social environment that would validate her words was still decades away.

Seven · Playing it again in the 30s and 40s

THE 1920s had been a sybaritic time for many: a pleasure-filled aftermath to a horrific war when hair had been let down – as well as cut shockingly short – and skirts taken up, and both men and women had begun to explore more liberal attitudes. The decade had seen women enfranchised on the same terms as men, the first Labour government and the flexing of trades union muscles in the General Strike. Society was changing ever faster; but the poverty under which the majority of the population struggled had not gone away, and class and wealth still divided an unequal nation.

The 1930s were, if anything, worse. Worldwide economic depression affected prosperity everywhere, tackled in America by initiatives such as Roosevelt's New Deal and resulting in Britain in demonstrations like the Jarrow marches. The decade was overshadowed, too, by the growing inevitability of another war with Germany, so soon after the previous carnage. Ironically, it was the final onset of the Second World War in 1939, after years of appeasement and vain hopes for 'peace in our time', that ended the depression. And the conflict, of course, dominated most of the 1940s, with the attendant 'live for the day' mentality of all wars, compounded by heavy civilian casualty figures as bombs and rockets rained down on both Britain and Germany. Women again took on men's jobs while they were away, and those at home sought to temper the danger and austerity with snatched happiness and hopes for the future. One of the most significant events of the decade was the Labour Party victory in the general election of 1945 after the war's end – for many a surprising rejection of Winston Churchill, who had proved an inspirational war leader. But the depression of the 1930s, combined with the privations of the war years, threw a long shadow: people wanted a different life, more and faster change and a more equitable society.

During these sombre years, people found their pleasures where they could. The London theatre scene during the 1930s and the war had a deserved reputation for wild behaviour. In 1932 the fortunes of the ailing Windmill Theatre in London had been dramatically revived when its manager, Vivian van Damm, persuaded its owner, Laura Henderson, to put on what he called the Revuedeville – a mixture of songs, dances, sketches and comic acts considerably enhanced by *tableaux vivants* featuring nearly naked women. To avoid the obscenity laws that forbade nudity on stage, the women were presented as motionless statues, clasping strategically positioned feathers, scarf or scenery. The ploy was highly successful and continued throughout the war years; the theatre's proud boast 'we never closed' was sometimes rendered as 'we never clothed'.

And then there were the movies. During the depressed 1930s and the threats of bombing raids during the war, cinema offered an escape route – a couple of hours with the stars away from the realities of life. The 1920s had been the heyday of silent movies, with vampish female actresses such as Louise Brooks, Clara Bow and Mary Pickford and brooding male leads like Rudolf Valentino, whose hooded eyes and smouldering looks entranced women everywhere. When talkies arrived many of the silent stars failed to make the transition: the career of John Gilbert, Greta Garbo's leading man and sometime lover, took a downward dive when his voice turned out to be high and reedy. Garbo herself held back from revealing her husky Swedish accent on screen for as long as possible; her final silent film for MGM in 1929, *The Kiss*, marked the end of an era. The stars of the 1930s and 1940s, male and female, are icons of the Hollywood legend: Marlene Dietrich, Jean Harlow, Bette Davis, Mae West, Lauren Bacall and Elizabeth Taylor, along with men such as Errol Flynn, Clark Gable, James Stewart, Henry Fonda, Humphrey Bogart and Gary Cooper.

The Hollywood publicity machine did its best to keep the lid on disreputable stories about the stars' private lives; many have emerged only years after the actors' deaths. It was well known at the time that Rudolf Valentino fell foul of Californian divorce laws when he married his second wife in 1922; his first marriage to an allegedly gay actress was said to have been unconsummated, but he did not wait the statutory year after the divorce before marrying again, and was prosecuted for bigamy and jailed. Yet on the other hand neither Clark Gable not Loretta Young acknowledged or publicly revealed during their lifetimes that they had had an illegitimate daughter in 1935; she herself did not discover who her father was until the widely known rumours were passed on to her by schoolfellows. Errol Flynn's madcap sexual escapades – mirroring in real life his swashbuckling behaviour on screen – were notorious: the expression 'in like Flynn' became slang for a successful sexual conquest, and his publisher later vetoed the title Flynn proposed for his autobiography – 'In Like Me'. But the secret lives of stars such as Garbo and Dietrich remained hidden until biographies published well after their deaths, in a more liberal and intrusive world, revealed all.

Greta Garbo is perhaps the greatest of the 1930s' screen icons, partly because of her ethereal beauty and partly because she withdrew from both the glamour of the film-making world and her own celebrity. After deciding in the 1940s to make no more films, she spent the last fifty years of her solitary life in New York, glimpsed occasionally hiding behind dark glasses during her long walks through the city. She herself claimed that she had never uttered her famous line, 'I want to be alone,' apart from in one of her movies, *Grand Hotel*; instead, she claimed, 'I only said, "I want to be left alone." There is all the difference.'

When it became known that she was certainly bisexual and predominantly lesbian, speculation had it that her withdrawal from society was due to sadness, and later bitterness, about her unrequited love for another Swedish actress, Mimi Pollak. Her response to the announcement that Mimi was pregnant was an unambiguous declaration in a letter to her: 'We cannot help our nature, as God has created it. But I have always thought you and I belonged together.' Among her lesbian affairs were relationships with fellow Hollywood luminaries such as Louise Brooks, Marlene Dietrich, Claudette Colbert and Joan Crawford, and also with the writer Mercedes de Acosta who had been Isadora Duncan's lover. Male lovers included Cecil Beaton, the photographer, who was otherwise homosexual, and she nearly married her co-star John Gilbert after conducting an affair with him; but she failed to turn up for the wedding.

Marlene Dietrich, too, kept her private life out of public view. She and Garbo shared many of the same female lovers, but she did enter into a marriage with Rudolf Sieber and had a daughter, from whom she was estranged for most of her life. Dietrich's male lovers included John F. Kennedy and his father, Joseph, but the love of her life was the French actor Jean Gabin. Vivien Leigh's most tempestuous love affair was with Laurence Olivier, with whom she embarked on a relationship when they worked together in 1937. The glamorous and sexy couple married in 1940 after their respective husband and wife agreed to divorces. Like many glittering stars of the period, however, Leigh suffered unhappiness and frustration in her private life.

The Oliviers' marriage was blighted, and ultimately destroyed, by her depressive illness — she suffered from bipolar disorder for most of her life — and the tuberculosis that killed her in 1967. Her magnificent performance as Scarlett O'Hara in the 1939 blockbuster *Gone with the Wind*, with Clark Gable as Rhett Butler, won her immense fame and an Academy Award. The film itself, with its themes of romance and destruction, survival and heartbreak, became the stuff of legend – a 'must-see' Hollywood extravaganza breaking through the storm clouds of impending war.

The power of the cinema, and the fantasies upon which it traded, are parodied in Stella Gibbons' brilliant comic novel of 1932, *Cold Comfort Farm*. The book is the story of Flora Poste, a young but level-headed orphan who goes to stay with her vast family of Starkadder cousins on their farm in Sussex and takes on the task of resolving their various problems and bringing them into the modern world. Young and raunchy, Seth Starkadder is obsessed with 'talkies' and with their female stars, and in an attempt to rescue him from a lifetime of small-town seductions, Flora introduces him to her movie mogul friend. Earl P. Neck, conveniently in search of the next Gary Cooper, recognizes Seth as 'exactly what he is, the local sexually successful bounder' and whisks him away to Hollywood to become a star.

The rich satire of *Cold Comfort Farm* has many targets, from romantic rural fiction of the period to psychoanalysis and the Bloomsbury Group. The language is a parody of rural dialect, full of sensuous made-up words, and the family is riddled with emotional entanglements: Judith has unnatural fantasies about her son Seth, whose favourite occupation, when not at the cinema, is mollocking with Meriam, the hired girl, who always ends up pregnant; the beautiful Elfine is the erotic fantasy of both cousin Urk and Adam, the cowman; and ruling over them all is the rarely seen Ada Doom, the matriarch, who terrifies the family with her reminiscences about seeing something nasty in the woodshed when she was a child. Flora herself has to negotiate the sex-obsessed writer Mr Mybug (whose name is really Meyerburg) and who drags her on long walks to admire breast-shaped hills, nipple-like buds and phallic flowers – in a wicked parody of D.H. Lawrence. She resists his approaches and sorts out the family with common sense and skill before marrying a normal, non-Starkadder, cousin. The glorious pastiche unfolds against the pungent, sickly-sweet scent of the sukebind – the spring flower which symbolizes the awakening of sexual urges in man and beast.

Back in the city, some of the British upper classes led lives as rackety as off-screen Hollywood stars. George, Duke of Kent, the youngest surviving son of George V, was bisexual and promiscuous; he was also addicted to morphine and cocaine. Noticeably more intelligent and cultivated than other members of his family, he was also dismissed by some of them as effeminate and smelling too strongly of perfume. His marriage to the striking Princess Marina of Greece and Denmark produced three children, and they were feted as a glamorous couple, but he had many affairs both before and during the marriage. Female lovers included black singer Florence Mills, music hall star Jessie Matthews, Poppy Baring of the banking family and Margaret Whigham, later to become the notorious Duchess of Argyll (p. 218). The prince is also thought to have had an illegitimate son with American socialite Kiki Preston, whom he shared in a *ménage à trois* with the bisexual son of the Argentinian ambassador to Britain. George's brother Edward believed that this son, who had been adopted at birth, was Michael Canfield, first husband of Lee Radziwill, Jacqueline Kennedy's sister.

George's male lovers included Noel Coward, with whom he had a relationship that lasted nineteen years. Anthony Blunt, later to be outed as a communist spy, was reputedly one of many others, and he was also said to have been blackmailed by a male prostitute to whom he wrote compromising letters. His death in a plane crash in Scotland while on active service in 1942 was also mysterious; conspiracy theories had it that he was involved in the events surrounding the flight to Britain of Rudolf Hess, and that another body at the crash site was Hess's. The man later tried and sentenced to life imprisonment at Nuremberg was (apparently) an impostor.

The aristocratic Mitfords, children of the second Baron Redesdale, were a family whose politics and sexual adventures embraced a variety of different ideologies and attitudes. To the far right was Unity, whose adulation of Adolf Hitler caused her to shoot herself on the outbreak of the war, though she survived until 1948. Of similar views was Diana, married first to Bryan Guinness and then to British fascist leader Oswald Mosley, and imprisoned for a time during the war because of her avowed support of Hitler. To the far left was Jessica, married first to Esmond Romilly, a nephew of Winston Churchill, with whom she travelled to Spain during the Civil War and who was killed in 1941, and then to radical American lawyer Robert Treuhaft. They were both members of the Communist Party at the height of anti-Communist feeling in America and were summoned to testify before the House Un-American Activities

Committee. The oldest sister, Nancy Mitford, initially pursued a hopeless relationship with a homosexual Scottish nobleman, and then married Peter Rodd. She worked in a Mayfair bookshop, George Heywood Hill Ltd, and during the war became an ARP driver. Nancy also started a long-standing affair with a French politician, Gaston Palewski, during the war. She followed him to Paris afterwards, but he later married someone else. The only boy among the seven Mitford children, Thomas, had a homosexual affair with James Lees-Milne while a schoolboy at Eton and was killed in the war.

Nancy's novels about her family, *The Pursuit of Love* and *Love in a Cold Climate*, are mocking portrayals of upper-crust behaviour in the years leading up to the Second World War. Sex frequently rears its ugly – and not so ugly – head; one of her heroines has a mother who left her when she was a baby and acquired a reputation as 'the Bolter' because she flitted from man to man with gay abandon. Another falls in love with her uncle-by-marriage and forces him to marry her after the death of his wife, before becoming bored and falling into the arms of another older man. Perhaps the most famous exchange is between Linda, heroine of *The Pursuit of Love*, and the love of her life, Fabrice, whom she meets while seated on a suitcase in the Gare du Nord in Paris. Amid floods of tears because her return ticket to England has expired and she has no money to buy a new one, Linda tries to pre-empt any attempts at abduction – 'I should like to point out that I am not a white slave. I am the daughter of a very important British nobleman' – but Fabrice is not deterred; he whisks her away to the Hotel Montalembert, where he predicts a happy and long-lasting affair.

Louis Mountbatten – known to his family as 'Dickie' – and his wife Edwina were a couple who weathered many storms and affairs during their marriage. Another glamorous pair, they proved incompatible from the start, but Dickie resisted a divorce which would have brought scandal down on the royal family, to whom he was closely related, and tarnished his naval career; moreover, he was relatively impoverished and she had the money. Both had affairs in the 1930s, but when the war started they threw themselves into war work and survived to become the final Viceroy and Vicereine of India in 1947, bringing the Raj to an end and handing over the reins of power to newly independent India's first Prime Minister, Jawaharlal Nehru. And it was with Nehru that Edwina was to find the strongest love and affection of her life. During the year or so that the Mountbattens stayed in India she became increasingly close to him, relishing the cool and peaceful veranda of the prime minister's home in the blazing Delhi heat. They were determined to put their official roles above private feelings, but after the Mountbattens left, she continued to write to him every day for the rest of her life. Nehru was a widower, a wise and subtle man, and for both of them the relationship was fulfilling and deeply rewarding. He described her in his letters as his inspiration, bringing him solace from the cares of office: 'You came and unlocked the doors and windows.' In return, she acknowledged the depth of their love, punctuated as it was by occasional meetings and long absences: 'You have brought me all I was yearning for, happiness, balance, misery even! But we know the reason and we would not change it.' When she died in 1960 while on a visit to Borneo, Nehru sent two Indian destroyers to accompany her body to the burial at sea that she had requested.

The scandal of scandals in the 1930s was, of course, the affair of the Prince of Wales and Wallis Simpson, an American divorcee. Edward was an undoubted playboy, happy to enjoy the advantages of his position while railing against its restrictions. He complained in letters to his lovers that the tasks he had to undertake as Prince of Wales were leading him to physical and mental breakdown, and although he did work hard, and was popular in his role, he was unwilling to settle down. He seems to have felt a particular attraction towards American married women, and several of them became his mistresses. One of the first was Freda Dudley Ward, who was separated from her husband and whom he met in 1918 when she took cover from an air raid at a house in London where he was present at a party. They were to remain an item until 1934, and she was the recipient of many of his letters complaining about the rigours of his life. Another was Thelma, Lady Furness, and it was she who introduced him to Wallis Simpson in 1931. It was not to be long before he and Wallis, a divorced woman married to her second husband, started an affair. As their romance developed, her total unsuitability did not diminish in establishment eyes, but nothing could deter the king from pursuing the relationship.

Meanwhile, Wallis's divorce from Ernest Simpson was proceeding, amid frenzied public curiosity and – once the decree nisi had been granted – determined efforts to prevent it becoming absolute. The King's Proctor, who would have the task of finalizing the divorce, was inundated by claims of collusion and adultery on both sides, which under the rules of the time would have made a decree absolute impossible. Edward himself did not give up his crown without a struggle; but the various solutions to the impasse which he suggested to the Prime Minister, Stanley Baldwin – such as entering into a morganatic marriage where his wife would not become queen and any children would not inherit the throne – were rejected out of hand. The result was an abdication, and the new Duke of Windsor broadcast to a startled nation (and indeed world) on 11 December 1936: 'A few hours ago I discharged my last duty as king and emperor… You must believe me when I tell you that I have found it impossible to carry the heavy burden of responsibility and to discharge my duties as king as I would wish to do without the help and support of the woman I love.'

The only English king in history voluntarily to renounce his crown, Edward was bitter about the circumstances and so were others in his family. He noted that his brother, the Duke of York, who had just succeeded him as George VI, '…has one matchless blessing, enjoyed by so many of you, and not bestowed on me – a happy home with his wife and children.' The sad comment is a little disingenuous, given that Edward had preferred to carry on affairs with married women during the whole of his adult life, rather than seek out the 'right sort of girl' with whom to settle down. His relationship with his father had been a stormy one, for that reason among others; indeed, George V is known to have hoped that his elder son 'will never marry and have children, and that nothing will come between Bertie and Lilibet and the crown.' That this actually occurred, less than a year after George died, rocked the monarchy and resonates to this day. Mrs Simpson's divorce proceeded – the Proctor finding no firm evidence to prevent it – and the decree absolute was pronounced on 3 May 1937. George VI's coronation took place on 12 May and Edward and Wallis married in France on 3 June, to begin a life of exile; never were the Windsors received into the royal family, and no reconciliation ever took place.

Among the less urbanized – and less exalted – ranks of society, behaviour such as that of the glitterati in the capital would have been considered thoroughly shameless. Marital breakdown was regarded as failure, as well as being socially disgraceful and economically disastrous: most unhappy marriages just had to be endured. For those who were religious, there was also the sinfulness in failing to observe the 'till death us do part' aspect of the marriage sacrament. Children of broken marriages suffered among their peers in the same way as illegitimate children did. And it was even more disreputable to be cited as the co-respondent in a divorce case. For women particularly, this was an igno-minious disgrace; as a result, many men tended to 'do the decent thing' and allow themselves to be exposed as the guilty party.

There were other ways to deal with marriages that had gone wrong. Despite tighter controls on public records, and improved communica-tion technologies, bigamy was still all too possible. In one case held in the National Archives [MEPO 3/966], the man tried to have it all ways. William Tennant Robinson had married Dorothy in 1935; he left her in 1937 and promptly took up with Mabel Gray. They almost immediately went to Gretna Green, where he signed his name to a declaration that they had been resident there for twenty-one days and the wedding took place. Two months later he left his new 'wife', whereupon his legal wife heard about the Gretna escapade and reported him to the police for bigamy. When the case was heard he was already in prison for non-pay-ment of a fine for a motoring offence, and on being found guilty of bigamy he lodged an appeal on the grounds that his second marriage was not legal because he had not met the residence conditions. Anxious not to let him disappear after his release from prison, the legal authorities and the Department of Public Prosecutions debated the validity of his claim and decided not to allow his appeal. He was re-arrested immediately on his release and imprisoned for bigamy.

It is clear in this case that Robinson's only reason for the so-called marriage was in order to have sex with his new woman. But she, too, must have been aware of the illicitness of the arrangement, despite her statement to the court: 'When the man Robinson took me to Gretna I thought I was going to be properly married and after the ceremony I was of the opinion that I was Robinson's wife and legally married to him. I saw [him] sign his name on both of the forms I now produce and on two retained by the blacksmith. I am not pregnant as the result of my associ-ating with Robinson. I have read this and it is true.'

Other preoccupations of the time were with war in Spain and impending war with Germany, leaving many young people determined to experience as much of life as possible while they still could. In his autobiographical novel *As I Walked Out One Midsummer Morning*, Laurie Lee describes leaving home with no fixed destination on a June morning in

1934. He was nineteen years old, footloose and fancy-free, escaping from 'the small tight valley closing in around' and seeking a wider world, full of possibility and adventure. Rained on and sighed at by cows during his first night in the open, he nearly turned back but could not face the ridicule of his brothers. In London he decided to go to Spain and, while waiting for the ship to sail, met and enjoyed girls – one of them, Nell, 'used to lie in my arms in the summer dusk, struggling to save us both from sin' and begged him to take her with him. But he was discovering that it was easier to leave girls behind than to stay with them, and in Spain he relished his solitary life on the road, earning money and food by playing his violin and meeting welcome and unwelcome acquaintances along the way. The languor of the hot days, the wine-befuddled evenings spent in music and talk, the girls he met and made love to – all resonate with the intense and febrile quality of those doom-laden years. The sensuality of his encounter with a girl in a brothel at the end of an evening is almost tangible: 'she put a long brown finger to the neck of my shirt and drew it slowly down my body…'.

Lee's love of Spain, and the Spanish people, created its own imperative. After being brought back to England by the Navy to escape the looming civil war in Spain, he realized that he had to return to fight, despite the attachments of the moment. Once again, women have to be left along the way, and the desolation of a final, passion-filled week with his married mistress under the mountains of southern France is an archetype of wartime farewells. In leaving with no hope of return, despair charges love to an almost unendurable pitch: 'a week of passionate farewell… A week of hysteria, too – embracing in ruined huts, on the salt-grass at the edge of the sea … the mountains were always in sight and the girl made it clear she thought I was going to my death. Our love was more violent than ever, as though we accepted this as its end and wished to leave each other destroyed.'

He returned alive and safe, only to face – like everyone else in Europe – the massive dislocation that war with Germany brought to every aspect of life. Almost the first sound Londoners heard after the announcement on 3 September 1939 that Britain was at war with Germany was the wail of an air raid siren – a grim reminder that in this war civilians would be targeted from the air. So there was fear – but there was also, as ever, a dogged desire to make the most of what life had to offer. The universal blackout, aimed at preventing enemy pilots from identifying what was on the ground beneath them, could also hide pleasurable goings-on and illicit meetings. Air raids could conceal snatched moments of intimacy, and love and lust would come to swift fruition, as did Bendrix's and Sarah's in Graham Greene's *The End of the Affair*: 'There was no pursuit and no seduction. We left half the good steak on our plates and a third of the bottle of claret and came out into Maiden Lane with the same intention in both our minds.' The 'end of the affair' is what the book is about – guilt and sickness conquering love and leading to emptiness and death. But the ardour and hedonism of a wartime romance encapsulate the thrill of a time when pleasure had to be seized in both hands and danger defied.

Mary Wesley's novels, too, are illuminating about relationships of the time. She was herself rather a scandalous figure, marrying Lord Swinfen and having two sons, but then leaving him and living a life full of affairs in London during the war before meeting her second husband, Eric Siepmann, a playwright and journalist. It was after his death in 1970 that she turned to fiction, partly to ease her widowhood and partly because she needed the money. Her first novel was published when she was seventy, and several others followed which she claimed were not autobiographical, but which certainly echo the rather scandalous goings-on during the 1940s that she had herself enjoyed. She admitted to an interviewer that the war had given her generation a very good time: 'an atmosphere of terror and exhilaration and parties, parties, parties.' Her characters are amazingly open about sexual matters, and their language would have appalled the proper mothers of the time. The cousins in *The Camomile Lawn* are typical: the beautiful Calypso, determined to marry for money and doing so, while taking lovers all along the way; Polly, lover of both of a pair of twin brothers who never know which of them is the father of her twins; sad little schoolgirl Sophy, who is being gently abused by her uncle and who later reacts to a flasher by pushing him off a cliff. Some of the characters recur in later novels, and are usually regarded with horrified amazement by the more strait-laced younger generation.

Wartime life overseas could also be full of opportunities. Olivia Manning's *Levant Trilogy* chronicles expatriate British life in wartime Egypt, where the perils of being far from home at a time of conflict only added to the need to grasp at fleeting pleasure: 'The English do become odd here. Ordinary couples who'd remain happily together in Ealing or

Pinner … think themselves Don Juans or tragedy queens and make scenes in public.' In both Cairo and Alexandria, as the German Afrika Corps advanced, stranded expatriates sought refuge both in the colonial splendours of clubs, where gambling and drinking went on day and night, and in the numerous brothels. The approaching Germans sent a message to the ladies of Alexandria: 'Get out your party dresses and prepare to defend your honour', and the nervous men awaiting the arrival of the enemy took their own full advantage of the sex on offer. Seedy terraced houses displayed advertisements for cures for 'all the diseases of love' and the promise to restore 'horse-like vigour' to the impotent, while in Cairo the narrow streets of the Esbekiyah thronged with women, poised in every doorway and leaning, half-naked, out of every window, while music pulsated from cafes and young boys offered their sisters. Outside the heady red light areas, affairs and infidelities had become part of the civilian way of life. Manning's heroine, Harriet Pringle, is reluctant to return on an evacuation boat and leave her husband alone in such a city: 'Inconstancy was so much the rule among the British residents in Cairo, the place, she felt, was like a bureau of sexual exchange.'

Yet the tensions of war did not always result in the abandoning of principles. The classic film *Casablanca*, released in 1943, starred Humphrey Bogart and Ingrid Bergman — and the now-famous song, 'As Time Goes By'. It takes its story from love gained and lost, and regained after a clash in the north African city between German officers, Free French authorities, a prominent resistance fighter and the owner of a bar. Arriving in Rick's bar with her husband, Ilsa Laszlo discovers to her shock that Rick is the man with whom she had fallen deeply in love years before, believing her husband to be dead, in pre-invasion Paris. Now Victor Laszlo, a heroic resistance fighter, needs to escape to Portugal to carry on the struggle, but cannot leave without exit papers which the corrupt French police will not let him have. Rick obtains the papers, while he and Ilsa fall in love all over again. She decides to let Victor go while she stays; but Rick, in an emotional final scene at the airport, nobly insists that she must do the right thing and leave with her husband. The importance of his mission must override all other feelings at a time of such peril.

Bogart and Bergman in the film were an all-time great double act, and the triumph of principle over love was an enduring message. Yet it was not to be long before Bergman suffered a major setback in real life for choosing love over principle. Celebrated for her roles in *Casablanca* and other major films, an Academy Award winner and married to Dr Peter Lindstrom with whom she had a daughter, she was at the height of her profession when she fell in love with the director Roberto Rossellini while working with him on *Stromboli*. The affair caused a world-wide scandal, particularly as she had become pregnant, and her divorce and quick marriage to Rossellini made no difference. *Stromboli* was boycotted, their later work together was ignored and for several years they were outcasts from the film world. Her triumphant, Oscar-winning return in the late 1950s coincided with the breakdown of her marriage to Rossellini, and for the rest of her life, until her death in 1982, she enjoyed both a happy third marriage and a series of noted film and theatrical successes, with her reputation rehabilitated.

Morality at home was a major issue for the authorities during the war. Bigamy was a particular worry, with the massive troop movements and general disruption making it all too easy for a potential bigamist to evade notice. A confidential letter in the National Archives was drafted by officials at the General Register Office in Blackpool to Superintendent Registrars in February 1941. It responds to concerns about the danger of bigamous marriages being contracted by members of the forces: 'As was the case in the last war, experience during the present war has shown the need for the utmost care being taken by a register officer attesting a notice of marriage of a member of the forces to satisfy himself that the man is free to marry' [RG 48/1690]. The letter went on to suggest that, if the registrar had any grounds for suspicion, he should ask the man to produce his Pay Book, although even this was not conclusive proof – no mention of a wife did not mean none existed.

It is clear from a reply to this letter, from the Deputy Superintendent Registrar, District Register Office, Wetherby, later in February, that they were facing a real problem: 'Bigamy appears to be one of the easiest of crimes to commit in this country. At the commencement of the Assizes in one of the large cities recently, the judge commented on the alarming number of cases before him of bigamy, in fact he referred to it as an "epidemic", and most of the cases shewed in evidence that the bigamous marriages took place in Register Offices. I quite appreciate your instructions ... but this procedure is of practically no use whatever to the official, because if a man is intending to commit bigamy he is usually a plausible lying fellow and does not hesitate to brazen the proceedings through, as the many cases before the judges testify.'

For women, too, the temptations offered by vast numbers of soldiers of all races passing through were often hard to resist, even when they were already married or engaged to someone serving abroad. The rates of illegitimacy went through the roof during the war years. Some estimates claim that at least a third of all the babies born during them were illegitimate, and many a man returned from a far-flung battlefield to find that his wife had been unfaithful and often had a baby to show for it. The women's magazines used their advice pages to offer words of censure or comfort to the many women who wrote in to ask for help. Situations were often clouded by the uncertainties of the times: the advice column in *Woman* in June 1944 related the case of a young woman whose fiancé had been reported missing at sea several months previously and who was now wondering whether she should accept the advances of another young man. Although still in love with her lost fiancé she was considering devoting the rest of her life to making the new man happy. The wise advice was that she should wait a while. Another wrote about her boyfriend who was a prisoner of war in Japan; while she wanted to be loyal to him, all her friends were going out with boys and she was horribly lonely. The advice was friendly but uncompromising: 'I am glad that you are keeping faith with your boy'; maybe the answer was for her to join a youth club or do voluntary work.

Isolated lapses were regarded as forgivable, whether by the man or the woman — though men's escapades always received a little more indulgence, particularly if they were in the forces. And the advice columnists were almost always hard on women with husbands or boyfriends serving abroad who wrote in for help about having met someone new or — worse — having become pregnant. Their main concern was invariably how the man was going to feel about it and how best to tell him. 'How you could do such a thing passes my comprehension. But now the main thing to do is to avoid hurting him, isn't it?' The mental health and well-being of those fighting and suffering abroad for their country were paramount. A robust piece in *Women's Weekly*, 24 July 1943, is typical: 'I think that you, and others like you, who seem to have a very sketchy idea of loyalty, need to face facts. Your husband has gone overseas. Do you realize what this means — danger, privation, loneliness, possibly pain and death? Do you realize that he and all those with him are facing this cheerfully and for your sake so that you, and all of us here at home, can live in safety and comfort? Do you think that you are worth it?

Above [28] ISADORA DUNCAN's free-flowing and expressive dance style, combined with her free-living lifestyle, is lampooned in this French cartoon showing the effect she could have on her audiences. **Right** [29] HAROLD NICOLSON and Vita Sackville-West had a long and happy marriage, despite their individual preference for homosexual affairs. Vita's explosive relationship with Violet Trefusis was a sensational scandal in the early 1920s, though her sons did not know about it until after her death, when her own account of it came to light. This photograph was taken in 1932 at their home in Sissinghurst Castle, Kent.

Above [30] THE WINDMILL Theatre famously boasted that 'we never closed' despite the air raids and bombs of the Second World War. Three of the Windmill Girls — Hula, Paddie and Pamela — relax in their dressing room during a break in the show in September 1940.

Left [31] MARLENE DIETRICH, shown here in a still from the 1932 film *The Blonde Venus*, was one of the most alluring stars of Hollywood in the 1930s. She had many affairs with both women and men during her long life, sharing several of her female lovers with Greta Garbo.

Above [32] Four of the Mitford sisters, daughters of Lord and Lady Redesdale, photographed in 1932. Unity (left) and Jessica are standing behind the author Nancy (left) and Diana. The Mitford girls' varied politics and love affairs were celebrated: their mother is on record as sighing that a headline 'peer's daughter' in a newspaper was bound to be about one of them.

Above and **top right** [33] Two DOCUMENTS from the National Archives file [MEPO 3/2138] on concerns about prostitution and American troops in London in 1942/3. The sensational article in the *Sunday Pictorial* alleged that London was rampant with vice, a charge that the police and the government were at pains to refute. The letter from 'A/Superintendent "C"' admits that ' there is a grain of truth in the article and Police would be the last to suggest that the position in the West End is all that could be desired… [But] to those acquainted with the true state of affairs, the article is unworthy of serious attention.'

A.1.Department (Thro' D.A.C.1.)

      The article headed "The Spider's Web of Vice" which appeared in the 'Sunday Pictorial' of the 23rd. August, 1942, is a highly sensational and exaggerated account of the state of affairs in the West End of London. Like all such journalistic efforts relating to vice there is a grain of truth in the article and Police would be the last to suggest that the position in the West End is all that could be desir' We know that so called dens of vice do exist, and have exist' for many years; also that there are a number of blackguards who are out to fleece service men and others, and do not min. how they make money so long as they do make it easily and without working for it.

      It is our purpose to deal with such establishments and persons as soon as evidence is available warranting action. It is only recently that our powers have been extended by Defence Regulations and we shall invoke these powers whenever possible.

      The record as disclosed in the above report by S.D.Inspector Gavin, who is specially employed on this work, shows that we have not been idle, and we shall do our utmost to close all undesirable resorts and deal adequately with the proprietors thereof.

      To those acquainted with the true state of affairs, the article is unworthy of serious attention.

14/9/42   A/Superintendent "C"

Left [34] GEORGE, Duke of Kent, fourth son of King George V, with his wife Princess Marina, in 1934. His parents were eager to see him settled down with a suitable wife in the hope that marriage would curb his erratic lifestyle.

Right [37] KENNETH
TYNAN, photographed here
in 1964, was a byword
during the 1960s for
decadence and louche
behaviour, as well as for his
sharp theatre criticism. He
was a vigorous opponent of
censorship in all its forms,
and was a co-writer of the
long-running sexy revue
Oh Calcutta!

Above [35] THE LAST WOMAN to be hanged in Britain, Ruth Ellis made no attempt to seek
a reprieve after she was condemned to death in 1955 for shooting her lover, David Blakely,
pictured with her earlier that year. The judge warned the jury that they must take no
account of her admission during the trial that she had committed adultery. **Below** [36]
MANDY RICE-DAVIES (left) and Christine Keeler (right), the call girls at the centre of the
Profumo scandal in 1963. It gripped the public with revelations about the immorality of high
society, the goings-on among prostitutes and their protectors, and lies told to Parliament.

Above [38] HIPPIES and teenagers gather in Hyde Park, London, during the 'summer of love' in 1967. They offer flowers as tokens of peace and love to a bemused policeman.
Right [39] As MICK Jagger's girlfriend and a successful singer in her own right, Marianne Faithfull was one of the icons of the 'permissive society'. Here she carries a newspaper describing her as 'NAKED GIRL AT STONES PARTY' after police raided Jagger's home for drugs in 1967.

Can you believe that you, and others like you, who have no idea of remaining loyal to their marriage vows, who talk lightly of "being in love" with another man, are worth the lives of all our gallant men? You certainly should not say anything to your husband about it; you don't want to add to his hardships.'

If the evidence of the affair could not be concealed because there was a baby, the advice was to wait until the husband was home safe before breaking it to him as gently as possible. In the case of a returning prisoner of war, the usual suggestion was that she should write to the matron of the hospital where he was being nursed back to health, or to his camp commander, to find a way of keeping the truth from him until his health was sufficiently robust; 'it might be the finish of everything for him if he knew it now.' One male advice columnist was harsh about women who tried to ease their own consciences by burdening their men with confessions while they were abroad; he knew that kind of letter well, he said: 'It begins with some such stock phrase as "I don't know how to write this to you." Well, why write the cursed thing? Keep it. Tear it up. Wait till the war's over – you may have learned more sense by then. Or if not, perhaps he'll have died happy. Cruel? Possibly. But not so cruel as the pen of a thoughtless woman. The amount of damage to morale and to the war effort [of such letters] is probably greater than that done by the whole of Dr Goebbels' propaganda machine...'. He also quoted a war correspondent: 'Are half the wives in Britain demented? Won't they realize the men out here have a job on that's more important than the heart-burnings and soul-searchings of all the silly females who have nothing better to do than pour out on paper their wretched "confessions"? Don't they know what they're doing to the morale of the men?'

Little consideration was given to the morale of the women who had also had a great deal to endure and whose contribution to the work of winning the war was considerable. As ever, it was the woman who had to remain chaste; and if she did not, and fell victim to an unwanted pregnancy, there was little she could do about it. Contraception was in its infancy and still unreliable; abortion was illegal and dangerous if back-street practitioners were resorted to; and adoption was impossible without the consent of the husband. The only sensible advice that could be offered was that she should be honest with her husband and hope for his forgiveness. Some men did indeed accept the cuckoo in the nest and raise it as their own; others were prepared to forgive and forget as long as the child was put out for adoption; but many others could not accept the situation and sued for divorce. Before the war the majority of divorce petitions were brought by the wives; afterwards most were brought by the men, and usually for adultery. Before the war they were running at about 10,000 a year; afterwards the number shot up to 25,000 or more.

The solution, for one advice columnist, was work. She accepted that many marriages had been entered into hastily on the onset of war and repented of later; she also accepted that the world was becoming more civilized about the needs and rights of the innocent children whose illegitimacy was not their fault; so the solution was to remove oneself from temptation by working hard for the war effort: 'Work till you are too tired to mope; work till you win the comradeship of the other workers around you; work till you forget how much you long for "him" to kiss you and put his arms round you. Work to help him come home again.'

Once the Americans had entered the war, the authorities began to get very worried about the vast increase in illicit sex offered by young women to the large numbers of American troops who were now in London. Mayfair had become a virtual American colony owing to the many buildings there taken over by American troops and their support structures; and Shepherd's Market, in the heart of Mayfair, was now being frequented not just by its traditional prostitutes, but by scores of girls who just wanted to meet the exotic Americans. These young British girls were out for a good time and for some of the fruits of the wealth the Americans brought with them – not only money, but also goods such as cigarettes and stockings. Moreover, many of them were ignorant of basic biology and believed that upright sex against a wall prevented pregnancy; hence the large numbers of 'knee tremblers' offered in dark doorways after the blackout to passing soldiers. And, as a senior police officer put it, these girls did not 'accost' men, but simply made it clear that they would welcome advances.

One Colonel Clark, who was a legal adviser attached to the US army, was insistent that new legislation was required to make picking up on the streets illegal, as it was in the USA, and to give police greater powers of control. The response from the British authorities was measured but firm, pointing out that immorality in itself had never been illegal in the UK and that the police were doing all they could within the limits of current regulations. At a meeting with the Attorney General, Clark appeared to be 'very persistent in his idea that the boys should be able to write home saying that they never saw a doubtful lady in the streets of London.' And though the British authorities resisted his over-zealousness on this occasion, it was generally agreed that the issue was a significant one. There were suggestions that some of the high pay enjoyed by American troops should be frozen, and that troops should receive regular lectures on the dangers of consorting with prostitutes and women picked up on the street, on the basis that 'while it is a waste of breath to talk to a hard case, it is not a waste of breath to talk to a decent boy.' The Americans themselves estimated that fifteen per cent of their troops would be unlikely to be tempted by casual sex, a further fifteen per cent would never be dissuaded from indulging in it and the remaining seventy per cent would be influenced by circumstances.

The American soldiers were characterized as both 'wolves in wolves' clothing' and 'oversexed, overpaid and over here'; but they were attractive, rich and available. As one British housewife put it, 'We were not really immoral, but there was a war on.' British fathers, husbands and brothers were away, women were doing hard war work and wanted to enjoy themselves when they could; and the Americans had plenty to offer. There were also problems, of course. The willingness of many white British women to consort with black American soldiers caused some trouble; blacks and whites were segregated in the US army, and certain white soldiers were incensed that their black comrades were forming relationships with women they regarded as their own territory.

Alongside the 'good time girls', the authorities also had professional prostitution to worry about in the fervid atmosphere of wartime London. A file in the National Archives deals with the response of the government and the police to a sensational article by Lester Powell in the *Sunday Pictorial* of 23 August 1942 entitled 'The Spider's Web of Vice' [MEPO 3/2138]. According to the article, the West End of London was a hive of vice dens where soldiers on leave were fleeced of their money, the white slave trade was rampant and innocent young women were trapped into a life of prostitution. He reported one tale of a pretty young girl from the north who came down to the capital to help the war effort by working in a munitions factory, only to meet and become engaged to a personable young man-about-town who established his respectability by introducing her to his aunt. Thrilled to be setting up home with him, she failed to challenge the fact that he set about ordering new furniture in her name – only to be faced with a massive bill for the articles after he disappeared.

On appealing to the aunt, she was told that the only way out was for her to join a troupe of 'entertainers'; a fake medical certificate released her from the munitions factory and she embarked, *force majeure*, on her new life. From now on, of course, she was ruined.

The journalist claimed to know 'literally dozens of travelling white slave circuses' of that sort, and to be able to provide the Ministry of Labour, should they require it, with a list of 'at least fifty addresses where useful man- and woman-power is going to waste' (in afternoon sex clubs). The police responded robustly to the charge that they were not in control of West End vice, insisting that the author's claims could be treated as his 'flair for sensational journalistic exaggeration'. They admitted that there was a grain of truth in the article, and that 'the position in the West End is not all that could be desired. We know that dens of vice do exist ... and that there are a number of blackguards who are out to fleece service men and others.' But they also pointed out examples of the action taken against the trade: fines of £308/12/- had been levied in respect of ten brothels, and two people had been imprisoned; and eight ponces had been proceeded against for living on immoral earnings.

Venereal disease was also an issue. An epidemic of it swept London – and, to a lesser extent, other centres of military activity – during the later stages of the war, and most of it, the authorities realized, could be laid at the door not of prostitutes, who knew how to protect themselves, but of the often ignorant and careless 'good time girls'. As one American senior officer told his troops, 'Any woman who can be "picked up" and "made" by an American soldier can be, and certainly has been, "picked up" and "made" by countless others. How much greater is the chance that she will have a venereal disease?' Combating such disease became an increasing priority, not just because of its effect on the soldiers themselves and their morale, but also because of the damage to the reputation of London and the British to those at home in the USA. The *Daily Mirror* of 3 June 1943 carried a report from New York about the shock that was sweeping America after stories of vice-ridden London reached there. 'Sensational charges made by the usually staid *New York Times*' alleged that venereal infection among US troops in London was at least twenty-five per cent higher than it was at home, and that the flocks of women soliciting in the streets around Piccadilly Circus were a 'tourist attraction'. 'There can be no doubt that the vast majority of American soldiers arriving in this theatre have never before been in a city where one of the most famous down-town streets is nightly transformed into an open market.'

During the First World War, the authorities had relied largely on solemn exhortations from the likes of Kitchener, and generally buried their heads in the sand; but times had changed. In the early 1940s, the Home Office set up a multi-disciplinary committee to consider the problem. One British civil servant agreed with what those at home apparently believed was the innocence of the Americans, though he obviously felt that naivety was a more appropriate word. A memo dated 11 November 1942 claimed that, 'Personally I would say that to anyone who knew Paris or even London in the last war, London at the moment is by comparison a well-conducted Sunday School ... I would suggest that the real difficulty is the quite remarkable inexperience of a large part of the American troops, who succumb to the most elementary tricks of the prostitute and confidence trickster class.' A handwritten comment next to that last sentence reads 'I wonder!'

Eventually, therefore, the prudishness displayed both by government ministries and the press about venereal disease was tackled. In 1937, newspapers had refused to publish health warnings about the problem; in October 1942, all the women's magazines carried a full-page statement from the Ministry of Health giving the facts about venereal disease and offering advice on how to deal with it. *Good Housekeeping* had an editorial on the opposite page, 'To All Thinking Women', putting the weight of the magazine behind the campaign. Along with information about the symptoms and directions on what to do about them, the health authorities stated, 'Professional prostitutes are not the only source of infection. Any free-and-easy sex behaviour must mean a risk of infection and cannot be made safe. Clean living is the only way – abstinence is not harmful.' The editorial pointed out that otherwise clean-cut and innocent young men were just as vulnerable as those who frequented prostitutes, that young girls who seemed on the surface to be admirable companions for such young men were frighteningly likely to be infected and that the best antidote was for wives and mothers to make their home life 'so warm and full and rich that husbands, sons, daughters, wherever they may be ... will feel its call stronger and more compelling than any temptation'. In addition, it suggested that they could welcome into these happy homes less well-placed young people working in the services or in factories who might otherwise succumb, through sheer loneliness, to cravings for excitement leading to promiscuity.

Despite all this rightful — if rather righteous — concern, it was undoubtedly the relief of being on leave and away from the front line that produced high levels of promiscuity among the armed forces. One calculation had it that the average US soldier who served in Europe from D-Day through to the end of the war had sex with twenty-five women. And after the surrender of Germany in 1945, there were inadequate supplies of condoms, which were rationed to four per man per month. German women were often eager to consort with American soldiers, despite an official policy of non-fraternization, because they had food and cigarettes. In Italy, too, at the end of the war, figures claim that three-quarters of US soldiers had sex with Italian women, paying with cash or food, and using condoms only sometimes.

It was not all promiscuity, of course. Many of the American soldiers and the British girls they met and dated formed happy relationships and got married. 'GI brides' were a phenomenon of the immediate post-war period, with many newspapers carrying photographs of ships laden with waving women setting off for the other side of the Atlantic. These marriages had often been arranged in the teeth of the US army authorities, who looked on British women as potential gold-diggers and discouraged fraternization; the girls' families were also likely to have objected, particularly when they were very young, and not just because they were unhappy about them going so far away from home. Whether or not the young man was a decent sort and in love with their daughter, parents knew that he was bound to be sent away to the war and might never return — if he was not killed, he might simply regret his impulsive action and disappear. They were also understandably worried about what might happen if a swift wartime romance went wrong once the couple were faced with real life back in the USA; the girl would be far from home, far from the support of family and friends and very vulnerable — particularly with babies to consider.

For some young girls, these fears proved all too real. Husbands did disappear never to be heard of again. Some women suffered the misery and despair of arriving in America, often with a baby in tow, to find that there was no one to meet them and that they were unwanted baggage from the past; or they suffered unbearable homesickness when they reached their new country, and gave up. Others found the bureaucracy imposed on them before they were allowed to set sail impossible to cope with, or succumbed to the impossibility of saying goodbye, perhaps for ever, to their loved ones.

For those who did leave, it was an anxious voyage. Many of the men were shipped straight home from the continent, leaving their wives to follow on ships specially organized by the army. Most of the women had not seen their husbands for some time, and they must have wondered whether they had made the right decision; whether the man was as good as he seemed; what his family were like and what they would think; when they would ever see their families again; what America was like – that vast, different country with so many strange customs and words and such different living standards. It was truly a journey into the unknown, however much they had learnt from magazine articles giving wise advice or schools set up to teach them American ways – one of them, ironically, in the Rainbow Club in London's Shaftesbury Avenue, once notorious for wartime sex. Unsurprisingly, many of these marriages did not endure; but many others were highly successful, and in both cases the women usually stayed in their adopted country and made a good life for themselves there.

The privations of the war years did not disappear after the exhilaration of VE Day and VJ Day. Rationing continued until the early 1950s, as economies all over Europe struggled to get back on an even keel. Men who had seen horrors all over the world arrived back in a country still in the grip of shortages. The winter of 1947/8 was one of the hardest on record. War had been a stimulus as well as a danger, and returning to everyday life entailed, for many, coming down to earth with a bump. A quote from Elizabeth Smart's prose poem *The Assumption of the Rogues and Rascals* sums up the exhaustion felt by people struggling on in the post-war years: 'Out of this weary landscape, girding your strengths around you, you are to step through a couple of decades with your children on your back, singing a song to keep them optimistic and looking to left and right ... Too late to desert. Too late to heave off your crippling kit and head for the hills. The problem now is how to put one foot forward ... On. Just keeping your feet from going numb. Just keeping them functioning.' Smart herself had had a passionate love affair with the (married) poet George Barker, with whom she had four children. The intense relationship inspired her most famous work, *By Grand Central Station I Sat Down and Wept*.

The spirit encapsulated in Noel Coward's *Brief Encounter*, filmed in

[199]

1945, was abroad. The unconsummated love affair between a housewife and the man she first accidentally meets in the railway station waiting room presents a crucial antidote to the immoral freedoms which some women enjoyed during the war years. The characters played by Celia Johnson and Trevor Howard are middle-aged, married and parents – and both are middle class, the moral backbone of society. Their failure to go beyond furtive cups of tea and meetings at the cinema as their love develops provides the tension at the story's heart; and their final decision to stop meeting stems from horror at the thought of betraying their spouses and their innate moral values. Such integrity chimed well with the climate of the times, desperate to return to the pre-war status quo where marriage was for life and divorce a disgrace. The final scene is poignant, as their miserable farewell is interrupted by a chattering friend; and their last glances at each other as his train arrives and she dashes on to the platform, perhaps with the idea of hurling herself in front of it, are memorable. He leaves, and she returns to her family, both determined to do their duty.

This new mood of restraint replaced the euphoria that took society by storm in the 1920s and created phenomena such as the flappers. But there was to be determined change. The returning ranks of service men and women tipped the balance in the 1945 general election, calling for faster movement forward and greater equality, hoping for a post-war world where there would be a better life for all. The victorious Labour Party promised a new welfare state, an excellent state education open to everyone, nationalization of the essential infrastructure of industry and society and an overall levelling up.

And even if the moralists disliked it, a massive change was indeed on the way. The Americans had imported more than millions of men and their cigarettes and nylons; they had also brought direct exposure to their lifestyle and prosperity. The pin-up girls they flaunted in their barracks and on their vehicles – Betty Grable, Rita Hayworth, Jane Russell – exuded Hollywood sexuality; their music – jazz, big bands, crooners – was exciting and raunchy; they spoke with the accents of movie stars; and they were rich. The British were prepared to put up with austerity in wartime, but were becoming increasingly impatient with it as the war receded and the 1940s drew to a close. The Americans had provided a breath of the air of a new, vivid life, and the 1950s would see it coming to Britain and being wholeheartedly embraced.

Eight · Making love and making waves

THE FIRST HALF of the twentieth century had been, in some senses, a prudish time. Traditional middle-class morality still governed the lives of the majority at the beginning of the 1950s with all that it entailed: chastity for women, the fear and disgrace of extramarital pregnancy, divorce a shocking failure, abortion and homosexuality illegal. Illicit sex had never gone away, of course, but for most people it, and its consequences, had to be kept under wraps.

Political and economic changes, however, were starting to challenge established attitudes, and louder questions were being asked about the morals and mores that previous generations had taken for granted. Why should women be subservient to their men? Why should they not have lives of their own outside the home, married or not? Why should a child born – through no fault of its own – to an unmarried woman be stigmatized as illegitimate for life? How is it that a man can get away with impregnating his girlfriend and then denying any responsibility for the child? And be regarded as a bit of a lad into the bargain?

At the same time the Labour government's reforms of health and education were permeating further downwards within society, opening up many more opportunities for ordinary people to better themselves – and to make money. The influx of all things American after the end of the Second World War was opening eyes to a more equal, and in many ways jollier, way of life. Technology was progressing ever faster, offering wider ranges of labour-saving consumer goods as well as a great many more leisure options. In 1950, few households had a television or a refrigerator; ten years later most did, and the same was true of indoor lavatories and bathrooms. In 1950 austerity was still the watchword, and rationing still in place. In the early 1960s the Conservative Prime Minister, Harold Macmillan, could pronounce without fear of contradiction his verdict on the times: 'You've never had it so good.'

In some ways sexual manners were bound to lag behind the rapid pace of change while morality retained its Victorian hue. Although the scent of greater freedom was in their nostrils, women were still to a large extent stuck in the past. Domesticity ruled and other options were limited, although even Cambridge University finally granted women the right to take degrees in 1948. The nuclear family was the norm: husband coming home from work to his pipe and slippers in front of the fire while his aproned wife busied herself with the supper and his clean, polite children played or did their homework. Smiles and respectability all round, family solidarity taken for granted.

But rebellion was in the air, and from within the family, too. Children had always been simply miniature adults, their clothes scaled-down versions of those worn by their parents, childhood turning into a quickly truncated youth as they joined the workforce as soon as they were able. But in the 1950s the teenager was born, bred in America but rapidly taking root in Britain and embracing behaviour that shocked the older generation. Teenagers had their own music, their own dance crazes, their own fashions, their own manners and morals – and they were the first to benefit from the new prosperity and to cock a determined snook at what their elders regarded as normal.

Their music was loud and sexy, their dances fast, furious – and sexy – and their clothes – yes, sexy too. The images are seductive: girls and boys both in tight 'drainpipe' trousers, skirts getting shorter, tops skimpier; 'teddy boys' with long, Brylcreamed hair and sideburns; girls with back-combed beehives lacquered to immobility. And eventually denim jeans, the unisex item of clothing taken over from manual labourers, began to conquer the world.

This was a new culture of youth, looking to America for its influences, increasingly captivated by the raunchiness and the sheer glamour of its music and films, and the actors and singers who performed in them. Amidst the greyness of austerity-locked Britain, and with the memories of real Americans 'over here' during the war years, this seemed truly a new world. Aficionados of jazz and swing had long known about the revolution in American music brought about by mainly poor black musicians from the south whose influence had spread over the whole continent; but this kind of music, and its developments, was now opening itself up to a wider audience – white middle-class kids on both sides of the Atlantic for whom it was a liberation from their parents and from the stultifying norms of the time.

Forget the crooners and the big bands; now there was Elvis Presley gyrating wildly to loud music with a heavy beat. His main influences were the black musicians in the still segregated deep south, where he came from, and his appearances on stage singing what white music impresarios regarded, in what was then common parlance, as 'nigger music' or 'devil music' were often curtailed or banned. The sexy ways in which Presley moved were also highly offensive to the powers that be. Preachers denounced him in their pulpits, and a judge once granted a performance licence on condition that he did not move at all on stage; he complied, apart from a gently wagging finger.

But the youth loved him and his music. The songs he sang echoed the themes of love and lust that had long been the staples of the jazz world, and he personified a sort of gently debauched teen scene which was eager to embrace a culture different from – and shocking to – that enjoyed by their elders. This was to become even more the case in the 1960s.

Elvis himself never performed in Britain; but he had his imitators by the score, and the music world ballooned into a full-scale industry, fuelled by ever-growing demands from young people for new sounds, new dances, new excitement. Cliff Richard, Tommy Steele and Adam Faith were home-grown entertainers with Elvis-like long hair and Elvis-like pelvic gyrations on stage. Smoky coffee bars and clubs such as the Marquee in Soho's Wardour Street were the new venues patronized by the teenagers. Dances echoed the beat of the music by being wild and uninhibited, the boys, with cigarettes hanging out of the corners of their mouths, swinging the girls around till their skirts billowed up to show their stockings and suspenders. It was a sexy time for young people. Diana Melly, in her recent autobiography *Take a Girl Like Me*, recalls making love on Hampstead Heath with George Melly on the day she first met him at Soho's Colony Club. She was twenty-four at the time, on her second marriage and with two children; he was a thirty-five-year-old jazz singer whose careers both in the navy and later in music had been marked by numbers of affairs with both sexes. After their marriage they both carried on with an open, free-love-based *ménage* in which lovers and children came and went.

Films were another source of glamour. The 1930s to the 1950s were the heyday of cinema, the entertainment of choice for a large proportion of the population on a Saturday evening. Many a first date was marked by tentative fumblings in the darkness of the back rows of the local Odeon while gazing in wonder at the screen gods and goddesses looming overhead, larger than life and ten times as sexy. It was the age of glamour and charisma, from the sparkling chemistry of Humphrey Bogart and Lauren Bacall (who married in real life) to the slick repartee of Rosalind Russell and Cary Grant in *My Girl Friday*, which brought romance into the hardbitten newspaper world. Several stars spanned the decades, such as Mae West, who had made a name for herself as a slinky, wisecracking blonde known for her bawdy doubles entendres, her big breasts and her swaying walk; her curves became legendary after they were celebrated by Allied soldiers during World War II in the name they gave their life-jackets – they were known as Mae Wests from their resemblance to her torso.

Her rude sexuality was legendary, too. Before her films achieved their huge – and enduring – success, she had written and staged a great many risqué plays and revues, and was once prosecuted on morals charges and sentenced to ten days' imprisonment for public obscenity. She was an early victim of the heavy censorship imposed on American show business in the 1930s, and suffered the closure of many of her ventures. But she was indomitable in her belief that talking about sex was a basic human right, and she was also an early supporter within American cinema of homosexual rights.

Her play *Diamond Lil*, in which she played a racy woman from the turn of the century, was an instant success on the Broadway stage when it opened in 1928, and she revived it several times during the course of her life. Her film version of it, *She Done Him Wrong*, made a star of Cary Grant and won an Oscar nomination for best picture. But it was one of the lines she uttered in her first film for Hollywood, *Night After Night* opposite George Raft, that made her an instant movie star: on her first entrance, in response to the exclamation of a hat-check girl, 'Goodness, what lovely diamonds,' her response was 'Goodness had nothing to do with it, dearie.' Memorable for many other devastating one-liners during her career – I used to be Snow White, but I drifted'; 'I generally avoid temptation unless I can't resist it'; 'Is that a gun in your pocket, or are you just happy to see me?' – she carried on working for most of her long life, one of her final appearances being as the sex-mad casting agent in the 1970 film of Gore Vidal's transgender novel *Myra Breckenridge*.

Marilyn Monroe is perhaps the most iconic blonde bombshell of the 1950s, remembered for her sultry beauty, her marriages and affairs, the unhappiness of her final years and for singing 'Happy Birthday, Mr President' to John F. Kennedy during what was her last significant public appearance. Originally regarded by studio bosses as a bit of a bimbo, she proved in some of her major films that she could be a comic actor to be reckoned with: her role in *Some Like It Hot* – regarded as one of the best films of all time – along with her performance of the song 'Diamonds Are a Girl's Best Friend' in *Gentlemen Prefer Blondes* and the skirt-blowing scene in *The Seven Year Itch* more than ensure her place in the Hollywood pantheon as an actress, not simply a beautiful blonde. It was during the filming of the skirt scene that her then husband, Joe DiMaggio, finally lost his temper over her public flirtatiousness, and the subsequent scenes heralded the end of their short marriage. Yet despite her later marriage to the playwright Arthur Miller, it was DiMaggio who claimed her body and arranged her funeral after she was found dead of an overdose of sleeping pills in August 1962. She had meanwhile had affairs with both John and Robert Kennedy – concealed from the public until long after both were dead – and those relationships, combined with her contacts with the Mafia through Frank Sinatra and his Rat Pack, have led to many conspiracy theories about her death. But she was in truth a troubled creature, despite her beauty, fame and success; and her tragedy is an inescapable part of her legend.

West and Monroe between them, along with their male counterparts such as Clark Gable and Humphrey Bogart, typify the glamorous escapism offered by movies, together with their sexuality and loucheness. The real lives of movie stars echoed those enjoyed by their screen alter egos, too, with their multiple marriages and divorces, their grand Californian homes and their international, millionaire lifestyles. Rock musicians soon began to emulate those lifestyles, and their fan base among the rebellious young often allowed them to behave in even more outrageous ways. There was a great deal of rich living on the one hand and bad behaviour on the other.

The British show business scene developed in a different direction, too – one in which sexual innuendo and doubles entendres formed the basis of films and comedy programmes on television and radio (still in the 1950s the main source of home entertainment). Radio programmes such as *Beyond Our Ken*, which ran from 1958 to 1964, and *Round the Horne*, which followed it in the mid-1960s, were full of such material. *Round the Horne* was credited with keeping radio comedy alive in an era when television was taking over, and it was only the sudden death in 1969 of its anchorman, Kenneth Horne, that killed it off. It is still a cult programme, remembered and listened to for the clever wordplay of its writers, Barry Took and Marty Feldman, and the interaction of its actors, notably – in addition to Horne – Hugh Paddick and Kenneth Williams as the double act 'Julian and my friend Sandy'. Williams played other parts, too, as well as interrupting scenes in which he was not involved with ad libs or manic off-stage laughter. His folk-singer, Rambling Syd Rumpo, was memorable for lines like 'I nadgered my snod...' and 'I'd whirdle with a fair young maid.'

But it was Julian and Sandy – playing two ex-chorus boys, now 'resting' actors – who regularly stole the show with their high-camp humour delivered in the gay slang known as Polari. This 'language', which had been around in one form or another for a couple of centuries, was much in use in the gay subculture of the mid-twentieth century, and Paddick and Williams were among early entertainers to introduce their listeners to it. While homosexuality was still criminal, this slang was a genuine way to avoid the attentions of the authorities – it was much safer to comment on a man's 'bona bagadja' than on his 'nice cock'. And it was a splendid vehicle for all sorts of innuendos delivered to an audience on mainstream radio who could often only guess at their meaning. 'How bona to vada your eek' was how they usually greeted each other ('How good to see your face') before launching into screamingly camp descriptions of their current doings accompanied by shrieks and 'oohs' and much virtual elbowing in the ribs. Funniest of all was when the straight Kenneth Horne tried to join in: 'Oooooh! He's bold. He's got all the palare', accompanied by giggles and sly digs as to how he came to know the jargon.

Many of the words have moved into the mainstream: 'bold' meaning 'daring' as opposed to 'shameless'; 'cottage' for a public lavatory and 'cottaging' for the use made of it by gay men; 'bitch' and 'butch' when applied to men and women of ambivalent sexuality; and 'naff' – spelt 'naph' in the scripts – for 'bad', now a frequently used substitute expletive. There is a 'Bona Riah' hairdresser in Brighton ('riah' being backslang for 'hair' just as 'ecaf' – shortened to 'eek' – was for 'face'), and Morrissey called one of his albums *Bona Drag*, meaning 'nice clothes', in 1990.

Julian and Sandy's overt homosexuality – enhanced because both actors were known to be gay – did not faze the studio audience or those listening on air. In the episode where they set themselves up as legal advisers, the undertones of their statement 'We have a criminal practice' was not lost on anyone; and once one knew that 'omi' meant 'man' and 'palone' meant 'woman', the meaning of 'omipalone' was all too obvious.

In the rest of the show, too, names and wordplay were omnipresent, aimed both at getting laughs and at titillation: when Syd Rumpo sang about a man called Reg Pubes, the writers were being disingenuous when they claimed that 'the filth was in the ear of the beholder'.

On screen, meanwhile, the *Carry On* series placed a similar reliance on innuendo and sexual ambivalence. And in Charles Hawtrey the films had a character, like Julian and Sandy, who was identifiably gay, leading to enhanced comic possibilities. Kenneth Williams, a staple of these films too, surprisingly often played a character oppressed by the unwanted attentions of a woman, frequently the statuesque Hattie Jacques. They, together with Joan Sims, Sid James with his filthy laugh and Barbara Windsor as the blonde bimbo, were the stock cast; and the plots revolved around unlikely pairings in everyday settings like hospitals, schools, holiday camps and the like. Once seen, it is hard to forget Barbara Windsor clutching her bare breasts after her bra has pinged off during a vigorous session of PT in *Carry On Camping*, or Kenneth Williams as Julius Caesar shrieking 'Infamy! Infamy! They've all got it in for me!' in *Carry On Cleo*.

The real lives of many of the actors were sometimes the stuff of comedy or tragedy. Barbara Windsor – who became the inaugural 'rear of the year' in 1976 – was married to Ronnie Knight, who had to flee to Spain to escape arrest for armed robbery, and also had flings with the gangster Reggie Kray and her co-star Sid James. Hattie Jacques left her husband John Le Mesurier – well known for his portrayal of the upper-class Sergeant Wilson in *Dad's Army* – for a younger man, and Le Mesurier then briefly lost his next wife to a love affair with the doomed comic, Tony Hancock. Sid James collapsed on stage with a fatal heart attack and Joan Sims suffered all her life from depression and alcoholism. Charles Hawtrey descended into booze- and fag-riddled illness, and Kenneth Williams – who, despite the exuberance of his radio *alter ego*, never came to terms with his homosexuality – led a lonely and unhappy life and died, possibly by his own hand, in 1988. He claimed in public to be celibate, but his diaries record a sad succession of unconsummated or unsuccessful encounters. The last entry in his diary reads, 'Oh – what's the bloody point?'

The glitz and glamour of showbiz, then, was not always all it seemed, though during the 1950s and 1960s the reality behind the glossiness was concealed from the fans and audiences in order to maintain the mystery.

Gay Hollywood stars, such as Rock Hudson, went through sham marriages so that their homosexuality would remain secret, and rumours
about the bisexual lives of other stars – even such luminaries as Laurence
Olivier and Marlon Brando – often only came out after their deaths.
Noel Coward refused to acknowledge his homosexuality openly and
forbade his biographer, Sheridan Morley, to mention it. Even heterosexuality could be problematic if a lusted-after actor or singer turned out to
be unavailable; Beatle John Lennon was initially advised to conceal his
marriage to Cynthia in case his fans deserted him. Some of these secrets
could not be kept and became public knowledge; and in many cases it
was only the harsh reality of the Aids epidemic that revealed the true
sexuality of many of those within the gay closet who succumbed to it.

But nevertheless, young people who gaped at these idols of stage and
screen wanted some of that glittering lifestyle for themselves; and the
socially mobile 50s and 60s offered all sorts of opportunities. Some
youngsters actually made it into the gorgeous world of showbiz and
achieved the fabled wealth and the luxury they craved; others in this
increasingly affluent generation got their kicks from the new glamorous
occupations that the widening world was making possible – air hostesses, for instance, jetting off to far-flung countries, even if only for a night
or two, and enjoying the new freedoms of life away from home with
their equally free colleagues. When air travel began to expand in the
1950s, before the women's movement began to take hold, it was never
questioned that the hostesses had to be young and beautiful, of a regula-
tion height and weight, splendidly made up and willing to accept a role
where appearance was everything. One woman interviewed for the job
in 1954 recorded having to lift her skirt for the male interviewer so that
he could see her legs. Hostesses were instantly sacked if they got married
or – heaven forbid – pregnant. And they acquired reputations to go with
the apparent glamour of their jobs: when the 1960s photographer David
Bailey was asked whether he slept with all his models, his response was
to ask whether airline pilots slept with their air hostesses. He clearly did,
he implied; so they did, too.

Air travel was rapidly becoming more accessible to customers, opening up the possibility of foreign holidays for all. The availability after the
Second World War of aircraft and pilots to fly them, combined with the
perceived cheapness of living in other countries, made resorts on the
Mediterranean coast of Spain, for example, available to the mass market.

And the growth of package holidays, where discounted flights – which the law at that time forbade the airlines themselves to offer directly – could be hidden within the cost of the whole holiday, began to attract people of all ages. Travel and illicit activity fuelled by exotic locations were no longer the preserve of the rich and their servants. Abroad was a place where the weather was reliable, where living was cheap and where inhibitions could be cast off with one's clothes. Romances which could be waved farewell after the two-week break was over became as much a part of the annual summer holiday as sun, sand and sangria. Shirley Valentine came later; but the fantasy of running away from the drabness and drudgery of daily life to a world of laid-back Mediterranean *mañana* had its roots in the late 50s and 60s.

Meanwhile at home, the post-war decades remained aggressively prudish, actively hounding male homosexuals rather than quietly ignoring anything not too blatant. Books regarded as obscene had always been banned, but now they were prosecuted as well. The jury in the murder trial in 1955 of nightclub singer Ruth Ellis, the last woman to be hanged in Britain, were told by the judge that they must ignore evidence that she was an adulteress and a loose woman. In fact, there was no doubt that she had killed her lover, David Blakely, and the jury brought in the only verdict they could under the laws of the time. But it is noteworthy that her morals featured in the case.

There were massive numbers of signatures to petitions for her reprieve from the death penalty, which the Home Secretary ignored. And there were many similar ways by which the public demonstrated to the authorities that they were starting to get tired of illiberal laws and what were swiftly becoming to seem outdated sets of principles and values. One of those occasions was when John Gielgud appeared on stage for the first time after being convicted of gross indecency for a homosexual incident in Chelsea; the whole audience stood up and gave him an ovation on his first entrance, bringing the play to a standstill. This was in October 1953, the year he had been knighted in the Coronation Honours list. He had tried rather feebly to conceal his identity under the name Arthur Gielgud in court, and the police sergeant had done his best to keep the proceedings secret by persuading a duty magistrate to come in early; but a reporter from the *Evening Standard* happened to be in court and the story appeared in the lunchtime edition. Despite the overt public support, Gielgud felt the humiliation keenly, and some of the press carried on pushing for greater vigilance against what they were touting as the 'homosexual menace'.

Alec Guinness had been luckier when he, too, came up in court in 1946 after being caught in a homosexual act in a public lavatory in Liverpool. He gave his name as Herbert Pocket, a character in Dickens' *Great Expectations* whom he had played on stage in 1939 and was about to play in a film. He got away with it, and it was only after his death in 2001 that biographers revealed that he had struggled all his life with his homosexuality. Gielgud eventually came to terms with his sexual orientation, living openly and happily for the last forty years of his life with his companion, Martin Hensler.

The purge on homosexuals in the early 1950s came in the wake of the Burgess/Maclean spy scandal. Homosexuals were notoriously susceptible to blackmail, so the CIA and MI5 seem to have decided to come down hard on them in the hope of lessening Russian recruitment of high-placed susceptible traitors at the height of the Cold War. Guy Burgess and Donald Maclean were the first of the so-called 'Cambridge five' to be unmasked as Soviet spies in 1951; alerted by Kim Philby, the third member, they fled to Russia ahead of their arrest and lived there for the rest of their lives. Philby followed them some years later, but the fourth member of the spy ring, Anthony Blunt, was not publicly named until much later. Blunt and Burgess were both homosexual, and it was Blunt who probably recruited the others in the 1930s, having become Burgess's lover. In 1945, Blunt was appointed Surveyor of the King's Pictures, a job he kept under the new queen until he retired in 1972, having been made Commander of the Royal Victorian Order in 1946 and knighted in 1956. It was only when he was about to be unmasked in a book due to be published in 1979 that he was officially named and shamed, and stripped of his knighthood. He died shortly afterwards.

The years 1953 and 1954 were to see a major witch-hunt against homosexuals. Police officers acted as *agents provocateurs* in public lavatories, hanging around until they were propositioned and then making an arrest. Claims of indecent assault were followed up rigorously, and some high-profile people found themselves victims. One of these was Rupert Croft-Cooke, a writer who lived in Sussex with his secretary, Joseph Alexander. After inviting two Royal Navy cooks, whom they'd met in a London pub, to spend the weekend, they were raided in the middle of the night by the police in response to allegations of indecency made against them by their visitors. The only evidence was the not altogether reliable word of the two cooks, who had anyway tried to withdraw their testimony, but it was enough to convict them; Croft-Cooke got nine months in prison and Alexander three. The actions of the police in the case and the prosecution evidence were sufficiently flawed to prompt Croft-Cooke to decide to write about it, only to find himself being warned off; when he asserted that he was going to expose the 'filthy witch-hunt' that was going on, he was told that indeed it was still going on, and a second conviction was always easier to get than a first. He nevertheless went ahead and published *The Verdict of You All* in 1955.

Higher profile still was the series of prosecutions brought against Lord Montagu of Beaulieu. He was first arrested, with film director Kenneth Hume, after they had taken a couple of boy scouts to a beach hut on the Beaulieu estate to look for a lost camera. He had reported the missing camera to the police, but when they arrived to investigate they showed more interest in what they believed had been going on between the men and the boys. After claims of indecent assault had been made by the scouts, Montagu and Hume were committed for trial – to be acquitted on the more serious charge of committing an unnatural offence but forced to face a new trial after the jury had failed to agree on the lesser offence of indecent assault.

Before this second case could come to trial, there were yet more arrests resulting from incidents in the Beaulieu beach hut. This time the victims were Michael Pitt-Rivers and Peter Wildeblood who, together with Montagu, were accused of indecent acts with two airmen, Edward McNally and John Reynolds, at a party in the beach hut in 1952 which the prosecution claimed had descended into a sort of Bacchanalian orgy. The fact that the two airmen had been involved in many other homosexual affairs and that McNally had a friend called Gerry whom he called 'my husband' cut no ice with the prosecution; the Director of Public Prosecutions had promised the witnesses that no action would be taken against them regardless of what came out about their other homosexual liaisons. All three defendants were subsequently found guilty and sentenced to prison terms.

There were some gay men – though they would not at this time have used the term – who were not prepared to hide behind a façade. One of these was Quentin Crisp, who actively cultivated his effeminate appearance by dying his hair, painting his fingernails and toenails, wearing outlandish clothes and affecting an outrageously camp manner – and in public, not just in private. He was often abused and attacked in the street as a result, but did not flinch from displaying his true personality. His attempt to join the army at the start of the Second World War failed after he was declared medically exempt because he was 'suffering from sexual perversion'; he stayed in London throughout the Blitz and the blackout, picking up American GIs and declaring that London was one vast paved double bed. The central London flat he lived in at this time was where he would stay for the next forty years until he moved to America; he famously never cleaned it, saying that the dirt didn't get any worse after the first four years. His memoirs, published in 1968, took their title *The Naked Civil Servant* from his years of working as a life model which, he said, 'was like being a civil servant except that you were naked.'

Joe Orton was another who boldly asserted his homosexuality. He and his lover, Kenneth Halliwell, whom he had met at RADA in 1951, were imprisoned for six months in 1962 for stealing books from Islington library and returning them with their covers or blurbs altered or defaced. A volume of John Betjeman's poems, for example, had its dust-jacket replaced with a photograph of an almost naked, tattooed middle-aged man. Orton began to write plays in the early 1960s which, despite their somewhat shocking nature, gained growing success on the London stage and on television; among them were *Entertaining Mr Sloane*, *What the Butler Saw* and *Loot*, which included a part he had written specially for Kenneth Williams. He, Halliwell and Williams sometimes holidayed together in north Africa, but Orton's relationship with Halliwell was becoming increasingly difficult as his professional career blossomed while Halliwell's stuttered. The tragic end came in August 1967, when Halliwell beat Orton to death with a hammer before killing himself with an overdose. The biography written by John Lahr, *Prick Up Your Ears*, was later filmed with a screenplay by Alan Bennett.

The police crackdown on gay men in the early 1950s had a result that they had probably not predicted. While some of the press continued to bay for the blood of 'deviants', others devoted articles to thoughtful debate on the issue, and there was pressure from members of the estab-lishment, including a group of clergymen, for consideration to be given to amending the law. The Home Secretary, Sir David Maxwell-Fyfe, was prepared to listen. In 1954 he announced the establishment of a commit-tee, chaired by John Wolfenden, which was to look into the laws relating both to homosexual offences and to street prostitution, both of which were regarded as having becoming worryingly more prevalent and overt since the end of the war. The recent court cases, and the rabid public attention they had grabbed, had only served to highlight the issues even more. The membership of the committee was wide-ranging and included three women; it sat for three years until its report was produced in 1957.

Crucially, they heard evidence from two prominent professional men prepared to be open about their homosexuality in order to support the case for decriminalization. One was Patrick Trevor-Roper, a distinguished Harley Street eye specialist and brother of Hugh, Regius Professor of History at Oxford. The other was Carl Winter, director of the Fitzwilliam Museum in Cambridge. They had come forward partly because they wanted to challenge the evidence of Peter Wildeblood, newly convicted and just out of prison. Wildeblood claimed that he and others like him were 'respectable' homosexuals who should not be hounded; but others in his view were not so respectable and gave everyone a bad name. 'Good homosexuals,' he said, 'want to lead their lives with discretion and decency, neither corrupting others nor flaunting their condition.' 'Bad homosexuals', it was implied, do corrupt and flaunt, and harm the 'good' ones in the process.

Trevor-Roper and Winter, on the other hand, argued that sexual orientation was innate and could not be induced by seduction or corruption. Homosexuals, they said, posed no threat to innocent heterosexual youth, and their sexuality was no more responsible for bad behaviour than it was with heterosexual people. Even more telling than the intelligence and good sense of their arguments was the light they shed on the life of gay men in a world where it was illegal. As they pointed out, the vast majority accepted their sexuality and led ordinary, well-adjusted lives within a community of like-minded others. They both indicated that their social lives were almost entirely in that world, and that they knew large numbers of gay men from all walks of life. As they made it clear to the committee, their sexual orientation did not prevent them enjoying a full and vibrant social and sexual life. Trevor-Roper argued for the same age of consent as for heterosexual sex, i.e. sixteen; and he made the further point that decriminalization would help to reduce the numbers of young gay men who were driven to commit suicide because of society's intolerance.

The Wolfenden Report was admirably advanced for its time; published in 1957, it came out strongly in favour of decriminalization. All but one of the committee signed up to the recommendation that 'homosexual behaviour between consenting adults in private should no longer be a criminal offence.' It further stated that, 'it is not, in our view, the function of the law to intervene in the private life of citizens, or to seek to enforce any particular pattern of behaviour' and went on to suggest an age of consent of twenty-one for male homosexuals.

However, it was to be ten years before the 1861 Offences Against the Persons Act was repealed and the Sexual Offences Act passed – the law that began the long, slow process of legalization. The 1967 Act, sponsored by Leo Abse, was limited in its extent and was passed only by a very narrow margin. Debate along the way had been tortured and sometimes acrimonious. One MP declared that incest was a more natural act than homosexuality, and others were anxious to keep gay men apart from the general public; the corruption of the innocent was still on some people's agenda. The new law permitted sex between consenting adults over the age of twenty-one in private, and it applied only to England and Wales, not to Scotland and Northern Ireland; nor did it include those serving in the armed forces. It was to be many years before it was extended to the whole United Kingdom and before homosexuals enjoyed the same freedoms as heterosexuals: in 1994 the age of consent was lowered to eighteen, and in 2000 gay men and lesbians finally attained equality with their heterosexual counterparts when it became sixteen. That Act also for the first time brought lesbian sex within the reach of the law when sixteen was established as the age of consent for gay women too. Society's recognition of same-sex relationships has now gone even further, allowing civil partnerships with most of the advantages of marriage.

'The corruption of the innocent' was almost as much a worry in heterosexual quarters in the 1950s. It drove the prosecution in 1960, under the 1959 Obscene Publications Act, of Penguin Books who were seeking to publish D.H. Lawrence's *Lady Chatterley's Lover*. Lawrence had written the novel in 1928 and published it privately in Florence. The National Archives file on the trial [DPP 2/3077] contains some rather telling (and indeed amusing) correspondence from the office of the Director of Public Prosecutions when they were trying to acquire enough copies of the book for the judge and prosecution team to read it before the trial. They eventually resorted to asking officials at Her Majesty's Stationery Office whether they would be prepared to copy it. The response from J.R.

Simpson of HMSO was rather grumpily reluctant: he complained that they had a great deal of business on for the government, and moreover, 'Another reason for my reluctance is that the copying process would have to be undertaken by a staff composed mainly of young girls.' This was, after all, the trial during which the chief prosecutor, Mervyn Griffith-Jones, invited ridicule when he asked whether this was the sort of book which 'you would wish your wife or your servants to read.'

The book was potentially scandalous – in legal terms 'tending to deprave and corrupt' – because of its use of four-letter words and its explicit description of sex scenes, and also perhaps because the liaison was between people of different classes. The plot has Constance, Lady Chatterley, left sexually frustrated after her husband has become para-lysed and impotent, so she starts an affair with their gamekeeper, Oliver Mellors. One passage which caused particular outrage was the one when Mellors approached Constance from the rear: 'and short and sharp, he took her, short and sharp and finished, like an animal.' Lawrence is known to have amended the book several times to tone it down before its original publication, and it seems that he may have left this passage deliberately vague; the ambiguity as to the form of sex being described remains.

At all events, the publishers evoked the clause in the new law which provided a defence if the book was of such literary, scientific, artistic or educational merit that its publication was justified in the name of the public good. Witnesses testifying to its literary merit included E.M. Forster (whose homosexual novel *Maurice* was not published until 1970, after his death) and the academic Raymond Williams. The jury brought in a verdict of not guilty.

The aftermath saw cartoons depicting queues round the block to buy the book as soon as Penguin issued it, and a certain lightening of atti-tudes towards such material; though the file also contains a letter from 'A mother of three children' asking the DPP to prosecute the publishers of Alberto Moravia's *The Woman of Rome* which had somehow found its way into her respectable home: 'I intend to put this copy on the fire but advise you to do something to prevent the publication of such so-called literature.' But others urged him not to pursue an appeal against the verdict on the grounds that 'our reputation for upholding cultural stan-dards has suffered in civilized circles abroad through this prosecution. Perhaps we may soon have the spectacle of twelve good men and true sitting in judgement on *Troilus and Cressida* or *The Rape of Lucrece*.' Philip Larkin's poem 'Annus Mirabilis' celebrates the beginning of sexual intercourse 'in nineteen sixty three … between the end of the "Chatterley" ban and the Beatles' first LP.' And in the 1970s Morecambe and Wise used the Chatterley plot in one of Ernie's 'plays wot I wrote' about a man 'who has an accident with a combine harvester which unfortunately makes him impudent.' As a coda to the story, there is – also in the National Archives file – a card dated 8 September 1960 (just before the trial) which reads, 'I understand that you may be requiring witnesses in the forthcoming case Crown v. Penguin Books Ltd. I place myself at your disposal. Yours faithfully, Constance Chatterley.'

It was by no means the last prosecution of material regarded as obscene. *Last Exit to Brooklyn*, by Hubert Selby Jr, included material such as gang rape, homosexuality, transvestism, drug use and violence, and was also vilified for its brutal prose style. When it was published in the UK it sold well, though there were complaints to the Director of Public Prosecutions about its content. He did nothing, but in 1966 an MP, Cyril Black, started a private prosecution before Marlborough Street Magistrates' Court which resulted in a guilty verdict. At that point the DPP did take it up and sent the book and its publishers for trial at the Old Bailey under the Obscene Publications Act. The jury was all male; the judge had decided that women 'might be embarrassed to read a book which dealt with homosexuality, prostitution, drug-taking and sexual perversion.' The verdict was again guilty, but it was overturned in 1968 in a ruling that did much to change the laws of censorship.

The 1950s started in an age of austerity and post-war shortages; the 1960s ended in an era of flamboyance and increased liberality and freedom. Typical of the 1950s was the situation in which the parents of the actor Phil Davis found themselves: she had married George Davis during the war, only to fall head over heels for his brother when he returned from fighting in the Far East. Brother- and sister-in-law had run away together and had two children; but, desperate for respectability, they did not tell their sons the truth until the law changed to allow what had previously been regarded as a legally incestuous relationship, and they were able to marry. The writer David Leitch discovered a similar scenario with his foster parents; because they were not married they were not allowed to adopt him, so they simply moved away and introduced him to their new neighbours as their son. Paula Yates, too, found out only on his death that her real father was the entertainer Hughie Green. And Kenneth Tynan experienced a shock when his father died in the late 1940s; he was not called Peter Tynan at all, but turned out to be Sir Peter Peacock, who had once been mayor of Warrington and had been living a double life for decades.

Respectability was the watchword of the middle classes in the 1950s. Many a young adult discovered that his or her 'mother' was actually the grandmother and the so-called sister was the real parent (Catherine Cookson was one who famously discovered her parentage through street gossip), and unjustified suspicion could fall on teenage girls in families that suddenly produced a late baby. While fathers largely escaped censure, and could even deny paternity if they were so inclined, unmarried mothers were sent away to special homes to have their babies and were often then persuaded, or forced, to give them up for adoption. After the law changed to allow adopted children to seek out their birth parents, there have been many cases of people finding whole new families in middle age, and women being reunited with the son or daughter they last saw when he or she was only a few days old. It was not, however, until 1989 that bastardy as a legal concept was abolished with the passing of the Children Act, and not until 2003 that paternal responsibility was granted to unmarried fathers provided their names appeared on the birth certificate. With the coming of DNA testing, paternity is less easy to deny or conceal; and there are few cultures today that stigmatize illegitimate children.

Meanwhile scandal continued to flourish among the more flamboyant sections of society, and many of the aristocracy maintained a traditional nonchalance on sexual matters. Fergus Linnane cites one madam of a London brothel in the 1950s who remembered a client descending the stairs of her establishment meeting his son coming up; they smiled at each other and carried on. Lord Lambton, who was forced to resign after a sexual scandal in the early 1970s, is on record as asking, 'Surely all men visit whores?' The politician Bob (later Lord) Boothby maintained a long-standing affair with Dorothy Macmillan, wife of Conservative politician and Prime Minister Harold Macmillan. Their daughter, Sarah, was brought up as one of the Macmillan family, but she had an unhappy and alcohol-riddled life and died aged only forty. Boothby's cousin, Ludovic Kennedy, is on record as stating that Bob had fathered at least three illegitimate children by at least two women. He was bisexual, too, and had a number of homosexual liaisons from his schooldays at Eton onwards; one of them was with the gangster Ronald Kray.

One of the most celebrated scandals of the time was that involving Margaret, Duchess of Argyll, and the 'headless' man. During her first marriage to Charles Sweeny, an American amateur golfer, she suffered a bad fall down a lift shaft which is said to have changed her personality and rendered her sexually voracious. She had already had several affairs, including one with George, Duke of Kent, and during her second marriage to the Duke of Argyll she carried on her illicit liaisons with man after man. When the duke petitioned for divorce in 1963 he cited affairs with eighty-eight men, said to include three royals and two cabinet ministers. Also produced in evidence were several Polaroid photographs of the duchess dressed in nothing but a three-strand pearl necklace; one of them showed her with a naked man whose torso and genitals were visible, but not his face. There was much speculation about his identity, and comparisons were made between the handwriting on the photographs and that of the five major suspects; this analysis pointed the finger at Douglas Fairbanks Jr, but he denied it to his dying day. Another name bandied around was that of Duncan Sandys, a son-in-law of Winston Churchill and then Minister of Defence. The judge was harsh in his comments while granting the divorce: the Duchess of Argyll was 'a completely promiscuous woman whose sexual appetite could only be satisfied with a number of men'. Nothing conclusive about the identity of the 'headless man' ever emerged and the duchess never revealed his name. The case has continued to fascinate to this day: *Powder Her Face*, a modern opera by Thomas Adès, includes an aria sung by the duchess while she is engaging in a sexual act.

There is a curious link between the Argyll case and the Profumo affair, the other major scandal of the early 1960s. That case also featured an unidentified naked man, known to be a high-level member of the establishment – rumoured even to be a cabinet minister – but never named to this day. Naked but wearing a mask, he would serve guests at the famous dinner parties given by Stephen Ward, and then eat his own dinner from a dog bowl.

The Profumo affair had everything: political sleaze; immorality in high places; call girls and pimps; Russian spies. At a time when society was waving farewell to the strait-laced 1950s and beginning to revel in the new era of sexual liberation that the 1960s were promising, it revealed a shockingly immoral world at the heart of government and the establishment. The photograph of Christine Keeler, the strikingly attractive call girl at the centre of the case, straddling a chair naked has become an icon of the era, and her pose is imitated to this day.

The scandal had its roots in the fact that Keeler was involved with both John Profumo, Minister of War in the Conservative government, and Eugene Ivanov, a naval attaché at the Soviet Embassy. This was when the Cold War was raging, and it was felt that British security was compromised by these liaisons. Keeler and another call girl, Mandy Rice-Davies, were protégées of Stephen Ward. A London osteopath, poised at the centre of a web of sleazy intrigue, he delighted in giving risqué dinner parties at his Wimpole Mews flat where he introduced unlikely people to each other. Lurid stories about these parties involved sadomasochism, two-way mirrors and orgies. But Keeler always denied that Ward was running a virtual brothel; influence and power were what he wanted, not money.

It was Ward who introduced Keeler to Profumo during a weekend party at Lord Astor's country house, Cliveden. They embarked on a passionate affair, which Profumo tried to deny when the press got wind of it. But he then made the crucial error of lying to the House of Commons about the affair, claiming that 'there was no impropriety whatever in my relationship with Miss Keeler.' A few weeks later he had to admit that he had lied, and resigned from the Cabinet and from the House. He spent the rest of his life working for charities and was eventually rehabilitated enough to be awarded the CBE.

Meanwhile Stephen Ward was charged with living off the immoral earnings of Keeler and Rice-Davies who, during the trial, uttered the memorable line 'He would, wouldn't he?' when told that Lord Astor had denied ever sleeping with her for money. The case ended when Stephen Ward committed suicide on the last day, before the jury was due to retire. Keeler subsequently claimed that Ward had been a spy for the Soviets and had asked her to get information for him and to be a go-between with the Russian Embassy. But nothing was ever proved, and Lord Denning's subsequent report on the whole thing came to the conclusion that there had been no breach of security. One is tempted to echo Mandy Rice-Davies: 'He would, wouldn't he?'

The 1960s witnessed an astonishingly speedy turn-around in public attitudes towards sexual morality, fuelled by changes in legislation and —

especially — the advent of the contraceptive pill. This had been developed in America in the middle of the 1950s and licensed for use there and in Britain in the early 1960s. It provided, finally, a foolproof method of birth control and freed up men and women, inside and outside marriage, to have sex without necessarily having babies. Within a very few years the centuries-old shackles of traditional morality, grounded in the need for legitimacy and therefore female chastity, were discarded. Phrases such as 'living in sin' and 'unmarried mothers' were consigned to history.

As we have seen, 1967 saw the start of the decriminalization of homosexuality. There must have been something in the Parliamentary water that year, because it also saw the laws about abortion amended and updated. The 1929 Infant Life (Preservation) Act had permitted abortion up to the twenty-eighth week of pregnancy if it was necessary in order to preserve the physical health of the mother; in 1938, the case brought against a doctor who'd performed an abortion on a young girl who had been raped extended the legality to psychological health. Now in 1967 David Steel's Abortion Act legalized it up to twenty-eight weeks for a wide variety of reasons, and also provided it free on the National Health. This was not quite 'abortion on demand', but it did make it more available.

It is said about the 1960s that if you can remember them you cannot have been there. It was a remarkable decade, one where prosperity grew greater while the world grew smaller as international travel broadened horizons and the mind, where the cult of youth embedded itself ever deeper into society, where the death of deference was making itself felt across the whole spectrum of class attitudes, where education for all who wanted it was leading to greater equality and more rigorous questioning of traditional norms. Clothes and hairstyles reflected this new exuberance: tiny mini-skirts, tight jeans, brightly coloured shirts, exaggerated patterns, complemented by loose bobbed haircuts for women and long bushes of thick hair in Beatle cuts for men. The music was loud and vibrant, and for the first time British acts conquered America. Television came into its own, with programmes such as *That Was the Week That Was* further challenging conventional manners. *Private Eye* was started, funded by the iconoclastic Peter Cook and underpinning the satirical feel of the times heralded by shows such as *Beyond the Fringe*. England even won the football World Cup.

The flamboyantly louche Kenneth Tynan was one of the many

figures who epitomized both the freedoms and the decadence of the 1960s. He had been unconventional all his life, supporting motions calling for the legalization of homosexuality and abortion during debates while he was still a schoolboy, and embracing a colourful lifestyle while at Oxford – including the heavy drinking and smoking that were eventually to kill him. He indulged in many affairs during his marriages and favoured sadomasochistic sex; and he was passionately opposed to censorship of any kind. It was during a live television debate on that subject in 1965, as part of the satirical show *BBC3*, that he became the first person to utter the word 'f**k' aloud on British television. The incident provoked outrage, indicating that the new freedoms were at most skin-deep and applied only to a small sector of urban society. The House of Commons issued no fewer than four separate motions of censure, Mary Whitehouse had more ammunition in her campaign for 'morals and decency' on television and the BBC was forced to apologize. Tynan was unrepentant, however, and went on to write – in collaboration with other notables of the time like Samuel Beckett, John Lennon and Edna O'Brien – the erotic revue *Oh! Calcutta!* which ran on the London stage and on Broadway for several years. The revue consisted of sketches based on erotic fantasies and featured several scenes where both male and female actors were totally nude. Its title was a pun on the French '*O quel cul t'as!*' meaning 'Oh, what an arse you have!' Predictably, it sparked a great deal of controversy, but that did not mar its enduring success both in Britain and in America.

Rock stars and their model girlfriends were the new aristocracy, along with the young actors and actresses whose flamboyance and outrageousness made 'swinging London' the place to be. Michael Caine and Terence Stamp, wannabee film stars, shared a flat, each ordering the other to be absent when he had a girl to stay. For a while Stamp dated Jean Shrimpton, face of the 1960s until she decided to retire from the modelling life and the gamine young Twiggy took over, stick-thin and tiny with her huge eyes and her schoolgirl hairstyle. Mick Jagger and Marianne Faithfull were the rock star couple *par excellence*, extravagance and decadence personified. Tales of their drug- and sex-filled lifestyle, along with the other Rolling Stones, The Beatles and the rest of the London *demi-monde* of the period, titillated and fascinated those on the outside who could only watch; though William Rees-Mogg, editor of *The Times*, could find it in himself to write a memorable editorial after

Mick Jagger was briefly imprisoned for possession of marijuana, questioning this 'breaking of a butterfly on a wheel'. Drugs were the order of the day. The Beatles later admitted to smoking a joint in the lavatories in Buckingham Palace while waiting to receive their MBEs – awards which resulted in a mini-deluge of medals returned in disgust by outraged colonels from the shires.

This was a time of excess and abandonment in many ways, fuelled on one hand by the freedom given by the contraceptive pill and on the other by the cult of prosperous, devil-may-care youth that had taken over. Marriage for some was out of fashion, but the 1960s were also an age of heightened social conscience, nurtured by the rebirth of folk music and the protest music that was grafted on to it. Bob Dylan and Joan Baez were the high priest and priestess of this movement for a while, until Dylan betrayed the faithful and went electric. The soaring ballads of Simon and Garfunkel and the sun-soaked Californian surfing music of the Beach Boys were complemented both by the guitar-smashing excesses of The Who and the brilliance of black Motown. And the 1967 'summer of love', with thousands of young people flocking to the Haight-Ashbury district of San Francisco to experience the free love, jiggling-naked-breasts culture of hippiedom, heralded a brave new world. Woodstock was its apogee, when five hundred thousand young people descended on a small town in upstate New York to hear music by some of the best bands of the time and to feel in tune both with each other and the world. They were the flower children in their brightly coloured flowing caftans, poking roses down the barrels of guns and preaching peace and love to anyone who would listen – and going home to their communes for happy sex romps under the heady scent of marijuana. Or so the legend has it!

There were downsides. The hard-living lifestyles of the new elite led to many premature deaths: Brian Jones of the Rolling Stones, drowning in his swimming pool in 1969; Jimi Hendrix, choking on his own vomit after an evening of drinking and taking sleeping pills in 1970; Jim Morrison of the Doors overdosing on heroin in the mistaken belief that it was cocaine in 1971; Janis Joplin, another drug-related death after a period of being clean. There was sleaze, too, such as the disputed and perhaps apocryphal episode involving Marianne Faithfull, a fur rug and a Mars bar into which the police apparently walked when they raided one of the Rolling Stones' country houses. And Altamont, only a few months after the glories of Woodstock, cast a dark shadow over the myth of the festival, with murder taking place under the eyes of the Stones on stage and the violence of the Hell's Angels, ostensibly there to keep order but laying about them with weapons and manhandling people off the stage.

Reliable birth control was complemented by a greater understanding of human sexuality from studies such as those published by Kinsey and Masters and Johnson. The combination was truly the genesis of a sexual revolution – one of the most radical shifts in social attitudes and behaviour since industrialization. And liberality was growing apace, too. A few more years saw the undermining of social and marital norms that had been around for centuries, with consequences not entirely beneficial. Middle-class morality was replaced by a hedonistic belief in pleasure as a right, and a competitive, fearful edge to sexual conquest – were you missing out on the lifestyle party attended by the rest of the world? Still, new legislation not only decriminalized homosexuality and abortion, but also began to establish equal rights for women, giving them new freedoms both in the home and in the workplace. Pros and cons can be endlessly debated; but the sexual revolution seems to be here to stay. Certainly someone living at the end of the nineteenth century would have been more in tune with the mores of the Middle Ages than with those that flourish – in all their glorious diversity, contradictions and absurdities – today.

Further reading

Beckett, Ian, *Home Front 1914–1918: How Britain Survived the Great War*, The National Archives, London, 2006

Behlmer, George K., *Child Abuse and Moral Reform in England 1870–1908*, Stanford University Press, Stanford CA, 1982

Black, Jeremy, *The British Abroad: The Grand Tour in the Eighteenth Century*, Sutton, Stroud, 2003

Bridge, Mark, 'A Tale from the Raj', *Ancestors*, 46, June 2006

Brittain, Vera, *Testament of Youth*, Fontana, London, 1979

Coote, Stephen, *Penguin Book of Homosexual Verse*, Harmondsworth, 1983

Coward, Mat, *Bona Palare: The Language of 'Round the Horne'*, www.verbatimmag.com

Dalrymple, William, *City of Djinns*, Flamingo, London, 1994

Davies, R.T. (ed.), *Medieval English Lyrics: A Critical Anthology*, Faber & Faber, London, 1963

Davis, Norman, *The Paston Letters: A Selection in Modern Spelling*, Oxford University Press, Oxford, 1983

Fraser, Rebecca *Charlotte Brönte*, Methuen London, London, 1988

Forster, E.M., *Howard's End*, Penguin Classics, London, 2000

Forster, E.M., *Where Angels Fear to Tread*, Penguin Classics, London, 2001

Frost, Ginger S., *Promises Broken: Courtship, Class and Gender in Victorian England*, University Press of Virginia, 1995

Gardiner, Juliet, *Oscar Wilde: A Life in Letters, Writings and Wit*, Collins & Brown, London, 1995

Gibbons, Stella, *Cold Comfort Farm*, Penguin Classics, London, 2000

Greene, Graham, *The End of the Affair*, Vintage, London, 2001

Greenwood, James, *The Seven Curses of London*, Blackwell, Oxford, 1869

Haller, Dorothy L., 'Bastardy and Baby Farming in Victorian England', *The Student Historical Journal*, 21, Loyola University, 1989–90

Halsall, Paul, *Internet Medieval Sourcebook*, www.fordham.edu

Harris, Barbara J., *English Aristocratic Women 1450–1550*, Oxford University Press, Oxford, 2002

Hartley, L.P., *The Go-Between*, Penguin Classics, London, 2000

Hattersley, Roy, *The Edwardians*, Little Brown, London, 2004

Heard, Stawell, *The Secret Life of Arthur J. Munby*; www.casebook.org

Hibbert, Christopher, *London: The Biography of a City*, Penguin, Harmondsworth, 1977

Hickman, Katie, *Courtesans*, HarperCollins, London, 2003

Hotson, Leslie (ed.), *Shelley's Lost Letters to Harriet*, Faber & Faber, London, 1930

Larkin, Philip, 'Deceptions', *Collected Poems*, Faber & Faber, London, 1988

Lee, Laurie, *As I Walked Out One Midsummer Morning*, Penguin, Harmondsworth, 1971

Linnane, Fergus, *Madams, Bawds and Brothel-Keepers of London*, Sutton, Stroud, 2005

Littlewood, Ian, *Venice: A Literary Companion*, John Murray, London, 1991

Malory, Sir Thomas, *Le Morte D'Arthur*, Oxford University Press, Oxford, 1971

Manning, Olivia, *Fortunes of War: The Levant Trilogy*, Penguin, Harmondsworth, London, 1982

Melly, Diana, *Take a Girl Like Me*, Chatto & Windus, London, 2005

Mitford, Nancy, *Love in a Cold Climate*, Penguin, Harmondsworth, 1954

Mitford, Nancy, *The Pursuit of Love*, Penguin, Harmondsworth, 1949

Moorcroft Wilson, Jean, *Siegfried Sassoon, The Making of a War Poet: A Biography, 1886–1918*, Duckworth, London, 1998

Nicolson, Nigel, *Portrait of a Marriage*, Weidenfeld & Nicolson, London, 1973

Norton, Rictor, various articles, www.infopt.demon.co.uk

Paley, Ruth, and Fowler, Simon, *Family Skeletons*, The National Archives, London, 2005

Quennell, Peter (ed.), *Byron: A Self-Portrait in His Own Words*, Oxford University Press, Oxford, 1990

Reynolds, Barbara (ed.), *The Letters of Dorothy L. Sayers 1899–1936: The Making of a Detective Novelist,* Hodder & Stoughton, London, 1995

Roberts, Alan, *A sixteenth-century scandal,* www.applebymagna.org.uk, 2000

Robinson, F.N. (ed.), *The Complete Works of Geoffrey Chaucer,* Oxford University Press, Oxford, 1974

Saki (H.H. Munro), *The Complete Short Stories,* Penguin Classics, London, 2000

Sassoon, Siegfried, *Memoirs of a Fox-Hunting Man,* Faber & Faber, London, 1975

Sayers, Dorothy L., *Murder Must Advertise,* Victor Gollancz Ltd., London, 1933

Smart, Elizabeth, *The Assumption of the Rogues and Rascals,* Paladin, London, 1991

Somerset, Anne, *Unnatural Murder: Poison at the Court of James I,* Weidenfeld & Nicolson, London, 1997

Stone, Lawrence, *The Family, Sex and Marriage in England 1500–1800,* Penguin, London, 1990

Townsend, Camilla, '"I am the Woman for Spirit": A Working Woman's Gender Transgression in Victorian London', *in* Miller, Andrew H, and Eli Adams, James, *Sexualities in Victorian Britain,* Indiana University Press, Bloomington and Indianapolis, 1996

Tresidder, Megan, *The Secret Language of Love,* Duncan Baird, London, 1997

Websites: those listed below were the main ones used, which then often pointed towards other resources which are too numerous to list.
• OLD BAILEY PROCEEDINGS 1674–1834 www.oldbaileyonline.org
• THE LESBIAN AND GAY STAFF ASSOCIATION OF LONDON SOUTH BANK UNIVERSITY www.knittingcircle.org.uk
• THE NATIONAL ARCHIVES www.nationalarchives.gov.uk
• www.Victorianlondon.org
• www.Victorianweb.org
• www.Wikipedia.org

Index

Numbers in **bold** denote a plate number

Acknowledgements

HUGE THANKS are due to Catherine Bradley, publisher at the National Archives, for commissioning this book in the first place and then for her detailed and caring editorial help. Also at the National Archives, Amanda Bevan and Ruth Selman were extremely generous in imparting their expertise and knowledge, Alfred Symons was of enormous help in sourcing documents and Cynthia Fraser was a greatly resourceful picture researcher. Ken Wilson has produced a typically elegant design and Liz Jones and Vanessa Morgan edited and proofread with speed and efficiency. Polly Allison and Jemma Underwood were magnificent research assistants, unfazed by the nature of some of the material they were asked to look for; Paul Thomelin was kind enough to share with me an illuminating incident in his own family history; Peter Marchant's historical insights were invaluable; Alan Roberts gave me permission to quote from his research into Appleby (chapter 2); Rictor Norton, who is a social historian specializing in gay history, was generous in allowing me to use his research. Many others have been encouraging and supportive when I got bogged down. Needless to say, any errors are mine.

The books listed in the Further Reading list were my main source and starting point for much of the basic material. Where I have made direct use of any of the contents I have cited the title within the text. The internet is, of course, an additional research tool *nonpareil*. Articles on specific topics researched via the internet are listed under their authors within the bibliography, and there is a further list at the end of websites used more generally. Many of the direct quotes from Victorian writers come from Lee Jackson's extremely useful website Victorianlondon.org.

Every effort has been made to trace and credit copyright holders; we will be glad to correct any unintentional errors or omissions in future editions of this book.

PICTURE ACKNOWLEDGEMENTS
in order of plate number:

[1] British Library, London, UK/Harley 4425 f.12v; [2] British Library, London, UK/akg-images; [3] Bibliotheque Municipale, Agen, France/Bridgeman Art Library; [4] Bibliotheque Nationale, Paris, France/Bridgeman Art Library; [5] Eileen Tweedy/British Museum/Art Archive; [6] TNA:PRO KB8-9m.3 (28 hen viii); [7] TNA:PRO PCI/I/170; [8] National Portrait Gallery, London, UK/Bridgeman Art Library; [9] Royal Society of Arts, London, UK/Bridgeman Art Library; [10] Corporation of London/HIP/TopFoto.co.uk; [11] Manuscripts and Special Collections, University of Nottingham/An/PB 369/12; [12] Victoria & Albert Museum, London, UK/Bridgeman Art Library; [13] Corporation of London/HIP/TopFoto.co.uk; [14] TNA:PRO C124/874/1; [15] akg-images; [16] Mary Evans Picture Library; [17] British Library, London, UK/Bridgeman Art Library; [18] TNA:PRO J90/1266; [19] Museum of London, UK/Bridgeman Art Library; [20] Mary Evans Picture Library; [21] Mary Evans Picture Library; [22] Art Archive; [23] Mary Evans Picture Library; [24] TNA:PRO COPY1/204 f.197; [25] Eileen Tweedy/Art Archive; [26] Bodleian Library, Oxford/Art Archive; [27] Topham Picturepoint/TopFoto.co.uk; [28] Mary Evans Picture Library; [29] TopFoto.co.uk; [30] Getty Images; [31] Paramount/Kobal Collection; [33] TNA:PRO MEPO 3/2138; [34] Mary Evans Picture Library; [35] Topham Picturepoint/TopFoto.co.uk; [36] Topham/PA/TopFoto.co.uk; [37] Roger Mayne Photographs/Mary Evans Picture Library; [38] Mirrorpix; [39] David McEnery/Rex Features.